From Ear to Ear

From Ear to Ear

A Pianist's Love Affair with Song

STEVEN BLIER

FOREWORD BY **ADAM GOPNIK**

W. W. NORTON & COMPANY
Independent Publishers Since 1923

Copyright TK

*For Alex, who made it all happen,
and Jimmy, who makes it all happen.*

Contents

Foreword by Adam Gopnik . . . . ooo

1: *Iolanthe* . . . . ooo
2: I Did It Sideways . . . . ooo
3: Alan and Martha . . . . ooo
4: University Without Walls . . . . ooo
5: Mentors and Tormentors . . . . ooo
6: No Career in Song . . . . ooo
7: A New Path Opens . . . . ooo
8: The History of My Legs . . . . ooo
9: Halfway Up Mount Rushmore . . . . ooo
10: Lorraine . . . . ooo
11: How the Sausage Gets Made . . . . ooo
12: Scheherazade Had It Right . . . . ooo
13: Arms and the Man . . . . ooo
14: Across a Crowded Room . . . . ooo
15: *Iolanthe 3* . . . . ooo

Acknowledgments . . . . ooo
Index . . . . ooo

Foreword

ADAM GOPNIK

THE MEMOIRS OF musicians are surprisingly instructive and humbling, especially for us literary types who imagine that only those schooled in writing can adequately articulate experience. Berlioz leads the pack, of course, but there are more recent hyper-readable memoirs by, among others, Stephen Hough and Jeremy Denk, not to mention the bewitchingly instructive letters of Beethoven and Mozart and the diaries of Ned Rorem. Jazz musicians, of course, have a library shelf of their own, from Art Pepper to Artie Shaw.

The idea that what musicians do doesn't translate into writing is false. The art they make may sit above and beyond language, but it isn't at all apart from conversation—and musicians, when you can build trust enough to get them talking, are the most unequivocally amusing of companions. Almost always they have tales from the road, and this type of story leads the pack when it comes to shop talk. At some happy level, such stories are always the same, whether it's about Schubert Lieder or Frank Loesser or Sondheim being sung in concert hall after concert hall: we expect, and enjoy reading about, the depredations of producers, the Sahara-like dryness of dressing rooms; we relish the details of torn gowns and sketchy hotel rooms and bad late dinners and suspicious spouses. The joys of the road.

But if all musicians have something to share, those who inhabit the higher reaches of classical concert performance have an additional element to offer, never more beautifully and amply illustrated than it is in this memoir by Steven Blier. For in that world there is a particularly extravagant counterpoint, comic and cosmic at the same time, between the elevated ambitions of the practice, and the daily realities of physical and mental labor that music-making requires.

If it were a more gnomic kind of fable, Blier's memoir might simply have been called "The Accompanist," for the beauty of this memoir is that, while its author is front and center, he is not always squarely in the center of the follow spot. Blier is not only a superior accompanist, but he has—despite manifold reservoirs of wit and stubbornness that his friends know very well—the accompanist's readiness to bend in service to others, the supple ego of the observer rather than the stiff one of the divas, of either sex. This makes him an ideal raconteur. So, along with the stories of concerts conquered, there are also tales of amused adjustment, slow-growing realization, and rueful second thoughts. It is a triumph of "point of view," a view from the piano bench, gazing at the broad back of a vocalist.

Throughout he amplifies, with delicate relish, an image fixed in our minds like a Steinberg drawing: the diva in her gown, with the accompanist seated nearby, almost invisible behind the keys, anxious page-turner to his left. We see his face only at the start, and then again at the end. It is an image of music-making as fixed in our minds as that of the frowning conductor or the triumphant timpanist. A born accompanist, no one has written better of its joys and humors than Steven Blier. "Judaism may not have addressed the central issues of my life—my bar mitzvah had come and gone, to my great relief—but making music with a grown-up singer (Valerie was all of twenty-seven), whose unamplified voice could fill large theaters, released something primal within me," he tells us early on. "She was my gateway drug.... I was the town pump, the pianist who would put out indiscriminately, and nothing was off-limits.... Poetry fired my musical imagination, song lyrics delighted me, opera librettos were my emotional education."

We meet many famous singers and musicians in these pages, from Jessye Norman to Renée Fleming to Lorraine Hunt Lieberson to Wolfgang Holzmair to Susan Graham, but we meet them uniquely right-sized—neither unduly adorned with praise nor maliciously belittled, understood not as divas at play but as artists at work. What makes this book irresistible is this uniquely Blierian combination of rollicking and self-deprecating humor, running alongside a casual confidence in the depth of his musical knowledge, as when he tells us: "While playing for instrumentalists carried a slightly more respectable status, accompanying singers positioned you at the bottom of the musical food chain. You were expected to squire a diva around, carry her luggage, make liberal use of the soft pedal, and play a déclassé repertoire of Handel arias and French art songs. With rare exceptions (like Gerald Moore), being a class-A accompanist seemed to be the musical equivalent of winning a tiddlywinks championship." Or when he says "I could easily be subsumed into another person's psyche. This proved to be a huge obstacle for growth as a human being, but it made me a dream accompanist. I could disappear, leaving only the song behind like the Cheshire cat's smile."

The concert world that Blier opens for us here—and I don't know of another book that gives a view at once so unhindered and levelheaded of that art—is now, perhaps, diminishing, as its repertory, like its audience, ages, and the habits of listening that for so many of us were an entry into adulthood—no longer seem to matter as crucially for the next generation. Yet to read this memoir is to be reminded on every page that the song repertory is one as fully emotional, as anti-academic, as any form of performance there is—not a way of mechanically carrying on a "tradition," but a way of organizing and communicating emotion that has no parallel elsewhere in human performance. A love of song, not as a professional engagement but as a way of life, shines through these pages and will relight in the reader a desire to listen again to music she may perhaps have thought to know too well.

But there are two additional elements in these pages that will—and no other word comes to mind—inspire the reader. One is of Blier's invention and long nurturing of the New York Festival of Song, a uniquely metropolitan invention with an almost four-decade track record. NYFOS treats song not as a junior version of concert music, nor in the depressing way of "pops" concerts, as an apologetic alternative to serious music-making, but as a form unto itself. The song may be a shorter unit of meaning than a symphony or an opera, but its artistic standards are as high and its meanings as rich. Blier has turned NYFOS into a place where Schubert entangles with the Beatles, to the benefit of both, where Richard Rodgers dances with Jacques Brel and Black spirituals intermingle with Dvořák. For those of us who revere songs, who see Paul McCartney not only as an offshoot of Chuck Berry but as the heir to John Dowland, Blier's invention—and the recordings that go with it—are an indispensable part of the life of New York.

Though his objective may be to extend the breadth of the world's song traditions, he has still another subject to share. Blier has, over the past decades, mastered an illness that would have plunged a man of less character and resolve into a depression, or into helplessness. His refusal of that helplessness is genuinely heroic, but the story of his body is offered here in a manner beautifully and directly matter-of-fact. If anyone wants to learn how to cope with a significant affliction without false bravado but also without complaint or depression, the lesson is in these pages.

That he tells this personal history with a touch as light as it is deft is a testament to his character. The bittersweet practicalities of finding a better wheelchair and the understated joy of still, against all odds, being able to smile ear to ear are indelible. It is perhaps as well a testament to the power of music to offer a life of feeling so absolute that it transcends even the limitations of the bodies that, as this book demonstrates, so beautifully make it. The Cheshire's smile is the cat, Blier shows us, indefatigable even when absenting itself, still radiant at rest.

From Ear to Ear

At age three on Shelter Island, just two months before I encountered a piano for the first time.

CHAPTER 1

Iolanthe

WHILE I GRANT you that waking life has its good points, there is nothing I like better than a vivid, Technicolor dream. For over fifteen years I have been keeping a dream log, filled with the absurdist scenarios that my unconscious mind whips up most nights: stocky female cops who have a side business giving hot-rock massages, a Canadian bank that promises excellent returns if I invest small blobs of oatmeal and polenta.

My best recent dream was also my shortest. In it, I am looking at my iPod, where I come across the following playlists:

>Iolanthe 1
>Iolanthe 2
>Iolanthe 1
>Iolanthe 2

And then:

>Iolanthe 2
>Iolanthe 3

I woke up laughing. I didn't need a therapist to analyze this one.

Iolanthe, of course, is an operetta by W. S. Gilbert and Arthur Sullivan. Between the ages of seven and ten, my brother and I listened to one act of a Gilbert and Sullivan recording every night during dinner. Though we were only a half-hour drive from Midtown Manhattan, for some reason we assembled our collection of LPs by mail order from New York's reigning record store of the 1950s and '60s, Sam Goody. When each clunky boxed set arrived I was in a frenzy of joy, reveling in Sullivan's melodic grace and Gilbert's verbal dexterity, even though some of the words were unfamiliar. I could tell that these operettas were supposed to be comedies, but was a little too young to understand that they were also social satires. I took them as a kind of fantasy-slash-kitchen sink drama, and as a result both my moral code and my conception of mating rituals had a strangely fusty, Victorian cast. So did my vocabulary. I used words like "compunction" and "indelicate" in everyday conversation. When a kid in fourth grade hit a home run in punchball, I turned to the boy next to me and exclaimed (with a grandiose rolled *r*), "Success has crrrowned his efforts!" My classmate didn't say anything, but I could tell that he now perceived me as a lunar creature.

Of all the Gilbert and Sullivan operettas I sponged up, *Iolanthe* has always held a special place in my affections. I first saw the show when I was around nine years old, from what is still my favorite theater seat in the whole world: Row A of the first balcony at City Center, on West Fifty-Fifth Street. Because of the peculiarities of the space, the mezzanine suspends the viewer just over Row J of the orchestra, and as a result you feel as if you are magically hovering over the stage. It's like being in an operetta spaceship, the perfect place for a kid to enter into one of Gilbert's topsy-turvy worlds.

Iolanthe tells the story of a young man who is very close to his glamorous young mother but a stranger to his barrister father. Essentially, it's Gilbert and Sullivan's version of *Oedipus Rex*. All the women in the show are wise, powerful, and immortal because they're fairies; all the men (with the exception of the romantic lead) are dunderheads, especially the pompous members of the House of Lords who make up the male chorus. For a preteen about to grapple with his homosexuality,

Iolanthe was a slice of heaven, a skewed, riotously funny vision of an adult world I eyed from afar. As Gilbert later wrote in *The Gondoliers*, "O, it's too much happiness!"

The leading man is an Arcadian shepherd named Strephon (which turns out to be the pastoral-poetry version of my own name). Early in the operetta he reveals the great dilemma of his life: he is half fairy, half mortal. To be more precise, he is a fairy down to his waist, but from his belt line to his feet he's human, subject to the laws of nature. As a result, he is a brilliant guy possessing feet of clay—as well as a healthy, human sexuality to which Gilbert alludes with sly indirection. Strephon has concealed the secret of his birth from his fiancée, a shepherdess named Phyllis. When one of the fairies observes, "Your fairyhood doesn't seem to have done you much good," Strephon lets loose with this outburst:

> *Much good! My dear aunt! it's the curse of my existence! What's the use of being half a fairy? My body can creep through a keyhole, but what's the good of that when my legs are left kicking behind? I can make myself invisible down to the waist, but that's of no use when my legs remain exposed to view! My brain is a fairy brain, but from the waist downwards I'm a gibbering idiot. My upper half is immortal, but my lower half grows older every day, and some day or other must die of old age. What's to become of my upper half when I've buried my lower half I really don't know!*

It was this speech that clung to my subconscious, enough to have me dreaming of iPods long after they'd gone the way of LPs. For my entire life I have been grappling with a rare form of muscular dystrophy; the exact moniker is fascio-scapular-humeral dystrophy, or FSHD for short. My mother and her two sisters had it, and each of them coped with declining mobility and strength in her own way. All three sisters lived long lives—FSHD isn't a killer, but it is a challenge and a constant preoccupation. Every little while I'm obliged to give up something else: first it was working out, followed by walking up and down stairs, then sitting in low chairs, then sitting in chairs without arms, and then standing, and finally walking. I can no longer do many of the things I used to love, most recently (and sadly) cooking. Every venture outdoors must be planned out in advance, since I now speed around in a state-of-the-art wheelchair and need to be sure to avoid tiny elevators, unforeseen staircases, and tight corners.

The one thing I have not had to give up is making music. I've made my living as a pianist since I was twenty, and my brain-to-hand connection seems to have dodged the muscular dystrophy bullet. I continue to give concerts even as I constantly adapt to my body's changing pockets of energy and strength. I consider myself uniquely blessed. A buddy of mine who has FSHD used to play classical guitar, but he had to give it up when the disease attacked his forearms. I was luckier—the disease hit my arms in the opposite direction. I am built like Popeye from elbows to wrists, while farther up my arm I am more like Olive Oyl. As a result, the muscles I most need for the piano remain largely unaffected. Another stroke of luck: since FSH can go after the muscles in your face, some of its victims are locked in an eternal scowl, but I can still smile. I consider that one of the greatest blessings I could receive.

Contrary to the playlist in my dream, *Iolanthe* doesn't actually have a third act. Gilbert and Sullivan cap off their second-act finale with a joyous waltz as both the fairies and the Peers are poised to levitate into the air; the entire House of Lords turns around to show that they have magically sprouted wings, and now *everyone* onstage is a fairy. It's a scenario that warmed the heart of a young kid who would take flight with his own gay wings in another decade or so.

Gilbert never addressed the issue of how Strephon would ultimately deal with the predicament of his immortal torso and aging legs. That would be the subject of *Iolanthe 3*, the theme of the life I am currently living. I am a smart guy with legs that are "gibbering idiots." It's not easy, but music is my fairy brain, the magic continues to course through me, and I still make use of my miraculous ability to smile.

Iolanthe | 5

Outside the Old Met after the final concert, April 1966–a few months after meeting Valerie Masterson. I'm already an inch taller since that evening.

Valerie Masterson in the mid 1960s, in her iconic role as Mabel in *The Pirates of Penzance*. She knew what to do with a parasol.

CHAPTER 2

I Did It Sideways

Y OU NEVER FORGET your first time.
   I was thirteen years old, fairly small for my age, and a quintessential introvert. But I had recently made a new friend in high school, a brash young man four years my senior named Matthew Epstein, an avid opera fan and fearless backstage Johnny. At that time he was studying singing, and in me he'd found a bar mitzvah–aged pianist who was happy to accompany him for hours. We'd already done a recital together—my first time onstage with a singer. Like me, he was a Gilbert and Sullivan aficionado, but unlike me, he made it his business to get to know the principal artists of England's premiere G&S troupe, the D'Oyly Carte Opera, when they were in New York. Matthew, already perfecting the art of power-schmoozing at age seventeen, would later become a force of nature in the world of opera.

In the mid-1960s, soprano Valerie Masterson was the crown jewel of the D'Oyly Carte—a leading lady with a killer high C, and enough charm and physical grace to demolish the resistance of the most curmudgeonly listeners in the top balcony. Somehow Matthew managed to get Valerie and her husband Andrew to have supper with the two of us at the Tip Toe Inn on the Upper West Side. Over pastrami sandwiches, I did my best to keep up my end of the conversation, even though I was so starstruck that I could barely speak.

I still cannot imagine how Matthew persuaded Valerie and Andrew to come back to his parents' place after our meal for an impromptu musicale. It was Valerie's night off, and she probably should have been resting her voice. Instead, this lovely young singer with piercing, bright blue eyes let me accompany her in a slew of songs and arias—Rossini's "Una voce poco fa" (from *The Barber of Seville*), which she knew in German, Verdi's "Sempre libera" (from *La Traviata*) and "Caro nome" (from *Rigoletto*), "I cannot tell what this love may be" from *Patience*, complete with her own choreography, and a rendition of the Fairy Queen's song from *Iolanthe* delivered in a hooty, fake contralto timbre—a mocking tribute to her first teacher, who had instructed her to sing that way. Perhaps Valerie relished the chance to dive into something besides the G&S roles she was performing night after night. Possibly she was intrigued by the idea of making music with a tiny pubescent Jewish boy. Most likely she, like the rest of the world, lacked the artillery for saying no to Matthew.

Valerie possessed the megawatt radiance of a star, but it was her voice that mesmerized me above all. The intense projection of her sound, especially in Matthew's petite Upper West Side living room, was the most glorious thing I had ever heard, invading my nervous system like catnip. Her easy, brilliant upper register made my ears buzz, my blood race, and my curly hair stand up even taller. Judaism may not have addressed the central issues of my life—my bar mitzvah had come and gone, to my great relief—but making music with a grown-up singer (Valerie was all of twenty-seven), whose unamplified voice could fill large theaters, released something primal within me. She was my gateway drug.

I HAVE been immersed in music for as long as I can remember. I was given a xylophone when I was a baby, and could tap out elegant renditions of "Old MacDonald" and "Three Blind Mice" by the age of two. When I began nursery school, there was a large piece of furniture in the room I had never seen before: it was an upright piano. I peered up at the keyboard and realized that its keys were laid out exactly like my xylophone. A quick experiment proved that they played the same tunes as the little metal toy I had at home, only louder. It seems I became a daily entertainer at my school—I have vague memories of sitting in a very high chair at the piano, surrounded by an audience of toddlers, some rapt, some somnolent. Family lore has it that the nursery school teacher came to our house—in those days teachers paid calls on all the parents to discuss their young charges. After touring our apartment, she looked at my mother in puzzlement. "But... where do you keep your piano?" "Oh," chuckled my mother, "we don't have a piano." "You don't? But... Steven plays piano for us every day!" Not long after, my mother had her childhood piano, lying unused at her parents' apartment in Brookline, shipped down to our place.

It is true that my mother—Josephine—didn't have any real understanding of music. The visual arts were her true passion. She'd worked in museums, tried her hand at painting. But her father, my Grandpa Berg, did possess a very refined ear, though he never had any musical training. Still, he would listen to orchestral music and whistle the viola lines, the oboe parts—not the big, obvious violin tunes, but the inner voices—and even at age nine I knew he was a kindred spirit. What my mother had was a gift for empathy that amounted to a kind of genius. She didn't size people up in an analytical way, but instead quietly took in their essence: their frailties, their beauties, their wounds. Grandpa Berg heard the inner voices of music; my mother heard the inner voices of people. She was generous, egoless, and to this day, decades after her death, my lodestar. She couldn't carry a tune, but she carried me through my life. I am scarcely egoless, but I did inherit some of Josephine's gift of intuition. My life's work has been learning how to use it properly.

By the time I met Valerie I'd had eight years of piano lessons, though my playing had more panache than technique. My saving grace was that I had quite a good ear. In sixth grade I was the pianist for several class musicals, including *Annie Get Your Gun*. To learn that score, I was sent home with an LP of the original cast recording and over the course of an afternoon I figured out how to play all the numbers, notating them with a strange system of arrows and primitive chord symbols I invented for the purpose. Apparently none of the teachers at P.S. 141 had any idea that there were published folios containing the principal numbers—even complete vocal scores—that you could buy. It didn't seem to matter. At that time I made little distinction between learning by ear and playing from printed music, and had no trouble reproducing Berlin's melodies and harmonies at the piano.

From then on, singers would line up outside my door once they heard that I would play anything in any key, for free. I was the town pump, the pianist who would put out indiscriminately, and nothing was off-limits. Later, at summer festivals where I was supposed to be learning chamber music and Bach partitas, I could usually be found bashing my way through art songs, opera scores, folk music, show tunes, and practically anything that involved piano and voice. Poetry fired my musical imagination, song lyrics delighted me, opera librettos were my emotional education.

I consumed music so voraciously that it was hard to slow down and learn the basics of piano technique. With my first teacher, Tessa Morgan, I was both a dream and a nightmare student, riding a Beethoven sonata like a Harley. I couldn't be bothered with the rudiments of hand position, the proper fingering of scales, the drudgery of arpeggios. Somehow the majority of the notes came out anyway. And I never really learned how to practice, since I could sight-read with so much ease. I shared the philosophy of Algernon in Oscar Wilde's *The Importance of Being Earnest*: "I don't play accurately—anyone can play accurately—but I play with wonderful expression."

It's hard to teach an idiot savant. My next teacher, Miriam Gideon, was a prominent composer on the New York scene. A tall, imposing woman, she towered over her diminutive husband Fred Ewen, a distinguished literary scholar. They lived together in the tiniest apartment I had ever seen, two narrow rooms on upper Central Park West, one of them colonized by a grand piano and the other lined floor to ceiling with books.

Miriam had some of Tessa's maternal warmth, and she gently tried to impose order on her coltish new student. Order meant two things: weekly instruction in music theory and a more conscious approach to the piano on a physical level. Unfortunately for her, I had already perfected the art of passive resistance, and I became an expert at fending off information about the Lydian mode or the intricacies of figured bass. Too much actual information about music, I felt sure, would sully my instinctive connection to the muse. But Miriam persisted and slowly I started absorbing the basics. Doing my homework on the A train to my lesson, I was probably the only person in the subway car turning out dodecaphonic tone rows, but putting the twelve notes of the scale down on a music staff in random order didn't strike me as a difficult task. I could write half a dozen of them between 168th and 125th.

Miriam was ultimately a more effective music teacher than piano instructor. For her, the motion of playing the piano began at the shoulder, engaging the upper body both for power and the release of tension in the forearm, wrists, and hands. Her method had some validity, but I never got it quite right, and my approach to the instrument grew somewhat effortful. Nevertheless, Miriam upped my game, and after three years she thought I was ready for a big-name New York teacher: a Juilliard professor named Irwin Freundlich.

Getting into Mr. Freundlich's studio was apparently like being welcomed as an honored guest at the tsar's palace. But my senior year of high school was a bad moment for me to embrace a new opportunity. I was a fifteen-year-old basket case—applying to colleges while nursing a secret, troubling crush on a male teacher, and running on the merest fumes of self-confidence. The razzle-dazzle of a star professor seemed like one more threat to my equilibrium.

For my lesson with Mr. Freundlich I brought the Chopin Nocturne in E Minor, which I had looked at for the first time just a couple of days earlier. After hearing a couple of pages he got up to mark the pedaling he wanted in red pencil. Catching sight of my music up close, he offhandedly remarked, "This Schirmer score's no good," he said. "What should I have gotten?" "Oh, the Mikuli Edition," he replied, as if it were the most obvious thing in the world. He ended the lesson by going to his stereo and playing a scene from *The Devils of Loudon* by Krzysztof Penderecki. His studio blazed with the sound of women screaming over a slithering orchestra. I must have told him I liked opera, but I meant *Aïda* and *The Barber of Seville*. This aleatory howling set my teeth on edge.

For that entire hour I had been holding my breath, as though I were trapped in an elevator where someone had gotten sick. Mr. Freundlich wasn't at all unkind or condescending. I'm sure he saw how skittish

I was and did what he could to put me at ease. But when it came to music, I was beyond thin-skinned, more like an open-heart patient. After the lesson, in spite of my parents' entreaties, I refused to go back. Some months later he called. "You disappeared," he noted. I floundered. "Um... I don't want to study piano anymore. At all." Pause. "Well, I do hope you'll think that over, and continue." "Okay," I mumbled.

A year later, in my first week as a freshman at Yale, I *had* thought it over and auditioned to take lessons at the Yale School of Music after I learned that piano study qualified for college credit. I passed muster and was assigned to the studio of John Kirkpatrick, an eccentric Charles Ives specialist. A birdlike man of sixty-three, he had a nervous tic that sent him into a paroxysm of eye-blinking every couple of minutes.

After I made my way through whatever piece I was offering as a calling card in those days (likely Robert Schumann's "Des Abends"), Mr. Kirkpatrick sauntered to the door of his studio and locked it. "Take off your shirt," he ordered, "I want to see your back." In a daze, I did as he asked. He ran his finger down my spine. "You have scoliosis. Do you know what that is?" I was too paralyzed to do more than grunt. "You need more strength. You need to do exercises for your back, sit-ups and frogs. Do you know what frogs are?" When I shook my head, he proceeded to whip off his green and orange checked sports coat, lie down on his back in front of the piano, and do a backbend, arching his pelvis while supporting his body on his hands and feet. He then jumped up, blood turning his face beet red. "Do you want to try one?" I found my voice, barely. "Later?" following up with a panicked, "Thank you for the lesson, I have to go." Unlocking the door, I sped into the hallway and down the stairs as fast as I could.

After my experiences with Mr. Freundlich and Mr. Kirkpatrick, brief as they were, it was beginning to dawn on me that I was not like other pianists. I feared that most teachers would try to change me into something I couldn't be. For the second time in two years, I decided to give up piano study altogether.

And that might have been the end of it, were it not for a college friend named Stuart Fischer, who seemed to understand my true relationship to the piano better than I did. He tried to woo me back by asking me to play for his spring production of *The Fantasticks*, to be performed in the Morse College dining hall. I told him I didn't play anymore, but Stuart was crafty, and devised a plan. He asked another freshman, Henry Schneiderman, to sign on as music director. Then, about a week after he'd started rehearsals, he scheduled an evening session without telling Henry about it, and called me in melodramatic panic. "We have an important rehearsal tonight and Henry can't make it. Would you *please* fill in for him?" I told him I would come out of retirement for one night only. The minute I got to the piano, of course, all my old passion for music came roaring through me, and I knew *The Fantasticks* by heart, having performed it in high school. Playing with the kind of enthusiasm and freedom a musician experiences only a few times in his life, I felt as if I were breaking the fast on Yom Kippur. Stuart released Henry from his duties, and I once again began to think about the piano seriously.

The next semester, an older and wiser sophomore, I realized that I needed help with my playing. In the classical repertoire I lasted about twenty minutes before experiencing alarming cramps in my arms. Instinct and intuition had carried me to a certain level of proficiency, but I had hit a wall. I decided to try once more with the School of Music. The piano department had just engaged Alexander Farkas, a kind and modest young man, to teach the undergraduates. And he was exactly the Zen master I needed.

After hearing me play, Alex observed, "You're like a bottle with all this music inside you. But the neck of the bottle is narrow, and it can't pour easily. We're going to work on widening that neck." He was nonjudgmental, worked with me no matter how unprepared or distraught I was, and I started advancing. I began to understand how energy flowed through my body, how to access strength without gripping my muscles, how to feel air under my forearms and tranquility in my palms. He used a fair amount of Alexander Technique, which I had never heard of. Since his own name was Alexander, I assumed this was his quaint way of describing his style of teaching. It was months before I understood the long history and profound importance of Alexander Technique, which would ultimately grant me freedom and stamina at the piano.

Alex would walk to the window as I played and stare outside meditatively. Without looking at me, he would say, "Let go of your left elbow." Or "Stay fluid under your right wrist." "What's the left side of your neck doing?" He could hear the tensions in my body before I was aware of them, with preternatural acuity. Here was a kind of spiritual intimacy I had never experienced—under his spell, I released huge amounts of physical tension and began to develop a sensitivity to the length and space of my spine, arms, neck, and legs. As I played, my body felt so elongated that my hands seemed to be six feet away from my head, like Alice in Wonderland after she ate the second half of the mushroom.

There was a small price to pay for this freedom: while I was still able to play popular songs like a maniac, my classical music grew a bit placid. It was a necessary step, one I have noticed in other musicians during their early forays into Alexander Technique. If my Schumann sounded a bit bland, I could at least make it all the way to the double bar.

Alex almost never solved a technical problem directly, and only about half of his instruction was focused on my hands and wrists. He possessed a genius for allowing my body to fix those problems by opening energy blocks elsewhere. At the piano, if nowhere else in my life, I was learning to operate like a unified being, a Steve who existed from his toes to his scalp.

WHILE STILL strangely indifferent to playing as a soloist, I always came alive when I was jamming with singers and actors. I had already coached my first opera in the summer of 1967 at age fifteen, when I was enrolled in the high school program at the Tanglewood Music Festival in Massachusetts—teaching a lovely soprano named Jeannette Walters the role of Alice Ford in Verdi's *Falstaff*. She was singing with Sarah Caldwell's touring company, opposite the Falstaff of the well-known baritone Peter Glossop ("Steven, that man is a *wolf*. Oh, my lord"). Jeannette was twenty-three but she seemed very grown-up to me, dressed in summer diva-wear and trailing a faint scent of perfume. Although my Italian was extremely rudimentary, it was nevertheless more advanced than hers. She learned much of her wordy role phonetically, memorizing it by syllables. "Let's see, *farfarelli*, that's far far away; and *diavoletti*, like the spaghetti sauce; and *pipistrelle*, well, pee-pee I can definitely remember." Somehow she managed to memorize the entire role, and eventually we both mastered the complex fugue at the end of the opera.

Three years later, at a summer program at Temple University in Ambler (Pennsylvania), I was again the toast of the singers and the runt of the pianists. When it came to vocal music, I would play anything anyone threw at me, I could transpose at sight, and I wasn't choosy about my musical partners. After I sight-read Paul Hindemith's thorny, atonal *Das Marienleben* for the soprano Rosalind Rees, she made a beeline to my door the next week—as did the mezzo-soprano Florence Quivar, with whom I stormed through Verdi's "O don fatale" (from *Don Carlo*) on a daily basis.

Meanwhile I was tanking in my piano lessons at Ambler, ostensibly the reason for being in the program. "I'm from the Russian school of piano," my teacher announced at the first lesson. "You have to make your fingers march like little soldiers." This was obviously the diametric opposite of what Alex and I were working on at Yale, but I gamely hied off to the practice room determined to whip my lazy hands into shape. Within thirty minutes I felt shooting pains in my forearms and stumbled off to the infirmary, where I was greeted with a patient smile and an eye-roll the nursing staff couldn't quite suppress. "Just rest for a day or two. And take it easy when you do go back to the piano."

Almost everything else in my undergraduate life was either bewildering or depressing. While I was getting excellent grades—academics seemed to be the one game I did know how to play—too much of my course work struck me as meaningless, I was grappling none too successfully with my sexuality; coming out of the closet felt like jumping from an airplane without a parachute. And though I'd always intended to major in music, I began to realize I was not cut out to study it with the cool distance of a scholar.

A course titled "Music of the Classical Era" seemed to promise a fragrant immersion into the beauties of Mozart and his no-doubt underappreciated contemporaries. Instead, we were subjected to dry harmonic analyses of obscure symphonies as the blackboard filled up with Roman and Arabic numerals. The breaking point came when the professor wrote the name "Toeschi" on the board. He was on a list of German composers, so I assumed that his name was pronounced "Tushy." Now, I might have been gay, but I did not want to major in "tushy." "Toeschi," I much later found out, did live in Germany but was Italian-born, and probably pronounced his name "toe-ESS-key." Still, the damage was done. For me, music was all about colors, passions, swirls of melody, slashes of drama—not numbers, and definitely not tushy.

At the last possible moment, 4 p.m. on the final day of my junior year, I changed my major. It was December 17, 1970, it was snowing, and it was Beethoven's two-hundredth birthday. When I soberly told Mr. Pallisca, the head of the department, that I wanted out, he surprised me with both his gentleness and his attempts to get me to stay. I was certain I had done nothing to make me worth fighting for, but I was touched by his attempt to hold onto me.

I needed to major in something I enjoyed, but that was not so close to my core identity. Since I liked novels, and I was willing to throw around the in-vogue academic jargon to analyze them, I made the switch to English. I was relieved to be in a discipline I didn't take so seriously. Two wonderful professors—Peter Brooks, with whom I did a tutorial on Henry James, and Paula Berggren, who was my advisor for a senior thesis on Shakespeare comedies—carried me across the finish line.

AS MY college years were coming to a close, I made the mistake of telling my parents that I wanted to be a musician, specifically an accompanist. My dad—Julius—was aghast. "It's a hand-to-mouth existence!" he exclaimed, his standard response to any life plan other than doctor or lawyer. To prove his point, he arranged a dinner with a longtime family friend, Seymour Solomon—a former violinist who had founded Vanguard Records, the label of the Weavers, Joan Baez, Odetta, and a horde of fine, if not A-list, classical musicians. When I told him I was thinking of becoming an accompanist, he snorted. "That's not a career. Anyway, who are the great accompanists these days? There's Gerald Moore, but who else?"

This was not a smart tactic. Though I said nothing in response, I was experiencing a rare moment of clarity: Seymour seemed to be saying that it was a wide-open field. If there's only one well-known accompanist in the whole world that this experienced professional can think of, surely there must be room for a few others.

Still, as an upper-middle-class Jewish son, I thought that I should at least make an attempt to take a traditional path, even to an untraditional destination. So I applied to the Yale School of Music's graduate program for solo piano. There were no courses of study for collaborative pianists in those days; at conservatories, being an accompanist was the equivalent of being a musical janitor. And everyone knew you didn't go to grad school to learn how to clean toilets or play Schubert songs, you just kept your head down went about your business as unobtrusively as possible. While playing for instrumentalists carried a slightly more respectable status, accompanying singers positioned you at the bottom of the musical food chain. You were expected to squire a diva around, carry her luggage, make liberal use of the soft pedal, and master a déclassé repertoire of Handel arias and French art songs. With rare exceptions (like Gerald Moore), being a class-A accompanist seemed to be the musical equivalent of winning a tiddlywinks championship.

As I was preparing for my audition, one of the sopranos in the master's program, Amy Catlin, asked me to play the second half of her graduate recital: five songs by Gabriel Fauré, and Manuel de Falla's *Seven Popular Spanish Songs*. I agreed, aware that it was unheard-of for an undergraduate—an *English* major!—to participate in a graduate school concert. About a week before the performance, Amy asked me to come to a coaching with one of the piano faculty, Yehudi Wyner. I trotted off to the Music School.

I knew that the Yale School of Music didn't look kindly on me. In those days there was a sharp divide between classical and popular music, and I had gotten too involved with the undergraduate musical theater scene for the piano faculty to take me seriously. A wildly successful campus production of *Jacques Brel Is Alive and Well and Living in Paris*, for which I'd been arranger and musical director, had made me into a hot commodity in Yale's acting community, but turned me into a pariah at the School of Music.

Professor Wyner wasted no time in going after me. "It's marked *piano*, can't you read?" "Where is the staccato, I see a staccato marking and you make *that* sound?" "There is a *ritardando* indicated, do you think it doesn't apply to you?" This went on for an hour, at the end of which he accused me of not being able to play the correct number of beats in the final de Falla song, "Jota." "It's in six-eight time! You're playing nine-eight!" I knew I couldn't fix this "problem" because I was actually playing it correctly. I had simply redistributed the notes between my hands in a way that made it easier (an adjustment I use to this day), and Yehudi's eyes had misled his ears. Afterward I stayed at the piano as Amy was gathering her belongings, quietly playing the beginning of "Jota"—"tapata-tapa-tapa-tapa-tapa-tapa,   tapata-tapa-tapa-tapa-tapa-tapa"—reassuring myself that I had not lost my ability to count the beats in a measure. Yehudi came over to listen, scrutinizing at the score. "Well. I guess you're playing it right. But it still sounds wrong."

My audition took place a few days later in front of the whole piano faculty (though not Alex, who was an adjunct teacher). I had brought two pieces: "Danza," by Louis Moreau Gottschalk, and the A-flat Major Nocturne by Fauré. For the panelists, who were expecting the virile meat and potatoes of Brahms and Beethoven with perhaps some Debussy for a touch of *folie*, Gottschalk's Cuban/Creole party piece had the nutritional value of a Tic-Tac. And no serious heterosexual pianist would have been caught dead playing anything as swishy as Fauré in 1972. Though dimly aware of their prejudices, I knew I didn't want to offer the same repertoire as everyone else.

For the Fauré piece, I went into my Alexander Technique trance, avoiding anything that felt like tension. The nocturne may have sounded somewhat bland, but that kind of smoothness is appropriate to Fauré and at least I didn't crash and burn. After receiving my Fauré like a plate of week-old tilapia, the panel asked to hear the Gottschalk piece. They were probably expecting one of his typical virtuoso barnburners, but "Danza" isn't a knuckle-buster. A flouncy suite of dance tunes, it is about as far from Beethoven as you can get. As I played, one of the panelists stood up and made a semicircle around me, staring at my hands as though they were tarantulas. As he returned to his seat, he was shaking his head.

There followed a sight-reading exam, whereupon I relaxed. If I possessed one skill, this was it. And I did fine with the first piece, but the next was written in some clef I had never seen before. As a pianist, I only knew the usual G (treble) and F (bass) clefs—there was no reason I would have encountered any other. After I expressed some consternation, they acidly informed me, "It's *tenor* clef." "Well, where is C?" "Everything is a step lower than the G clef," they explained, as if stooping to put training wheels on my bicycle. I poked at the piano in a desperate attempt to make sense of the score. And then, it seemed the audition was over. As I stood and regarded the gray-faced panel, Ward Davenny, the spokesperson, declared: "Mr. Blier, we are not accepting you into the School of Music. And please understand this: you will never play the piano *anywhere*, with the lid up or the lid down, except for your children."

My instinct for self-preservation silently asserted itself in that moment. "We'll see about that," I thought, secretly relieved by their rejection. After being bullied by Mr. Wyner, I hadn't expected a bear hug from his colleagues, nor was I raring for two or three years of study with a faculty who seemed to dislike me. But I also knew that there was a community of singers and actors who couldn't get enough of me. I'd survive.

There was one tiny silver lining: the panel heard my audition before I had completed the application process. I still owed the school a fifty-dollar fee, which I never did pay. Ever since then, whenever I make a self-indulgent purchase, I imagine the bank interest my fifty dollars has accrued over the years. And I bless the Yale School of Music for the magenta socks or the cool fountain pen.

I might have been written off by the piano faculty, but I was still set to accompany Amy in her graduate recital. So a week later, I borrowed a suit from my first boyfriend—off-white, wide-wale corduroy, the height of chic in May 1972, even if two sizes too large for me—and played at Sprague Hall. Performance nerves weren't yet afflicting me in those days, and our songs went quite well. As I was leaving the stage in a glow of satisfaction, a tall, white-haired man hustled down the aisle and stood in my path. Ward Davenny was regarding me with the oddest mixture of anger, chagrin, and bafflement. It was the look Max von Sydow gives Linda Blair in *The Exorcist* as her head rotates.

"That was... very good. Very good," he stammered.

"Thank you," I slowly replied.

"Who taught you how to do that?" he almost shouted.

I wanted to give a smartass answer—"*I studied at the school of hard knocks,*" an old maxim of my dad's—but thought better of it. "I took a couple of the songs to my teacher Alex, once, a few weeks ago," I hazarded.

Clearly not satisfied, he narrowed his gaze: "Can you *always* do that?"

"I guess so." Repeatability was a new concept.

"I see. Well, I want to wish you the very best of luck. Yes, the very best of luck." Then he turned and walked up the aisle shaking his head, having evidently witnessed a phenomenon that overturned all his preconceived notions of the natural world.

Alan Titus in the autumn of 1972, fresh from his success in Bernstein's *Mass*, and wearing the only suit he owned at the time.

CHAPTER 3

Alan and Martha

IN SEPTEMBER 1972, fresh out of college, I returned from a summer theater gig on Hilton Head Island with a deep tan, an overgrown Jewfro, and no idea about what to do next. I didn't have to wonder for long. My high school buddy Matthew Epstein called to tell me that they needed a pianist that week at the Manhattan Theatre Club for a few rehearsals of *The Barber of Seville*. It seemed that the regular guy couldn't be there for a couple of days. (The "regular guy" was the now-famous writer Ethan Mordden, a deeply eccentric man who could never be described as regular in any other context.) Could I fill in from two to four on Tuesday and Wednesday? I could. I had nothing on my calendar for the entire month of September.

The opera was scheduled for a November opening in Cocoa Beach, Florida, but the cast was New York–based: Neil Rosenshein as Almaviva, Alan Titus as Figaro, and Frederica von Stade as Rosina. David Alden, a college friend of Matthew's, was directing. Of the four, Alan could claim the highest profile. A year earlier he had sung in the premiere of Leonard Bernstein's *Mass* at the opening of the Kennedy Center in Washington, DC, and a slightly distorted picture of him was splayed across the cover of the two-LP boxed set. He was a hot property at twenty-seven, an assured actor, a promising singer, and a handsome, zaftig young man who was not averse to appearing onstage wearing nothing but a thong. Frederica, or "Flicka" as she was known to her friends, had made her Met début as the Third Genie in Mozart's *Magic Flute* a couple of years earlier. She too was twenty-seven, and already displayed the disarming combination of modesty, assurance, and vulnerability that would endear her to audiences for decades.

Then there was Neil, whom I already knew through Matthew. A fellow standee at the Met, he was just twenty-four and a rookie, but miles ahead of me in confidence and experience, familiar with the ways of the musical world—and the ways of the world in general. He also had a reputation as a roué, which he did little to defuse, mixing playful innocence with a serious libido like a cuddly baby satyr. Surrounded by rising stars, I was twenty but looked about twelve, a bespectacled deer in the headlights.

In those days, the Manhattan Theatre Club was located in a five-story brownstone on Seventy-First Street between First and Second Avenues, with ironwork staircases and large wood-paneled rehearsal rooms. The building pulsated with the weary vibration of all the banquets, rehearsals, and meetings it had hosted since 1896. It gave off the smell of an old primary school, with just a hint of greasepaint.

I was the first to arrive for the rehearsal that Tuesday, and Alan was the second. Finding himself alone in a room with a pianist he didn't have to pay, he did what any opera singer would do: he took his big aria out for a run. "Hey, would you mind playing the 'Largo' for me?" He wasn't referring to the well-known piece that opens Handel's *Xerxes*, but to Figaro's entrance aria "Largo al factotum" from *The Barber of Seville,* most famous from its appearance in a Bugs Bunny cartoon. I was unfazed. As Matthew Epstein's pianist of choice during my teen years, I had accompanied him in the "Largo" about a hundred times. Tensing my wrists and pummeling the piano like a pile driver, I attacked Rossini's repeated chords like a bat out of hell. It may not have been technically correct, but apparently it was impressive.

After Alan had belted out his last high Gs, there was a brief silence. "That was good!" he finally said. "Wow." Another beat. "Look, I have a recital next February up in Massachusetts, just one performance with Community Concerts. You want to do it? I don't have a pianist yet." I felt as if the Pope had just invited me out for pizza. In a daze, I said yes.

For the next few months Alan took me on as his pet project. Not only was there a recital to prepare, but he was about to assume the role of Nero in two productions of Monteverdi's *The Coronation of Poppea*, one of them with New York City Opera. I needed someone to show me the ropes, and Alan must have needed a mascot. Who better than me, with tons of free time, a willingness to play anything for a mere pittance, and a puppy-like devotion to any good-looking man who paid attention to me? So we palled around New York as that Indian summer turned into autumn, rehearsing mostly in the basement of what was then called the New York State Theater, but sometimes at my parents' place in Riverdale where I was still living.

A man of great charm, Alan possessed the suave veneer of a snake oil salesman who admits that his product is a sham—and still manages to sell you a bottle. I have long wondered why he chose to spend five months with someone who had nothing to offer except a tireless ability to accompany him. His motives were certainly not sexual, though he did have a knack for manipulating gay men. One day when we were walking down Broadway, he referred to the bass-baritone Donald Gramm as "queer as a three-dollar bill." The expression wasn't new to me, and I silently chafed. In the days before the word "queer" had been reclaimed by the LGBTQ community, it was unquestionably a slur. I let five seconds go by before asking, "Don't you mean 'Gay as a three-dollar bill'?" It took him a moment to register my irony and see that I wasn't playing along. "Well, you know, there are a lot of homosexual men in the business," he informed me paternally. "But I'd be very surprised if you were homosexual." Maybe his taunt was meant to force me to come out to him. I gave him the best answer I could at the time: I clammed up. Eventually the awkward moment passed, and the subject never came up again.

Over and over again I played the Nero-Seneca duet from Monteverdi's opera for fifteen dollars an hour—as Alan flashed imperious anger at an imagined adversary. It never occurred to me to take the score of *Poppea* home for study or to listen to a recording, since I could sight-read the accompaniment and sing the other parts without any extra effort. Here in a nutshell was the upside and the downside of my skills: rapid absorption, thin scholarship. While I eventually understood that this was not a viable modus vivendi, for the moment I was a dependable Monteverdi jukebox, with the good sense not to interfere with Alan's process of learning the role.

The City Opera premiere was a success, and Alan received excellent reviews. After the run was over, we began work on the recital: art songs by Paolo Tosti, Ernest Chausson, and Haydn, folk songs in Benjamin Britten's settings, and for an encore "Simple Song" from Bernstein's *Mass* (Alan's calling card at the time). He was an elegant singer with a special knack for phrasing and musical style, and an instantly recognizable silvery sheen in his timbre. Yet his expressive gift, like his interpersonal dealings, was more about seducing the listener rather than exposing his emotional depths. He was rarely vulnerable onstage, but he was polished, persuasive, and easy to love—a classy vocalist with a shiny exterior.

While he could effortlessly replicate foreign accents, Alan was somewhat prone to incongruous language errors. If you didn't speak French, he could convince you he was a Parisian boulevardier; if you did, you might be puzzled by his occasional wordburgers. Fresh from eight years of high school and college French and prone to bursts of moral outrage, I was appalled by the repeated slipups in the Chausson songs—leaving off the final *s* of *fils* (son), for example, so that it became *fille* (daughter). Alan's mistakes assaulted my ear with the force of a car alarm. Through trial and error, I began to learn the Realpolitik of coaching singers. Rule No. 1: identify what I call "beet stains," errors that no amount of washing will ever remove. Rule No. 1a: learn to smile benignly onstage when you hear the mistake in performance, even when you've done your best to bleach it out. Yes, it may be a linguistic kidney stone, but it's not *your* kidney stone. Rule No. 2: get over yourself. In mainstream America nobody else cares, except other coaches and diction teachers.

The recital took place in Weston, Massachusetts, not far from Boston. Since my mother was born in Boston we had many friends and family members in the area, and they all turned out for my professional début. In 1973, full-regalia white-tie was not out of place for a recital, even in suburban Massachusetts. Alan, of course, was set. He already owned elegant formalwear—or at any rate knew the best place to rent it.

In a fit of Blier-family insanity, my father decided I should wear my grandfather's old set of tails, which had already been remade once, probably for my father's wedding in 1941, and were now altered to fit me. Amazingly, the fabric still retained its nap after all those decades. Grandpa Sam had been short and rotund, but Dad and I were both just short of six feet tall. Somehow everything was made to fit except the white suspenders, which my father insisted that I wear in spite of my vociferous objections. They constricted my shoulders and drove me crazy all night. When I came offstage after the first half, I let out a barrage of four-letter words as I tore off my coat to lower the straps. Alan found me in the wings half-dressed and hissed, "For god's sake, put your clothes on! We have to go take a bow!"

Although I wasn't nervous, having rehearsed for months, I was still keyed up: here was an important milestone, my recital début with a professional singer. It had arrived more quickly than expected. I remember almost nothing about the performance, but I don't think anything went awry. Since my missed notes are usually the *only* thing I register after I play, there were probably no serious boo-boos that night. My problems had to do with remembering tempi, especially when agitated. I was prone to beginning a song at a maniac's clip, only to have to slam on the brakes when the singer made his entrance. So it was that night: "Simple Song" skidded out of control until Alan pulled on my leash when he began to sing.

After that night Alan headed off to Corpus Christi for another *Barber of Seville*, and then to Washington, DC, for another *Poppea*. I was no longer required, and the days suddenly were empty. It felt like the end of an affair. Alan had been a large and confusing presence in my life, a temporary big brother, a maze of promises and dead ends, always attractive and always off-limits. For all the complexities of our relationship he provided me an entrée into the professional world, playing the sophisticated Henry Higgins to my fledgling Eliza Doolittle. I'm eternally grateful to him.

Martha Schlamme and me around 1974, the honeymoon period of our collaboration.

MY NEXT gig happened the following May, again at the Manhattan Theatre Club: my friend Stephanie Cotsirilos was singing at the company's first fundraiser. Having begun our musical partnership in that production of *Jacques Brel* when we overlapped at Yale, we were still going strong as we both began our careers in New York. Stephanie was beautiful, a diminutive Greek American, high-waisted and olive-skinned, and I'd had a mad crush on her from the day I first saw her. Admittedly it was the safe kind of hetero crush gay guys allow themselves, a passionate devotion to an unattainable woman. Stephanie had an intellectual objectivity that set her apart from most singers, and her performances sometimes bore the mark of careful planning rather than inspired spontaneity. There are some artists I think of as "dry ice performers"—so cold that they're hot. Stephanie was my first dry ice performer.

For the MTC benefit we offered two of our old Jacques Brel standbys, "My Death" and "Marieke." I arrived early at the hall, and although I was only playing two songs I felt the need to warm up as if I were tackling Rachmaninoff's Second Piano Concerto that night. After all, this was the first performance I would ever give in New York City. As I bashed away at a rickety upright piano, I was interrupted by a middle-aged blonde woman with an air of wounded mystery. "Would it be possible for me to have the stage for a moment?" she asked. I took in her elegance, her foreign accent (London tinged with Vienna) and barely concealed anxiety. And then I recognized her: Martha Schlamme, a fixture of my childhood who had first come to prominence during the folk music boom of the 1950s. With her pure soprano voice, elegant musicianship, and ability to reproduce the cadences of almost any foreign language with authenticity, she had risen to the top of a crowded field. Her music was an ethereal, European counterpoint to the folksy American style of the Weavers or the bluesy wail of Odetta.

Martha's age (forty-nine) and angst (suppressed but tangible) trumped mine (twenty-one and under control). She seemed both interested in me and locked in her own world, in need of an audience while craving privacy. She wanted to warm up but appeared not to know how—her voice seemed to baffle her. Sensing her anxiety, I paid her homage: "Oh, what an honor to meet you, I grew up with your records!" She gave me a wan smile as I yielded the stage, making my way to the cramped dressing-room area. There I found the other performers gabbing away, luminaries like Barry Bostwick, Richard Maltby Jr., Camille Saviola, and Raúl Julia. Since I was a kid, an outsider, and moreover a mere accompanist, they ignored me. As a beginner I was practically invisible. I knew that it might be years before I would be of any interest to artists of that stature. After a brief flash of resentment I settled down, simply glad to be along for the ride.

Our Brel songs went fine, though I remember playing "My Death" with the kind of fervor one might bring to the last act of *Tristan und Isolde*. Martha's performance also went well—two Kurt Weill numbers, "Surabaya Johnny" and "The Bilbao Song," accompanied by a terrific pianist I also knew from Yale, Bill Westney. Her voice was no longer the pure, steady soprano I remembered from her records, but a collection of slightly unsteady sounds cobbled together from her various registers—an uncomfortable mash of Joan Baez, Mabel Mercer, and Lotte Lenya. Yet somehow the wavering thinness of her high notes and the gulley of register breaks lower down lent authenticity to the Weimar classics, and she made those warhorses sound as if she had made them up on the spot.

Everyone else may have been ignoring me that night, but not Martha. Apparently she listened to our Brel songs from the wings, because after the concert she asked me for my phone number. Four months later she finally called, in desperate need of a new pianist. Bill Westney was moving on to the greener pastures of a solo career, and she was faced with a smattering of upcoming concerts and no accompanist. These gigs were pretty small potatoes for a former headliner at folk music festivals, but she was only just returning to the world of cabaret, attempting to catapult herself to stardom one more time. Anyone who played for her would need not only to be able to improvise in a wide range of styles, but to make her vocal frailties seem like virtues.

That person would also have to deal with the antediluvian condition of her music: three spiral-bound books containing handwritten arrangements of Yiddish songs, international folk songs, and Kurt Weill songs. Also some annoying specialty material, including comic pieces like "Crazy Barbara" (originally made popular by Danny Kaye on an LP called *Mommy, Gimme A Drinka Water!*) and a faux-Handel aria whose final line proclaimed in baroque cadences that men were "a pain in the ass." Martha's pianists would need to flip quickly from the blue book to the white book to the mahogany book, as well as a few stray Xeroxes on card stock. Some songs had been written in the black italic of a copyist, others in blue ballpoint pen, one in orange Magic Marker. Almost none of them contained lyrics. And there was exactly one copy of everything.

Like Puccini's Tosca, Martha lived for Art. (When I met her, she even lived *with* Art—in the person of a sweet, rubber-faced gay actor named Art Howard.) Her songs often overwhelmed her with their emotional weight. Even a simple folk song she had sung a thousand times would sound fresh and urgent, no matter how wobbly the singing. There was a Spanish ditty about a woman who bought a chicken at the market, but suddenly had qualms about separating the hen from her newly hatched chicks; had anyone ever thought to plumb the melancholy pathos in the third verse like Martha?

Like many experienced singers, Martha did not like to rehearse numbers she had sung for decades. She longed for a pianist who could figure it all out quickly and catch on to her rhythms—her *nuances*, as she called them, using the French pronunciation. Her needs fit perfectly with both my skill set and my deficiencies. I had not yet formed a strong musical will of my own, nor was I weighed down by the armature of graduate school training or any clear concept of boundaries. I could easily be subsumed into another person's psyche. This proved to be a huge obstacle for growth as a human being, but it made me a dream accompanist. I could disappear, leaving only the song behind like the Cheshire cat's smile. "You were wonderful," I was often told during my early accompanying years, "I didn't even know you were there."

My début with Martha took place in September 1973 at the Universalist Unitarian church on Central Park West and Seventy-Seventh Street. My dad drove me down to the Upper West Side and came in to hear the performance. Her 11 a.m. concert was folded into the worship service, a wonderful if somewhat bizarre idea. (If Riverdale Temple had thrown some Brel and Weill songs into their Shabbat Torah readings, I might have been a more observant Jew.) Martha's music wasn't generally hard to play, and I took special care not to assault innocent folk songs with an excess of youthful energy. The true difficulty was flipping from spiral book to spiral book as she introduced her next song. When the concert was over—could she really have sung Weill's raucous "Bilbao Song" at a church service?—Martha informed the audience that this was my first concert with her, and asked them to give me a special round of applause. I had passed the test. On the car ride home, I couldn't quite tell what Dad was thinking, but I imagine he was making peace with the direction in which my life was heading.

In fact, in the space of just a few months I had set the course for the rest of my career, which has happily straddled the worlds of classical and popular music. Nowadays that kind of versatility is accepted, if not commonplace. But in the 1970s it was both a selling point and a stigma, like someone who plays Brahms and also deals drugs. When classical singers wanted to dip into the marijuana of American popular song, I was likely to get the call. But for the really highfalutin gigs on classier art song series, I was not even on the short list. I knew I might have to make some choices in a few years. At age twenty-one, I was delighted to be accepted as a commodity on any stage, any rehearsal room, any audition hall.

Unlike Alan, whose goal was to sell the song to his audience, whether he was offering them the champagne of French art song or the Budweiser of American folk music, Martha was outraged by the very notion of selling a song. Once, when she overheard one of her students use the expression, she became so unnerved that she reverted to German, a rare occurrence: "Nein! Nein! Man *verkauft* kein Lied! Man *bringt* ein Lied!" You don't sell a song, you *convey* a song. You *bring* a song to *life*. When Alan sang an inward, intimate piece like Haydn's "She never told her love," I sensed that he wanted us to admire just how inward and intimate he could be—a simulacrum of sensitivity. Martha, on the other hand, was guided by her inner life. Her child's sense of fantasy allowed her to imagine scenarios so real that they filled the theater. True, conditions had to be just right for the magic to work. A casual listener at a nightclub, expecting an hour of pleasant background music, might be irritated by her insistence on high art, left-wing politics, and linguistic virtuosity. She needed an attentive audience, and her singing voice required a bit of indulgence. But the rewards were plentiful. She took possession of a song and made it into the monologue of a specific—and fascinating—person.

My relationships with both artists were tinged with a young person's skeptical misgivings. And I played out parallel dramas with them: as time went on, I was quietly jealous of all the other pianists and conductors Alan worked with, while Martha was less quietly jealous of all the other singers I worked with. But I loved and learned from them both. Neither Weston, Massachusetts, nor the Universalist church on Seventy-Seventh Street was exactly a Carnegie Hall début, but they were safe venues for a pair of experienced musicians to give a rookie a chance.

I ONCE had a dream in which I was watching an old black-and-white TV. On the snowy screen, *The Ethel Merman Show* is on air, and Ethel's guest in the dream is the soprano Elisabeth Schwarzkopf. They're a crazily incongruous duo: the American Broadway star who belted out Gershwin hits to the back row, and the ultra-refined German Lieder singer famous for the exquisite detail of her phrasing. The two women are seated on stools doing a bit of scripted patter between songs. Schwarzkopf's hair is gathered in a chic chignon, while Merman's curls are lacquered in place on top of her head. Schwarzkopf is in immaculate pale satin, Merman in an explosion of sequins.

Merman turns to Schwarzkopf and brassily declares, "You know, Lizzie, it's not how you *sing* a song, it's how you *sell* it." Schwarzkopf lets a moment pass and answers with almost pained condescension, "*Nein, Liebchen*. It's not how you *sell* a song. It's how you *say* it."

Fade to black.

It's a dream that has haunted me for years.

It turns out you have to be clever enough to sell a song, and you also have to be eloquent enough to say it with depth and conviction. It would take me several decades and a lot of experience to blend the best of what I learned from Alan and Martha into a coherent philosophy. Confusing as it sometimes was, I was lucky to work with two experts of those twin crafts at a very young age: Alan, the salesman, and Martha, the oracle. Each of them picked me out of the crowd and took me under their wing. And thanks to them, I was off and running at age twenty-one.

Me with big hair in Nantucket, summer of 1973—one of my only glam shots from that decade.

CHAPTER 4

University Without Walls

THOUGH MY CAREER had gotten off to an unexpectedly rapid start, I knew I had a lot to learn. My folks, of course, still thought I could profit from my Ivy League trifecta—Phi Beta Kappa, summa cum laude, an honors degree in English literature. Dad had given up on trying to talk me into med school, which was lucky because I had not taken a single science course at Yale. Instead, he floated the idea that I apply for a Fulbright to study the acoustics of concert halls in Europe, since I "liked music so much." Nothing in my previous four years of study indicated that this had any basis in reality. All the while my mother could see that I was pretty bashed up emotionally from my college years, and that I needed some time to stabilize myself. The subject was dropped. Though I had figured out how to work the system at school, I did not wish to go to school ever again.

I was hungry to understand the mysteries of music. I just didn't think that's what conservatories taught.

My quest for knowledge had begun in my childhood and accelerated when I discovered *High Fidelity*, a monthly magazine devoted to stereo equipment and record reviews. In the third week of every month, I made a beeline for the magazine room in our building's lobby, anxiously awaiting the latest issue. Rereading those back issues, which are now archived online, I am astounded at their high level of scholarship and critical thinking. Though much of it was above my head at the time when I was eleven, I wolfed down every article about opera and art song.

My obsession had started, of course, with G&S. But the seminal moment, the *coup de foudre*, arrived when I reached the ripe age of ten. My Aunt Ruth had given me a recording of Mozart's *The Magic Flute*, which I eyed warily for a few months, still clinging to the familiar comfort of *The Mikado* and *H.M.S. Pinafore*. Finally, one lazy Sunday afternoon I pulled the boxed set off the shelf and played Side 1. I wasn't sure how I felt about the overture, which struck me as somewhat ponderous and lacking in tunes. (Full confession: I still do.) But I was bowled over the instant the opera proper started. Tamino, the hero of the story, rushes in, pursued by a snake, and he is rescued by a trio of women who have a long, multipart number. The intricate close harmony of the Three Ladies, as they are named, sounded to me like *The Mikado*'s "Three Little Maids from School" heard while tripping on peyote. Though somewhat creeped out by the German dialogue I kept going, mesmerized by the tenor and baritone solos that followed.

Then came the Queen of the Night's virtuoso aria, ending in scads of rapid-fire coloratura and an ascent to high F. Can one note change your life forever? That is what it felt like to me—my first peak experience. I'd never heard anything so dazzling in my life. In an instant I was done with the mocktails of G&S and wanted the hard stuff. I became an operaholic.

It wasn't long until my father took me to my first live opera. To strengthen our father-son bond, my dad and I used to go out on Sunday excursions. Since he was a doctor, this usually meant waiting for him while he visited his patients in the hospital. He hoped this would make me want to be a doctor when I grew up, though sitting around in a parked car or the lobby of Mount Sinai had the opposite effect. Medicine did not look like an appealing profession. But I did absorb something meaningful from our Sunday drives: there are no days off when people are depending on you.

After accompanying my dad on a particularly lengthy series of Sunday hospital rounds, he turned to me and said, "Ste, you've been so good, so patient. Tell me, is there anything *you* want to do?" This was a question he had almost never asked. Without stopping to think, I blurted out, "Yes, Dad—I want to go to hear an opera at the Met." My father and I sped down to Thirty-Ninth Street where he bought tickets for the next available date, February 15, 1963—*Fidelio* with Jon Vickers. We had obstructed view seats, which placed us smack behind a floor-to-ceiling pole. I spent the evening teetering from side to side like a metronome, trying to catch sight of the performers and make sense out of the German dialogue. It was heaven.

From then on I caught as many live performances as my parents would allow, and never as many as I wanted. I heard Joan Sutherland in her dizzying prime, Renata Tebaldi battling through the ups and downs of her late career, Franco Corelli at his most brazen, Zinka Milanov on her last legs, Renata Scotto in her glorious early days, Birgit Nilsson making mincemeat of a hundred-piece orchestra.

High Fidelity became my music textbook, due in large part to its lead writer on vocal music, Conrad L. Osborne. I consider him one of my most important early teachers. "C.L.O." was himself a trained singer and actor with a deep technical foundation in both fields. His analyses were clear and vivid, peppered with carefully chosen details that conjured up the sounds of that month's LPs. Nothing escaped his critical ear, yet he wrote with respect and objectivity.

I practically memorized his articles, though I occasionally misunderstood them. Reviewing Maria Callas's 1964 recording of *Carmen*, he wrote that while a lyric tenor like Nicolai Gedda might have an easier time than a brawnier voice in the first two acts of the opera, he might find himself comparatively underpowered for the second half of the role of Don José—and then he might as well "peddle his Duparc." I assumed that Duparc was a French bicycle manufacturer, and that Gedda would have to pedal his way off, presumably into a neighborhood with less strenuous repertoire. One day twenty-five years later, I finally realized what Conrad meant: the sweet-voiced tenor would be better off selling—peddling!—his wares in lighter fare, like French art songs by Henri Duparc.

For a decade, Conrad's reviews opened my ears to the balance and function of the voice, with an emphasis not only on the upper register (unlike many other critics, who seemed fixated on high notes) but the entire range. He was also alert to vocal inflection and verbal eloquence. Conrad welcomed all kinds of singers, from the arty (Scotto and Schwarzkopf) to the primal (Nilsson and Corelli). Solidity was his sine qua non: a column of balanced sound on a cushion of clear vowels. Tricks that thrilled the opera audience didn't impress him. He wasn't taken in by a phony pianissimo produced by dropping all the core support out of the voice, or a successful high climax trumpeted out after pages of disorganized braying. He also understood the musical and dramatic structure of opera, and he could explain complex things succinctly enough for me to grasp them.

Even as a kid I could see that Conrad had his blind spots. He might look the other way when Tebaldi landed way south of a high C, and he was far more lenient toward singers who mangled the French language than I, a budding Francophone, could ever be. But disagreeing with this brilliant man was as much of an education as agreeing with him. We later became friends, and I continue to revel in his writing—now through a modern medium (his blog) but with his analytic mind if anything sharpened by time. And to this day, few things make me feel as intelligent as disagreeing with Conrad.

Since I was studying French in school, I was comfortable with songs and operas in Romance languages. But I was developing a block about German and Austrian vocal music, and became convinced as a teenager that German Lieder held unfathomable secrets that I would never unlock. This probably stemmed from an interview in *High Fidelity* with one of the genre's *monstres sacrés*, the German soprano Elisabeth Schwarzkopf, who proclaimed: "No one can sing the word *'Wald'* in a German Lied until she has spent months walking in the Schwarzwald." I took her words to heart. If you weren't allowed to say "forest" without a grueling trip to Baden-Württemburg, what other words were off-limits? And what phoneme would give you away as an imposter—was it the *w*, the *l*, the vowel? One thing was clear: I would never be worldly enough to play Schubert or Schumann. I was not ready to go camping in the Black Forest for my art.

These feelings have dogged me for my entire life.

The same magazine featured an interview with another art song giant, French baritone Gérard Souzay. Asked about the difference between French and German vocal repertoire, he answered, "German music is like a kiss on the forehead. French music is a kiss on the neck." Though my first kiss on the neck was years away, I took comfort from Souzay's imagery. I wouldn't say my French art songs improved dramatically after I acquired a little more sexual know-how, but he celebrated something I did understand instinctively: the sensuality of music. And he made it sound like a source of pleasure, not a Labor of Hercules.

Since *High Fidelity* arrived only once a month, I started reading other music reviews in order to widen my perspective on the new sounds invading my ears. Even as a preteen I could see that the *New York Times* critic Harold Schonberg tended to take a condescending tone toward the performers, even the ones he admired. Irving Kolodin in the *Saturday Review* was often acerbic, always fascinating. I gasped as he wielded his knife on the week's Met's performances. "Dorothy Kirsten sang her practiced Tosca and Ettore Bastianini practiced his Scarpia," went one verdict—a sentence that has stuck with me for over five decades. Both men shared a tendency to describe singers as if they were children, sometimes brilliant, often wayward.

I parroted their words in a no-doubt obvious attempt to sound sophisticated. At the intermission of a 1965 *Traviata* at Lewisohn Stadium (uptown on the campus of CCNY), I airily dismissed Calvin Marsh's Germont as "just a meaningless vibration of air." The phrase must have been stolen from Kolodin, and it sounded especially snooty coming from the still-alto voice of a thirteen-year-old. My comment rankled a man seated nearby who leaned over and put me in my place. "Calvin Marsh happens to be a very good singer with a strong technique." He was about to go on but he must have seen me blush with shame because he contented himself with an eye-roll and a glare.

There is nothing unusual about a young musician immersing himself in recordings, live performances, and books, though I never met anyone else in my field who went to the University of Conrad L. Osborne like me. But I was not in the market for a new flesh-and-blood teacher. After my audition at the Yale School of Music I was gun-shy about continuing my piano studies with anyone besides Alex Farkas, and I shunned the idea of getting a master's degree at a conservatory. Yet through an odd series of events I managed to get myself through the doors of The Juilliard School.

DURING MY first year out of college, my high school friend Matthew Epstein was working as a high-level artist manager at Columbia Artists Management and would send occasional work my way—mostly playing opera auditions for his singers. After a season of this, he threatened to stop helping me unless I enrolled in Martin Isepp's class at Juilliard's Evening Division. Matthew could see that I was clinging to my childhood, and that I would benefit from a mentor in the highest echelons of the musical world. Martin fit the bill: he was the head coach at Britain's prestigious Glyndebourne Festival, he accompanied the legendary mezzo-soprano Janet Baker in recital, and he was moving to New York to lead Juilliard's opera program. The school had also roped him onto the faculty of their extension classes, where Martin was offering a course in art song interpretation for both singers and pianists. It was open to all comers who could make it past the entrance audition. I tried to argue with Matthew, but he had me over a barrel: work with Martin Isepp, or forfeit my only useful connection in the music business.

The school had moved into its Lincoln Center home four years earlier, and the new building still emitted the glacial ambience of a sci-fi movie, an Alphaville for Steinways. I was nervous before auditioning for Isepp, but he welcomed me with low-wattage warmth. He was a handsome, stocky man of medium height with a florid complexion and a shock of black hair. That afternoon he wore the strained smile of a man who has spent too many hours listening to amateur singers and pianists. He asked me to play something. After I had rippled through a Fauré song while he supplied a droning ad hoc vocal line, he asked me to sight-read something—and this time there was no doubt about my skills in that department. I aced the exam and went downstairs to get something I thought I'd never possess: a Juilliard ID.

I soon found out why Martin was so quick to pull me in for his class.

The other singers and pianists were filled with good intentions but stymied by clumsy fingers and rusty vocal cords. I was the youngest person in the room by a good twenty years, and the only one with even a fledgling professional career. When the semester was over, Martin relinquished his duties with the Evening Division, but he engineered a way for me to continue my lessons with him by adding me to the pool of Juilliard's staff pianists. Suddenly I was being paid five dollars an hour to crash the voice studios at Juilliard—a sweet deal. And Martin kept me on as a private student for the entire spring semester.

It wasn't difficult to get the handful of professional singers I knew to come to my lessons; they all jumped at the chance to sing for the head coach of Glyndebourne. But I also brought in some of the not-ready-for-prime-time singers I worked with, unaware that they were not up to his standards. Occasionally I saw him wince at their attempts to sing Mahler or Poulenc.

Since my classical music-making was a strange cocktail of impulsiveness and inhibition, Martin did his best to impose a sense of structure. He showed me how to balance the sonorities of the piano differently to complement male and female voices—more low sonorities for sopranos, more brilliance for baritones. And he awakened me to the pictorial elements of Lieder. In Brahms's "Von ewiger Liebe," he likened the open fifths under the words "Eisen und Stahl" (iron and steel) to the sounds of a forge. "Just a fancy of mine, I guess," he softly said. Fifty years later, I still give those open fifths their special Isepp-clang. More than anything, I picked up his way of establishing a tempo without rigidity, a feeling of music-as-river. I came to understand that an ongoing suggestion of rubato—tempo variation—was a way to signal strength and flexibility simultaneously to a singer. It was like saying, "I favor this tempo, but I'm not doctrinaire about it"—the way a waiter might divulge that "the chef suggests medium-rare for the lamb."

Yet when the new school year started the next fall, I instantly sensed that something had changed. Instead of the avuncular welcome I'd come to expect from Martin, his greeting was strangely cool and evasive. I pushed my luck, unwisely assuming he'd offer me the support of a father figure and spilled my guts about some colleague who I felt had done me dirt. Too late, I realized that I had trespassed Martin's boundaries. The damage was done. I might have been a talented pianist but I was becoming a handful. Our relationship was over, and there would be no more lessons.

Thankfully, I still had my Juilliard ID and my staff position, and soon got a gig playing hours of German diction classes and high-level voice lessons. It was a safe and cost-effective way to rip through a huge amount of vocal repertoire, and four semesters of German class finally gave me a leg up on Schubert, Brahms, and Schumann. Most of the voice teachers had outsize personalities (with egos to match). They were intent on putting me through my paces, while secretly wanting my approval. Beverley Peck Johnson spent the beginning of mezzo-soprano Faith Esham's lesson coaching me on Schubert's "Die Forelle"—the trout. "I don't see the little fish jumping!" she squawked. I tried again. Still no flying fish. After eight attempts I simply threw myself at the instrument hard, channeling all my exasperation into my hands. This finally got a reaction. "Ah! There! There are the little fish!"

I learned from everyone I worked with, but the real magician at the school was a professor named Daniel Ferro. After a decent if somewhat limited singing career, Dan had found his true calling as a voice teacher. Blessed with an exquisitely refined ear for the human voice, he was rapidly becoming the go-to guy for some of the biggest names in opera. Matthew Epstein, now a bit of a *macher* in the music world, sent almost everyone on his burgeoning roster to study with him. Dan had recently saved the soprano Evelyn Lear from a vocal crisis that could have finished her career. She'd been in obvious distress at the Met's 1970 revival of *Ariadne auf Naxos,* but under Dan's guidance she returned to triumph in their 1974 *Rosenkavalier.* Now she was the toast of the town, and Dan rose to fame as her Svengali—a role he played with grandeur.

Dan had recently lost the pianist who played his lessons, and he must have taken a shine

to the shy, gawky twenty-two-year-old with wild hair and less than perfect skin. I soon became the pianist for all his lessons at Juilliard.

Dan took a painterly approach to the voice, informed by a keen sense of color and weight, light and shade, scale and depth. I experienced a kind of synesthesia at his lessons: voices took on the shapes of sculpture. He had a way of molding the sound, lining it up into its most suitable proportions. He didn't advocate a single method for everyone. One mezzo was allowed to barrel into her chest voice—the thrilling, belty low register you need for Verdi—while another was encouraged to find a gentler, less obvious transition as her voice descended. "That is her *natura*," he told me, never one to use an English word if an Italian cognate came to mind.

"I may not be smart, but I'm talented," Dan once commented to me. Of course he was quite intelligent, but I could see what he meant. He was a creature of impulse and instinct, backed up by years of Italian training. He had developed some theories about the voice, and he used certain techniques and vocalises for all his students. But his true genius kicked in when he heard someone sing a song or an aria. His command of vowel modification was like Monet's control of pigment. There are infinite ways to sing an "ah" vowel—from sunshiny, bright Italian to hooty, covered British—and Dan could structure vocal positions the way great audio engineers fine-tune multitrack recordings. When he did, the voices would become radiant and free, soaring without pressure, shining with a halo of resonance and bolstered with a compact core. The sound seemed to break free of the body and fill the room with overtone.

Younger students were easily intimidated by his grand, old-school manner. If they were lazy or unprepared, or if he suspected they were burning the candle at both ends, the temperature in the room dropped ten degrees. He took singing seriously and expected students to do the same. But I also remember how sensitive he could be with the slender voices who were unlikely to enjoy a major operatic career. "That is not their *natura*," he would gently comment after they left. Most of all, I'm grateful for how he trusted and encouraged me, and nurtured my passion for singing.

No voice teacher is uncontroversial, least of all the most successful ones, and Dan's critics claimed that he offered nothing but a bag of tricks, producing special effects without substance. "He doesn't teach support," was one line of complaint; "he doesn't explain about the physiology of singing, the cricothyroid engagement," was another. I got him onto this subject once without challenging him openly. "Look, Steve, you can support and support and support, but if you're not singing with good registration, you're still going to sound lousy. If you get those balances right, the support simply emerges." While this argument may be a bit of a dodge, it does contain an element of truth. Dan may not have been analytical about breathing, but his singers still learned how to use their air with economy and artistry. Other Juilliard voice studios may have produced louder voices, but Dan had the market cornered for beauty. As for the cricothyroid (a little muscle that controls the larynx), Dan made quick work of it. "Singers work through sensation. Do you really think Caruso and Ponselle were consciously flexing their cricothyroid when they made those sounds?" Case closed.

While I was initially put off by Dan Ferro's Olympian hauteur, so unfashionable in the waning days of the Age of Aquarius, I soon realized I had arrived at the inner sanctum of singing, an honor offered only to a select few. In the three years I spent in his studio, Dan taught me to hear, an aural education no normal curriculum could have supplied. He lifted me from Conrad Osborne's intellectual realm into something that blended Realpolitik and alchemy. When a singer was tuned in to his wavelength, Room 572 became a magical laboratory. Over time I began to grasp how his spells worked—the subtle ways that sounds could be thinned, amplified, rounded, deepened, lightened, or darkened. I could hear the vocal positions he wouldn't like even before he waved his hand to interrupt a Donizetti aria or a song by Richard Strauss. His bel canto aesthetic became the basis of my own, and I've built on that foundation for the last five decades. I still hear voices as three-dimensional, sculptural objects: Häagen-Dazs (Renata Tebaldi), crème brûlée (Leontyne Price), pliant clay (Teresa Berganza), baseballs (Birgit Nilsson). Or liquids: red vermouth (Cesare Valletti), cassis syrup (Cesare Siepi), battery acid (Mick Jagger).

Dan was not the only powerful guru in my early twenties. My freelance existence contained multitudes, and as time went on I found my way into some of the most prestigious studios in Manhattan.

A mecca among them was Frank Corsaro's acting class, and every few months a director or a singer invited me to accompany a scene they were preparing for it. Established stars, neophytes with their first contracts, and New York wannabes all sat at the great man's feet. Frank's productions at New York City Opera had breathed life into Verdi and Puccini warhorses in unforgettable ways. Using traditional sets and costumes—Frank didn't need to set *Rigoletto* in Las Vegas to evoke pity and terror—he examined every nuance of the opera's music and libretto. With a sensibility forged at the Actor's Studio, he brought to the opera house the same kind of detailed scene work he used when directing straight plays. Arias and duets that in other venues might waft by in a generalized wash of emotion and vocal onanism suddenly revealed their depths. I don't think I'll ever see a greater production of *Faust* or *La Traviata*.

Frank was mercurial, one moment an elfin court jester, the next a spluttering Rumpelstiltskin. In class he played the role of provocateur, pummeling his students with questions. Many of them were rhetorical. "Who *says* you can't take a tempo liberty in a Fauré song?" he bellowed at a timid mezzo-soprano. The answer, for the record, is pretty much everyone, starting with Fauré himself. "Who cares how you *sing* it?" he thundered at a singer overly concerned about her voice. The real-world answer? Most people, particularly the soprano's auditioners. But received wisdom concerned him less than his students' flexibility of action and imagination. Anything that inhibited them, including good taste, could be thrown to the wind for a few hours. You didn't have to sing well in his class, and many didn't. But you had to step out of your comfort zone and let it rip.

I only saw Frank lose his temper once, when a student made a choice too daring even for him. She happened to be his wife, the mezzo-soprano Mary Cross Lueders, who asked me to accompany her in a scene from Massenet's *Werther*. She served as her own director, and during the lengthy introduction to the Letter Scene she played with fire. Literally. She held a piece of paper—one of Werther's letters—so close to the flame that she risked igniting it, along with the table, her hair, and her clothing. She also let the match burn practically down to her fingertips—several matches, as I recall. I had seen her working some of this business out during our rehearsals, but I figured it went along with

Frank's general ethos. It did not. I was used to hearing Frank yell but I'd never seen him at that level of fury. "How *dare* you put us through that? There's no opera, there's just a race to get the *fire* extinguishers!" His face looked apoplectic, but he allowed himself only a short rant in public. He was muttering to himself as he left class that night, and we all assumed that when Mary and Frank got home more sparks would fly—and not from a box of matches.

Breaking all the rules is exciting, but if you want to go down that road, it's helpful to know what they are in the first place. I was fortunate to work with a few teachers who made the parochial seem sexy. One was Janine Reiss, the reigning vocal coach in French repertoire during the 1970s and '80s. Once again, it was Matthew Epstein who sent me her way for a series of lessons in the winter of 1976. She was in town coaching the Met's new production of Meyerbeer's *Le prophète*. Janine had the lively presence of a French movie actress, and I had to remind myself not to look at her midriff in search of subtitles. At first I was brought up short by her outspoken distaste for some of the Met's cast members. "*Oh là là*, has he really sung like that for the past thirty years?" she clucked about one Met icon. "And his French—*épouvantable*!" About another, in a lowered voice, "I went to the head of the music staff and said, 'Are you actually going to allow her to make those noises onstage? *C'est pas possible!*'"

While French may be the language of love, French repertoire is often taught with the strict discipline of a Dickens schoolmaster: no unwritten tempo variations (no matter what Frank Corsaro says); firmly defined open and closed vowels, at the risk of having a Francophone fall on the floor laughing when you make a gaffe; the five nasal vowels clearly differentiated without sounding as though you're coming down with a cold; and a firm legato line bound together without the help of Italianate portamento slides.

Janine could see that I was blocking my natural musicianship, constrained by the rules that had been drummed into me by previous French coaches. And I was at the mercy of another powerful inhibition: when I played art song in those years, I was constantly trying to conceal my skills in music theater and cabaret. If I let go, I feared that my Ravel might emerge with the pelvic swing of Gershwin, my Schubert with the faint aroma of a klezmer band.

After Janine heard me play a few songs, she leaned toward me and said: "Steve, you have a marvelous quality. You know where not to go too far." It sounded especially alluring in French—"*Vous savez où ne pas aller trop loin.*" "But a French song is like a woman. It is good to be respectful. But if you do not soon kiss her, she will begin to ... *wonder.*"

Janine had a sweet singing voice with a rapid, Piaf-like vibrato. When she wanted to illustrate how a song went, she accompanied herself at the piano as she sang it to me. I can still hear her delicate voice in phrases from those sessions forty-five years ago: the perfect, liquid grace of "Et les oiseaux rasant de l'aile la colline" in Duparc's "Phydilé," the sudden stab of wounded pride in Gounod's "Ô ma belle rebelle" at the line "Me puisse-je un jour, *dure*!" Other singers have sung those pieces more luxuriantly, but none has ever matched Janine for those flashes of musical expressivity. With only a thread of sound she could make her voice smile or weep.

We worked on the introduction to Fauré's "Clair de lune," a famously difficult passage to get right. The downbeats are in the right hand, and it's easy to bonk the first sixteenth note of the left-hand pattern (an offbeat), turning the moonlight into a floodlight. There is also a spot just before the vocal entry where the "no unmarked ritardando" rule is almost impossible to observe without sounding like a constipated Kapellmeister. After my first attempt to spin moonbeams, Janine gestured me aside. When she played it, the music flowed. Her articulation was clear but she seemed to have no bones in her fingers. Sounds emerged from the piano without any obvious attack. And when she got to the transitional moment which I had dutifully tried to play in tempo, she gently applied the brakes for a brief, graceful slowdown.

"I thought you weren't supposed to take a ritard in Fauré!" I earnestly objected.

"That was not a ritard," she countered.

"But ... "

"That was *souplesse*. Suppleness. You cannot play Fauré without *souplesse*."

With that single word Janine set my music-making in a new direction. Lacking academic credentials, I was always anxious about my legitimacy in classical music. That anxiety could make my playing somewhat dry and careful, which I mistook for the sound of a bona fide conservatory graduate. The irony was that I had avoided music school precisely in order to preserve the fire and liquid freedom of my playing. Janine not only encouraged me to follow my musical instincts, she also gave me the vocabulary to reframe the rules. The premiere French coach in the world, a woman who had known Francis Poulenc personally, reminded me that classical music should be sexy, vivid, and flexible. If it is not, "it will begin to... wonder."

Without realizing it, I had cobbled together an ingenious apprenticeship, a way to learn from strong personalities who might have overwhelmed me in a formal school program. Each contributed to my growing musical refinement. And yet I also learned a tremendous amount in a voice studio where practically no one ever sang a note.

In the winter of 1974 I got a call from Martha Schlamme. Someone in her acting class was looking for a pianist. "His name is Mark Zeller, he teaches at NYU." She paused. "I... don't know what you'll think of him. But he needs a pianist this coming semester. Here's his number." I went to Mark's place and auditioned by accompanying him in a few show tunes, including a sweet song by Kander and Ebb called "The Happy Time." Apparently I passed muster, and he took me on for the spring term in 1975.

Mark was the most methodical of all the professors I'd worked with. He had constructed a set of exercises for teaching actors how to sing a theater song. For example, they had to say each word of the song on an upward inflection, as if asking a question: "I? Could? Have? Danced? All? Night?" This was to activate the upper register—the so-called head voice—and lift the sound out of the throat. I was tasked with playing the notes as they spoke, subconsciously teaching them the tunes—many of them could not read music. Mark's gridwork helped an actor get the rudiments of vocal placement, learn a tune, and delve into the lyrics. For a rabid sight-reader like me, it was torturously slow work. But for someone without any musical training, it could be a godsend.

One of Mark's exercises made an especially deep impression on me. The students were told to recite the lyrics of their song—once again, very slowly—but they were not to utter a word until they had formed a distinct visual image for it. When they did, I would play the corresponding melody note(s) for that word. It could take ten minutes just to get through "The Heather on the Hill": (long pause) "Can't (long pause) we (long pause) two (long pause) go (long pause) walking (long pause) together (long pause) . . . " I observed something fascinating: the essence of the song, its atmosphere and story, its inner life, magically began to permeate the room. No one knew what the student was seeing in those pauses, but when he or she said the word, it detonated. Simple, familiar lyrics took on the weight of Shakespeare. One day a young woman brought in Carole King's "You've Got a Friend," and by the second line we were all in tears.

Once in a while the exercise would backfire. Another actress was working on the song "Mira" from *Carnival*. She worked her way through the opening lyrics—"I came on two buses and a train . . . can you imagine that, can you imagine that, two buses and a train"—and pretty soon the entire class was doubled over in laughter.

Mark's work was meticulous, technical, and uniform—the opposite of the divinely inspired Dan Ferro, the brilliantly chaotic Frank Corsaro, the multifaceted and sensual Janine Reiss. But he had hooked into a formula for revealing the hidden depths of song lyrics. In the process, he provided me with a solution to the Schwarzkopf dilemma. You don't have to go camping in the Schwarzwald to sing the German word for "forest." You just need an image drawn from your own imagination, and the more powerful the better. It could be the California sequoias, or the tree outside your childhood home, or even the tangle of a lover's hair. Nobody needs to know. Save your airfare and spend it instead on a good course in German diction—your American *L* could use work.

While Mark's method was rigid and seldom included any actual music-making, his class did possess a powerful element of sensuality—in the person of Paul Oertel, one of his students. Paul was always the first to get up and work each week because he had another class later that afternoon—and I made sure to be on time. He was smart, handsome, and visionary—a man who could induce a dizzying bliss. I fell pretty hard for Paul, and we enjoyed the kind of passionate love affair you can only have when you're twenty-three. It was Paul who finally delivered the "Souzay kiss" I'd read about ten years earlier. Alas, at the end of the semester he was leaving New York to get married to a woman in Colorado, and I was heartbroken when our romance ran its course.

Still, I'll always be indebted to Paul. He remains one of my greatest teachers—just not about music.

Martha Schlamme, exuding charm in the late 1970s with her trademark smile.

CHAPTER 5

Mentors and Tormentors

WHILE I PLAYED for many artists during the first dozen years of my career, Martha Schlamme was always the refrain. My time with her ran the gamut from the heights (a Carnegie Hall début and a sensational night at the Pavilion of the Ravinia Festival) to the depths (soggy evenings at suburban cabarets in front of a smattering of comatose audience members).

I was twenty-one when Martha and I met, she was almost fifty—"approaching middle age" as she put it. ("From which end?" my mother wondered.) I was a beginner; she was a divinely gifted, one-of-a-kind cabaret artist trying to rekindle a career that had flamed out.

In the 1950s Martha had been on top of the world. By the end of the decade, she had sung over a thousand concerts in the United States and appeared alongside the biggest folk-music stars, legends like Pete Seeger and Joan Baez. Having been one of the *Kindertransport* children relocated to England from Vienna before World War II, she was not afraid to sing about the peril of European Jews. Her status as a triumphant refugee brought a note of hope to an audience hungry for comfort. But her star began to wane as a new, more militant wave of performers rose up to confront the issues of the 1960s—particularly the Vietnam War, which claimed the lives of well over 58,000 young Americans. One day she walked into a record store and asked the sales clerk if they had the new record by "that marvelous singer Martha Schlamme." "Yes," the clerk replied without looking up. "Well, where is it?" "Where do you think? She's in the Jewish bin." It was a sign: it was time to climb out of the Jewish bin.

Thinking that the theater could serve as an escape route, Martha took classes with the renowned teacher Uta Hagen and became a devoted acolyte. Yet her second career as an actress was only a qualified success. She did some replacement work on Broadway, most notably a few months as Golde in *Fiddler on the Roof*, as well as several straight plays at the Long Wharf Theatre in New Haven, Connecticut. But hers was an intimate, personal art. She could tailor her solo concerts to her strengths, a virtuoso display of vulnerability and moral fiber. Without the safe backdrop of a grand piano, though, Martha could look as if she were floundering. When the big dramatic moments came, she tended to jab the air with a schoolmarm's pointed finger as her voice turned to a rasp.

Years later, a sophisticated director friend, Peter Schifter, dismissed her airily. "Martha? She's simply not a professional." I now understand what he meant. Her artistic fervor was born out of a sense of what was truthful, and this was the source of her greatness. But it was also the source of her limitations. If a director asked her to do something she considered false, she lacked that indispensable reserve of stagecraft, or stage artifice, to come up with a believable facsimile. Unlike many performers, she never planned her gestures—they emerged spontaneously each time in the heat of the moment. "I can't think about my hands," she once confided. "The minute I look at my hands, I feel phony. I think, Oh my god, whose hand is *that*?"

By the time Martha and I connected, she was mainly back to her singing career. For the first few years of our collaboration, everything went smoothly enough. She landed some gigs at the more prestigious clubs in town—Reno Sweeney, the Ballroom. One night my teacher Martin Isepp came to hear us and he brought along soprano Kiri Te Kanawa, the toast of the town after her sensational début at the Met in *Otello*. The two divas held a love fest after the performance. "I wish I could do what you do!" gushed Kiri. "Oh, but what you do is so thrilling!" Martha returned, without complete sincerity. She mistrusted people who sang well, particularly women.

Meanwhile I was beginning to be wary about being tied down to a single singer. After the initial joy of being hired to accompany an established artist, I grew tired of playing gigs in out-of-the-way nightclubs and community centers. More than anything I longed to be taken seriously in the classical world, despite all the strikes against me. And Martha, alas, appeared to be the biggest strike of all. In the caste system of New York's music scene of the time, a cabaret pianist who played Jewish folksongs for an aging chanteuse was disqualified from the upper echelons of art song.

What I did not understand was how much I was learning from Martha. Even as I was trying to wriggle free, she was providing the greatest gifts a mentor can offer: a clear set of ideals and what amounted to a user's manual for artistic intuition. For one thing, she was a terrific programmer. She could put together material from entirely different genres to explore a big subject like marriage or war, effortlessly bridging all the divergent styles. One of her medleys linked a Jacques Brel song ("Sons of...") with a poem by Edna St. Vincent Millay ("Dirge Without Music"), ending with an Irish folk song ("Johnny I Hardly Knew Ye"). In her hands it became an antiwar collage of startling power, performance after performance.

The power Martha summoned was born out of a deep respect for the songs she chose, no matter their provenance, and an uncanny awareness of which songs would detonate for her. When we read through a stack of potential new pieces, I knew we'd hit pay dirt when Martha began to cry. She would get up from the piano bench in search of Kleenex, and when she finally emerged from her bedroom, red-eyed and sniffling, she would stammer, "Oh, it's going to be a *wonderful* performance!" At the time I dismissed these outbursts as self-indulgent, but they were actually teaching me another valuable lesson—it's good to cry during rehearsal. Let the emotion sweep through you. It will be money in the emotional bank when you take the song to the public.

I could never predict what songs would please her. She sometimes opened her show with "Come In From the Rain," a sentimental ballad by Melissa Manchester which Martha invested with Chekhovian weight. But she disdained a Noël Coward song I brought her, "This

Is a Changing World," though I'd been certain she would gravitate to its wise, philosophical advice about the passage of time. In retrospect, I probably should have found a more appropriate recording than the swoopy, mush-mouthed rendition by Joan Sutherland. The cut ended and Martha gently said, "Oh Stevie, nobody needs to hear a song like that." Although Noël Coward and Joan Sutherland were superstars, revered by millions, for Martha the song sounded hollow. "Pretty," she called it—a slur in her lexicon.

Her terse dismissal opened the floodgates of my critical acumen, and I began to question all received wisdom about music. I could no longer assume a piece of music was "great" simply because others had decided it was. Half a century later, certain canonic works evoke the same response in me: nobody needs to hear a song like that.

Though fragile, Martha was a survivor, and her sureness of purpose could be breathtaking. Early in our partnership we performed a Sunday afternoon concert at a church on Manhattan's East Side. Everything was going well until the end, when a woman started screaming from the back of the hall. It was hard to understand what she was saying—could it have been a rant about the Rosenbergs? The Irish Troubles? An antisemitic diatribe? As she charged toward the stage, guards caught the woman and ushered her out of the room. There was a stunned silence as we all looked at Martha. She took a deep breath and announced, "I have found that the only response to things like that is to answer with love. And so I'd like to close with a song by Jacques Brel, 'Quand on n'a que l'amour,' 'If We Only Have Love.'" She turned to me: "Stevie?" And just like that, she lifted a turbulent corner of the world into a realm of peace.

It's not surprising that Martha could be somewhat messianic in her belief that song could change the world. Music had been core to some of the great social movements she had lived through, and in her prime she had been at the forefront of them all. The problem was that her purity as an artist was inextricably tangled with an intense neediness, a void in her soul that needed to be filled. She wanted her music to offer clarity and a sense of purpose to listeners, but in exchange she needed the audience's love to keep her own demons at bay. She was prone to singing seven or eight encores, tantamount to another half-program after the ostensible finale. For her adoring fans it was a feast, but the feast could turn into an embarrassment of riches. One evening as we returned backstage after encore number seven, she excitedly proposed another. It was our second show that night, the clock said 12:30 a.m., and I cautiously suggested we call it quits. She looked stricken. "But I wouldn't want to rob them of my 'Surabaya Johnny!'" I sighed at this quintessential Martha moment, knowing that after the sadness of the Kurt Weill lament we'd bow again, and she (after a "Well, I can't leave you there, can I?") would launch into a cheerful up-tempo number, which I could only pray would be the last.

With Martha the good and the bad were so intertwined that it was easy for me to undervalue what this passionate artist was teaching me. To be fair, I had a lot to synthesize in those days. At my Juilliard gig, Dan Ferro was promoting a kind of vocal refinement Martha considered intrinsically lifeless. In a studio ten blocks south, Frank Corsaro was throwing caution to the winds and tapping into the wild power of the id, while downtown at NYU Mark Zeller was harnessing the quietly judgmental aura of the superego to corral his students into artistic discipline. Martha was more Jungian in her approach, guided by an infallible instinct for what material would work for her and how it would fit into her carefully honed program. Though it wasn't clear to me at the time, it was Martha's sensitivity and iconoclasm that would most inform my own guiding principles in the future.

Our collaboration took a dramatic turn in 1975 when Martha introduced me to Alvin Epstein, her co-star in a Kurt Weill show she had first devised in the 1960s with the singer-actor Will Holt. Martha had been smitten with Alvin when they first worked together in 1968, only to discover that the only thing they had in common sexually was a preference for men. By the time I met them, they'd settled into a competitive brother-and-sister relationship, built on a delicate balance of dependence, love, and grievance. *A Kurt Weill Cabaret,* Martha and Alvin's first collaboration, had served as the opening show of the now-legendary Yale Cabaret, and they were reprising it seven years later to kick off the Cabaret's 1975–76 season. As Martha's regular accompanist, I was at the head of the line to inherit the Kurt Weill gig from the now-unavailable Bill Westney. The show featured some of the composer's most famous songs from his years in Berlin, Paris, and New York ("The Bilbao Song," "September Song") as well as a few rarities, including one scrawled in that infamous orange Magic Marker. Martha and Alvin had constructed a gritty love-her-and-leave-her narrative from the material, a relationship that developed over the course of the evening.

We went up to Alvin's Connecticut home to rehearse, where we found Alvin flu-ridden, unable to go onstage. Martha filled in with performances of her solo show on Thursday and Friday. By Saturday Alvin was well enough to leave his house, and that night I made my *Kurt Weill Cabaret* début, on an upright piano with the tonal richness of a vacuum cleaner. Those two performances were the first of hundreds I eventually played, including a national tour and a run on Broadway at the Bijou Theater during the 1979–80 season. The show required a strong pianist: both singers favored breakneck tempi for songs like "Oh Moon of Alabama" and "Mack the Knife"; Alvin needed hurricane-force energy for his solos, while Martha wanted the lightest sound possible. For their duets, I did my best to shift between first and fourth gear.

I'd seen Alvin onstage for years at the Yale Rep—brilliantly creepy as Molière's Don Juan, a maelstrom of inarticulate anger as Büchner's Woyzeck. By then he was already a theater legend, having made his Broadway début in 1956 as Lucky in the first New York performances of Beckett's *Waiting for Godot*, alongside Bert Lahr and E. G. Marshall. He followed that triumph playing the Fool to Orson Welles's King Lear, and even landed a role in Richard Rodgers's 1962 musical *No Strings*. Alvin was the most cultured person I had ever met, and I started to fall for him.

Our relationship began about a year after those first Kurt Weill shows at Yale. Martha smiled through her tears when she learned of it: "I'll dance at your wedding," she sniffled. But the honeymoon lasted just a few months. Alvin was not what I'd call an easy boyfriend, nor was I. His propensity to abrupt rages could be terrifying, while my lack of self-awareness must have presented huge challenges to him. His friends, more than twice my age, saw me as a boy toy. In most social gatherings everyone gravitated to Alvin, while I faded into the woodwork—except

The very complex Alvin Epstein in 1977,
getting a moment of R & R at his house in
Southold, Connecticut.

when we were with people my own age. Then he was the odd man out, a fifty-something surrounded by a bunch of kids. We didn't look alike, but when we traveled, everyone assumed we were father and son because of our obvious intimacy. At our infrequent best, we were like those classic Greek pairings of young lover and wise master.

Our incompatibilities began with the age difference and fanned out into a dazzling array of logjams. For one thing, we were often living in different cities over the six years we were together. Alvin first was based in New Haven, then took up residence in Minneapolis for an unhappy year running the Guthrie Theater. After a few seasons in New York, he relocated to Cambridge for the inauguration of the American Repertory Theater. I tagged along when I could, but nothing seemed to be adding up. It became more and more difficult to be with a partner twice my age as I moved into my late twenties.

Yet, being in a relationship with Alvin probably saved my life. My previous attempts at romance had led to nothing but failure, and I felt threatened by the gay *vida loca* of the late '70s. When the AIDS crisis began making its inexorable attack on the gay community I needed a refuge more than ever. Even if my home life with Alvin was not peaceful, it offered a safe haven from the sybaritic party downtown—a party that would end all too soon.

What Alvin and I did have in common was powerful enough to hold us together for over half a decade: a passion for music and theater that I have shared with few others. Did we also have a passion for one another? Yes, in our way. We were deeply entrenched in each other's life and work over the six years we were together, and profoundly devoted to one another in spite of our blood-curdling arguments.

Although he himself never went to college, Alvin was like a one-man graduate school for me. At the Met or New York City Opera, I was routinely treated to his running commentary. When the soprano in Tchaikovsky's *Pique Dame* walked onstage, Alvin muttered, "Wrong shoes." "What?" "You don't wear little pumps like that in a Russian winter." At a City Opera *Fledermaus,* Beverly Sills was camping it up in the role of Adele. "That's not a lady's maid," hissed Alvin. When Johanna Meier entered as Rosalinde, he leaned over: "And that's not a lady."

A 1982 Met performance of *Lucia di Lammermoor* starring Joan Sutherland and Alfredo Kraus was a major occasion; Sutherland had been away from New York for a number of seasons, this was her signature role, could she still sing it? When they came to the famous Act II sextet, everyone went into what we call "park-and-bark" position: plant your feet and deliver the goods to the back of the hall. I can accept a certain amount of park-and-bark at the opera, but not Alvin. This time he held his comments until intermission, when he exploded. "It looks like they're all waiting for the *subway*! All it needs it for Sutherland to take a step forward and peer into the wings to see if the *train* is coming!" This was accompanied by a devastating imitation of the diva's posture and facial expression—admittedly the strongest acting performance of the evening.

This was nothing compared to going to a play or a movie with Alvin. If I had the temerity to have enjoyed something he found wanting—like Lanford Wilson's *Fifth of July* or Robert Altman's *Three*

Women—we could have fights that emptied restaurants. (Though usually, the restaurant was already empty, since Alvin was the slowest eater I have ever known. When he was done with a T-bone steak or a lobster, you could practically place the remains in a vitrine at the Museum of Natural History.)

Very occasionally, Alvin would step in to coach me at the piano. After a dress rehearsal for a concert in Aspen, I asked him whether I'd been too loud or too soft. "Steve," he said, "you weren't loud enough *and* you weren't soft enough." Those few simple words changed my music-making forever, knocking me out of my safe middle ground to search for a bolder spectrum of colors and dynamics.

Alvin's process as an actor was mysterious; he rarely explained it, and it was the product of so many sources. As a teenager he attended New York's High School of Music & Art, where he dreamed of being either a painter or a pianist. His adult mentors included the theater designer and theoretician Gordon Craig and modern dance legend Martha Graham. When he studied with the great French mime Étienne DeCroux, Marcel Marceau was one of his classmates. As a result, Alvin was able to see and hear with uncanny precision, and his repertoire of physical gestures appeared limitless. His verbal delivery ran the gamut from the deliberate to the breakneck, from the hushed to the thunderous. In the Kurt Weill show, I never tired of hearing him introduce the "Mandalay Song": "Mutter Goddam's *Puff* in Mandalay . . . oh what *Puff* that was!" he murmured. The timing of that little pause, the sense of wonder and regret and memory in those few seconds! No one needed to be told that a *Puff* was a bordello. The explosion of air on the initial *P* and lingering on the final *F* said it all.

One day I walked in on him as he was working on a new role. The script was in his lap as he repeated the words like a high-speed mantra. Though aware that I might be trespassing at the wrong moment, I had to understand what I'd seen him doing. He answered me with surprising gentleness. "You have to say the words over and over and over again until they're *your* words," he explained. "And then you have the character." It seems simplistic until you grasp what he meant by "your words"—an ownership that wells up from your soul.

At Aspen, he guided singers through the well-memorized texts of their songs and arias until they were actually saying what they were saying. Pretending to be a very slow, hard-of-hearing dolt, he'd keep asking his student, "What? Where? I don't get it," and looking confused until they grew completely exasperated. I'll never hear the "Seguédilla" from *Carmen* without remembering Alvin's half-crazed face trying to make sense of the lyrics: "Near the walls of... where? "Seville!" shouted the increasingly frustrated mezzo. "Huh?" "SEVILLE!" Your friend... who? "Lillas Pastia." "I don't catch you, who?..." "LILLAS PASTIA!" You're going to drink... what?" "Manzanilla. MAN-ZA-NI-LLA!" When he finally allowed her to sing the aria, she delivered it with clarity and—an added bonus—a kind of feral sex appeal I'd never before seen in her.

Martha and Alvin were my Art Parents. I may have placed myself in a kind of gay Oedipal situation—sleeping with my father and, while not killing my mother, sometimes wanting to—but they provided a sanc-

Me outside the Bijou Theater in 1979 before a performance of *A Kurt Weill Cabaret*, surrounded as always by Alvin and Martha.

tuary when I needed one. For all her excesses, Martha taught me the essentials of performing concerts in a way I could never have learned in a conservatory, while Alvin educated my eye and ear, sharpened my sensitivities, and refined my taste. By my early thirties, though, I was feeling the need to assert some independence from both parents without losing them as friends and colleagues. Severing romantic ties with Alvin was not easy; immediately after we had The Discussion, he seemed to forget everything I had just said. We had to repeat the whole ceremony a few more times before he was able to understand that we'd morphed from partners to friends. Still, it was a relatively peaceable breakup after six-plus years as a couple. He was busy in Cambridge by then, and it was not unreasonable for me to want a partner I could see more often.

The break with Martha was far more dramatic. It began one evening in 1981 at the Guggenheim Museum, which was opening an important show of German Expressionist art. The museum's gala committee thought a program of Kurt Weill songs would be just the thing to entertain their wealthy patrons, and who better than Martha Schlamme and Alvin Epstein, fresh from their acclaimed performances on Broadway? The Guggenheim had been specific: "Just thirty minutes, shows at 8:30 and 10." Now, it was nearly impossible for Martha to program a thirty-minute set. "No one will complain if we are generous," she assured me as she loaded the program with their biggest hits. Technically speaking, she was correct: the audience did not complain. They simply walked out. We started our first show with a full house, but soon we found ourselves performing to a sea of retreating backsides as everyone but twenty-four people (mostly our friends) left the hall in search of things they preferred—booze, paintings, their buddies.

The second show was even worse, a smaller initial crowd thinning down to nine die-hards, all of them people we'd invited. Normally our Weill show ended with a bravura gesture: Martha, Alvin, and I each took a shift at the piano to play "Mack the Knife" as one of us took a solo bow. At the early show our bows had felt like dancing a minuet on the *Titanic*. By evening's end it seemed ridiculous to grandstand for the nine friends who had stayed in the hall. Catching Alvin's eye after the last song, I signaled a desperate "Can we just get out of here?" with my eyebrows. He nodded assent, I rose from the piano, we bowed as a group, and the whole soggy event was over.

After belting back some of the Guggenheim's white wine, the three of us piled into a cab. Alvin was quietly disgusted, I seethed in silence. This unfortunately left the floor open to Martha, who launched into a diatribe about rich, entitled people who don't recognize Art when it's staring them in the face, who show neither manners nor respect for Kurt Weill and his greatest living interpreters. As we rounded the corner to my apartment, Martha finally laced into me. "And then, *Herr Professor Blier* decides to take matters in his *own hands* and *cuts the bow*! As if it were *his* decision! An attack from the *inside*!" At this point I heard a disturbing growl, like a jaguar about to devour an ocelot. It took me a moment to realize that I was the source of the noise, and what's more on the verge of throttling Martha. Alvin grabbed me just as I leaned over to go for her throat. Opening the cab door, he practically threw me onto the sidewalk, and the cab zoomed off.

Being attacked for making the one sensible decision of the evening had ignited a firebomb within me. While Alvin didn't condone my behavior, I got the feeling that he was grudgingly impressed by the sudden appearance of my id at full blast. No one had expected the most passive-aggressive member of the trio to bust out in the back seat of a cab. Still, lunging for a colleague's throat after a concert *can* lead to a period of awkwardness. Martha and I had a gig a few days later, just a couple of songs at a midtown luncheon. After first approaching each other like ambassadors from warring nations, we managed to entertain the crowd in spite of our lingering rancor. Eventually I was able to apologize, and Martha responded with her classic mixture of insight and misunderstanding. "I talked to my therapist about what happened and he told me, 'Steven's anger wasn't about you. He was expressing an entire *lifetime* of anger.'" The first part of that statement, at least, sidestepped the truth: Martha was indeed driving me nuts.

I persuaded her to take on another pianist for gigs I couldn't play, an easier ask after nearly punching her in the head. Eventually two other pianists came on duty—Richard Bower and Harry Huff, fine musicians and easygoing guys, able to roll with all the punches of Martha's wide-ranging repertoire. When time permitted I continued to work with both Martha and Alvin, and once I was freed from exclusive servitude, my heart opened to them again. They rewarded me with some first-class gigs: a long run at the Harold Clurman Theater in 1984, and an engagement at the Jerusalem Festival in the summer of 1985—both the *Kurt Weill Cabaret* and Martha's one-woman show. The Israelis were less interested in Brecht-Weill than we'd expected ("This Marxism stuff, ach, we've heard it all before, and Brecht was awful to women, wasn't he?"), but they loved Weill's Broadway songs, as well as Martha's eclectic repertoire and eager charm.

After Israel, Martha went off to teach at the Chautauqua Institute in upstate New York, where she was also slated to do her one-woman show at their most important venue, the outdoor amphitheater. Our relationship by then had reached a golden period, especially after her success in Jerusalem. When I joined her in Chautauqua, I found that as usual, she had bonded strongly with the students, who worshiped her. But she was in an agitated state. Her father had just died, and there was no way she could get to the funeral in London. It would have meant canceling her appearance in the amphitheater, which had taken on mythic proportions for her.

I also learned that Martha was embroiled in a feud with her boss, the famously tactless Cynthia Auerbach. As the director of the opera program, Cynthia had felt free to make substantial changes in Martha's student cabaret show—to make it, in her words, more "audience-oriented." This was no trivial matter for Martha. She felt her work had been violated, and that her relationship to her students had been compromised.

This was why Martha had attached so much significance to her Chautauqua concert. It had to be a triumph that would justify her absence from her dad's funeral, and it also needed to be a vindication of her artistic principles, the most important thing in her life. She looked especially soignée that night—one of the makeup artists had worked her magic on Martha's face—and there was a fierceness about her that I had not often encountered. The show got off to a good start, and she spoke to the crowd about her father's passing before singing a *nigun*, the traditional wordless Jewish prayer that she always included. We were more than halfway through Act I when we arrived at Bernstein's "I Am Easily Assimilated," from *Candide*, which she had added to her rep fairly recently.

The song is about being a survivor, a multilingual immigrant who imagines she can slip into any culture and blend seamlessly into her new surroundings. After the second verse we had inserted a short piano break, during which Martha improvised a kind of folk dance. It was the only moment during her program when I could dig into the piano without worrying about volume. I piled into Bernstein's tango with gusto as Martha clapped her hands over her head and sashayed around the stage. Suddenly she stopped and darted a look of fear my way. She lurched toward her chair. My first thought was, "Oh God, I'm playing too loud, she's angry."

"Stevie, I'm fainting," she whispered.

Martha was such a spontaneous performer that I blurted out, "For real? Or for the song?" "For real," she rasped.

I walked immediately to the mike. "Is there a doctor in the house?"

Three men came racing down the aisle, took one look at her, lifted her up, and carried her to the theater's back porch where they laid her down on a long bench. All at once there was a small crowd of people—a few staffers, some friends—trying to help. One woman insisted that Martha was having an allergic reaction to her new makeup: "I saw this before with another friend. You *must* take off her makeup!" Martha, fighting for her life, fixated on this idea and demanded they wash her face. One of the doctors made a motion to remove the kibitzer. Pretty soon they called an ambulance. Martha drifted into unconsciousness before our eyes. She had suffered a stroke.

Four of us trailed behind the ambulance to the Jones Memorial Health Center in Jamestown. There was nothing to do but wait. We barely spoke. Finally a doctor emerged at one am. The stroke was serious, located in the brain stem. It was as though someone had pulled the plug on her very being.

She remained in a coma, and I traveled up to visit her four weeks later. In her hospital bed she looked serene. I realized that I had never seen her face without furrows of tension and stress. Her friend Valerie

Van Winkle was tending to her. "Take her hand, talk to her. She can hear you."

"She can? How do you know?"

"Please, just believe me."

I wish I'd had the presence of mind to say something profound and heartfelt to resolve all our past discord. But I was too freaked out, and felt inhibited by Valerie's presence. I'm afraid my words were generic and brief. So here is what I should have said: "Martha, you showed me my life's mission. You were uncompromising. You believed in the power of art, and you fought like a trouper. I am going to do the same, and use everything I learned from you. You were a piece of work, but you taught me better than you ever realized."

After two months in a coma, Martha departed this world. I was devastated by her death, which coincided with my father's downward slide into the cancer that would claim his life two years later. I remained in contact with Alvin, who had taken up residence in Cambridge for the American Repertory Theater, and our friendship took on a lovely patina as the years went by. He generously reached out to help me in the aftermath of a particularly brutal breakup, and I was touched that he was there when I got married in 2012. (I thought back to Martha's promise to dance at my wedding thirty-seven years earlier.) Even so, staying in touch with Alvin got to be a laborious process. In his later years it could take weeks to locate him. Although he owned a smartphone, he tended to lose it or let messages pile up to the point where no one could get through. As for email, he did check it regularly, if "regularly" meant once a month.

In 2019, wanting to be in contact around the holidays, I started the process of calling Alvin in late November, and after a few weeks managed to get through. His mind was still razor sharp, but there was even more dead air between sentences than usual. By then he had moved to an assisted living residence. I wanted in particular to ask him about a piece of advice I often use in my teaching. "What I tell my students is: first you work on a song, then you have to let the song work on you. Is that right?" Long silence.

"Say it again." I did. Another Alvin-length pause.

"Yes. Exactly. That's amazing."

"Alvin, I learned that from you." "You did?" "That, and practically everything else I know."

It was my last conversation with him. He died a few weeks later, and I received the news at the worst possible moment. Idly checking my phone ten seconds before going onstage for a Christmas cabaret show, I saw an email notification from my high school friend Katrin Peck. The abbreviated subject line read "Alvin Epstein, 94, Known for Beckett..." and her message began, "I think you knew this guy." I didn't need to open the mail. Alvin was gone, and I had to play a comedy show for a crowd of Brooklyn hipsters. I remembered Martha's braving it out after she'd lost her father. And I could hear Alvin's voice urging me on: "Stevl"—his nickname for me—"go do your thing. You'll have plenty of time to mourn me." So I did, and we had a pretty good night in front of an audience that grew more and more raucous as they kept drinking.

I never experienced the cathartic crying jag that Martha's death had provoked, maybe because Alvin is still alive within me. Every time I speak to an audience, I feel I am channeling him. In a recent dream, he called to say he was coming over to see me before taking a cross-country trip, relocating from San Francisco to Boston. Nonplussed, I eventually asked, "I don't mean to be rude, but are you alive or dead?" There was an Alvin-length pause before the answer came: "It's complicated."

Patricia Brooks, operatic sorceress, in *Puritani*.
© *Beth Bergman*

CHAPTER 6

No Career in Song

IN THE FIRST decade of my career, I nourished a dream to be the pianist on an LP of art song with a famous singer, preferably with my face splayed on the cover next to theirs. Being a successful cabaret pianist felt like winning the booby prize, and no matter how much I was learning from Martha and Alvin, my work with them felt like a holding pattern. Of course, I had no concrete plan for ascending the musical food chain. And for the first few years I was content just to be accepted as a professional musician in the rough-and-tumble world of Manhattan. After the Yale School of Music's decisive kick in the teeth, every gig, no matter how insignificant, felt like a sweet victory. In the classical world, I made my way with a talent for the non-Teutonic fringes of art song, a flair for French and Italian opera, and a fearsome ability as a sight-reader. These, along with my knack for the popular music of any nationality, had set me up as a working pianist. So did my willingness to play anything that got thrown my way.

Outside of my cabaret work, my concert opportunities were mostly limited to Sunday matinées in libraries, the occasional tour with Community Concerts, and début recitals with singers who had won competitions. This was how, in 1982, I was able to play at what was then called Carnegie Recital Hall (now Weill Hall) with a soprano named Maria Russo. Having taken first prize in the long-vanished East-West Artists Competition, Maria presented a program of traditional art songs that ended with two arias: one from *I Capuleti ed i Montecchi*, Bellini's setting of *Romeo and Juliet*; the other from Boito's *Mefistofele*, a barn-burner that would become a staple of her European career.

After the concert a tall, distinguished gentleman approached me. "I am Lorenzo Alvary," he intoned, his sepulchral, Hungarian-accented voice instantly recognizable from Metropolitan Opera intermission broadcasts. Alvary had been on the Met roster for thirty-one seasons, and his Magyar cadences permeated the company's English-language recording of *Così fan tutte*. By age seventy-one he had stepped into the role of impresario-at-large, judging competitions and dispensing advice. It was in the last of these capacities that he extended his compliments.

"You played the Boito aria very well. Who taught you how to do that?"

It was a question I was becoming familiar with, along with the puzzled, somewhat crochety look that accompanied it. "I grew up with opera," I told him. "I love playing the Bellini too," I offered.

"No. The Bellini, not right. But the *Mefistofele*, very good."

"Thank you," I said, as I tried to figure out what I'd done wrong. "I play Bellini like Chopin," I ventured, a remark that may as well have been in Martian.

"You should come to Europe. You could play in the biggest aria competitions, like the one in Barcelona, the Viñas. I could speak to them. You'd do very well."

This was like telling me that I could be a line cook in a respected diner, when I aspired to be a chef in a five-star restaurant. Other pianists might have jumped at the encouragement, but I demurred. I played opera arias all the time when singers were auditioning for roles, but I didn't think of it as very exalted work. I was essentially a functionary at someone else's job interview. "Actually, I want to focus my career on song," I confided.

His reaction was instantaneous, and violent. "Song? *Song*? There *is no career in song*! Even Elly *Ameling* cannot sell out Carnegie Hall!!" By now he was screaming, and his face had reddened. "You—vill—play—OPERA!" Then he turned and loped away in high dudgeon. It was as though I had refused the princely hand in marriage, while I waited for my dream husband—a unicorn.

I had my reasons. Pianists who work in opera houses usually begin by toiling in rehearsal rooms, cranking out hours of orchestral reductions for stagings and sessions with the conductor. It can be strenuous work, especially pounding out the accompaniments for the chorus and the ballet. I have many friends who love that job, which can eventually lift you into the upper echelons of an opera house as an administrator or assistant conductor. But since few opera orchestrations actually include the piano, I would never get to be part of the show I'd just prepared. For me, that was the deal-breaker. Line cook? More like prep cook.

The waning ticket sales of an art song icon like Elly Ameling seemed like an arcane metric for a major career decision. But there was a more concrete reason Lorenzo Alvary's words fell on deaf ears. By the time of Maria Russo's recital, I had learned that playing opera arias and working for an opera company are completely different things. I spent the summers of 1975 and 1976 as an apprentice coach at the Wolf Trap Opera Company, one of our country's best programs for budding opera singers. It proved to be my début and my swan song in opera. I was miserable in the job, in both senses—unhappy and inept. At the end of the second summer I was so tied up in knots that I landed in the emergency room with severe stomach cramps, which I feared might be appendicitis. The fact that it was merely trapped gas in my guts did nothing to comfort me. Opera companies and I were done.

Still, Alvary did have a point. Back in the 1940s and '50s, voice recitals had been an intrinsic part of the New York concert scene. If you sang a début concert at Town Hall, you could get six or seven reviews, and you might pull a glowing quote from one of them to feature in your publicity material. A few positive words from a newspaper might lead to more concert work for both singers and pianists. But by the 1980s the traditional début recital was becoming a relic, and no major critics would review a singer they'd never heard of. Arts journalism was starting to shrink—fewer newspapers and magazines covered classical music at all, and space was disappearing in the ones that did.

Blind to this, I pressed forward haphazardly. Besides competition winners, my concert opportunities tended to come in two other categories: opera singers on the rise who were able to book tours with

Community Concerts, a New York–based operation that scheduled performances throughout the United States; and big stars no longer in their first youth who could still fill a hall.

Of these, the competition winners provided me with the most interesting artistic opportunities. I was lucky enough to form partnerships with two gifted baritones, Christopher Trakas and William Sharp, both of whom had won the Young Concert Artists competition (Bill in 1982, Chris in 1983); Chris went on to share first place in the 1985 Naumburg Competition with Dawn Upshaw, and Bill walked off with the top award in the Carnegie Hall International American Music Competition in 1987.

Bill and Chris provided me with the thing I needed most: a profusion of recital dates with first-class partners. The Naumburg prize included a concert for Chris and me at Alice Tully Hall, where megastar conductor James Levine prowled around the auditorium at our dress rehearsal to "fine-tune the balances" (though I actually received no comments from him). We also got a recording contract, though neither the cover art nor the liner notes included my picture. John Musto, then at the beginning of an illustrious career, wrote us a beautiful song cycle, *Shadow of the Blues*, which we premiered on the disc.

The American Music Competition came through with even more dazzling prizes—a recital in Carnegie Hall and another recording contract, issued on both CD and LP. As a voracious record-listener since childhood, I treasured catching vinyl's last gasp before it succumbed to the invasion of compact discs. Our program included yet another Musto premiere: the opulent three-song cycle *Recuerdo*. I'm happy to say that both Musto works have now joined the standard rep.

Carnegie and Naumburg may have been the most prestigious competitions in the 1980s, but Young Concert Artists actually provided the most important benefit: not merely a New York début, but several years of concert bookings thereafter. The fees were low—I made two hundred dollars per recital—but all expenses were paid. We booked our own travel (often on People Express, who would fly you to Buffalo for nineteen dollars); the presenters found us hotels; and we submitted expense sheets to YCA on Xeroxed squares of paper. Geographical logistics were not YCA's strong suit: at one point Bill and I had to travel back and forth across the country on three consecutive weekends for concerts in Idaho, Montana, and Washington State.

Our audiences ranged from art song snobs to art song beginners. At universities we sometimes encountered enthusiastic, full houses eager to cheer us on. But other times we'd be met with an indifference bordering on rudeness. In Bozeman, Bill walked offstage after the first half with a strange expression on his face. It seems that the student who was doing our lights was also doing his girlfriend in the lighting booth. After intermission our already small crowd of listeners was even smaller. We later learned that our concert was part of a class assignment, but students only had to stay for the first half to receive credit. Bill and I trudged to the double bar as the lighting guy enjoyed a postcoital smoke.

Apart from recitals at the 92nd Street Y in New York and the Kennedy Center in Washington, DC, YCA concerts didn't offer much in the way of glamour. What they did provide was a way to learn what worked with audiences—and what didn't. In metropolitan areas the public could be snooty, as if they wanted to protect art song from unwanted intruders. They came to judge, not to enjoy, and sometimes they let you know the verdict right on the spot. At Bill's concert at the 92nd Street Y, I was pouring out my soul in the postlude to Schubert's famous "Ständchen" when a lady in Row C said "very sentimental" in a stage whisper loud enough for me to hear. The microphones picked it up too: her pronouncement could be heard on the broadcast.

Elsewhere, listeners were less prone to compare Chris and Bill with other art song singers. Instead, we were competing with performers from the entire range of musical genres. Those who loved classical music generally preferred instrumentalists, while those who didn't would rather have heard U2 or Madonna. For many, a concert with only one unamplified voice and a piano seemed like an order of potato peels, and it was up to us to convince them otherwise. At one school we were scheduled for a Q&A with the football team the day after the performance. Although the jocks were on good behavior, the gist of their questions was "What the fuck WAS that?" We did our best to draw back the curtain on our process, talking about the poetry, the subtle relationship of words and music. But it was rough going. At one point I heard someone comment to his friend, "God, what a faggot." He was not referring to Bill.

Still, the YCA tours were a valuable gift—my first chance to play art song repertoire over and over again, as I had Martha Schlamme's cabaret program. I began to understand the arc of a recital, usually by making bad choices. On one tour I was determined to start the evening with three sixteenth-century lute songs. Bill was skeptical about performing such delicate material on a modern piano, but I whined until I got my way. In concert, the songs had the crash-and-burn effect of the *Hindenburg*. A lute would have conjured the right soundworld for their Renaissance lyrics; with the piano, they came off as impossibly antique.

After years of respecting Martha's demand for super-soft dynamics and somewhat mushy textures, I expanded my color palette. I learned how to fashion a decent first date with a new piano, and which adjustments to make for a hall's acoustics. And this lifelong New Yorker was able to travel the country and meet people from practically every state.

Occasionally there were language problems I'd never before encountered. The gentle, soft-spoken gas station attendant in Tennessee leaned into the car to wish Bill Sharp and me a "nah snot." It took me several minutes to realize he wanted us to have a "nice night." This happened half an hour after I'd asked our waiter if the salmon special was a filet or a steak. "No, sir," he patiently replied, "it's a fee-ush." No doubt he is still telling his friends about the city slicker who didn't know what salmon was.

To make it onto the Young Concert Artists roster, all the musicians—vocalists, solo instrumentalists, and chamber ensembles—had to run the gauntlet. At the first two rounds of auditions, the singers were heard by a panel of song specialists. Qualities that won the day in opera competitions—volume, big delivery, high notes that make your fillings vibrate—might alienate this panel, who were seeking refinement and delicacy. But at the final round everyone was thrown together to compete against each other in front of a large, mixed panel. Now the singers required the approval of string and wind players on the panel, who often warmed to instrumental voices with narrow vibratos and perfect tuning, as well as the buy-in of the singers on the panel, who looked for personal expression, technical freedom, and command of language. As a result, there were many years when no singer was chosen at all.

The artistic bar for Community Concerts was not as high. Professional singers could audition for a committee of presenters in New York who, if they liked your act, would add you to their roster for the season—which meant you could find yourself performing anywhere from Kohler, Wisconsin, to Kennebunkport, Maine. Individual managers might also arrange recitals for their more established artists, bypassing the cattle call. Community Concerts was a godsend for musicians without national brand-name recognition, offering one of the last dependable outlets for solo performances. The only catch was that the talent pool was largely restricted to the roster of Columbia Artists, its parent company from the 1930s till 1999.

The organization was founded in the 1920s (it died a messy, bankrupt death in 2003), when it was difficult to bring classical music to underserved audiences. With its subscription-based business model, even small cities scrambling to put on concerts wouldn't lose their shirts if a performance got trumped by a big sporting event, bad weather, or the audience's unanticipated indifference to a particular artist. It was able to bring top-ranking performers to remote parts of the country, forming a classical-music replica of the vaudeville circuit. Leontyne Price, Beverly Sills, Richard Tucker, and Robert Merrill all took to the road in the early years of their careers.

My experiences with Community Concerts ran along similar lines to those with YCA audiences, fluctuating from the heartwarming to the bizarre. We usually played to decent crowds, but the singers I accompanied were often the only solo performers on the series. The presenters called recitalists like us "singles," and I learned that we were considered a risky proposition in many places. A vocalist (or violinist, for that matter) could get sick and cancel. This wasn't a problem they would encounter with the New Shanghai Circus or the Von Trapp Family Singers. And many people didn't like, or thought they didn't like, classical singing. On the other hand, we were comparatively inexpensive, perhaps our strongest selling point.

"Once," confided a presenter in Harvey, Illinois, "we were supposed to have Risë Stevens for a concert." I raised my eyebrows, impressed that they had engaged the Met's premiere Carmen to sing in this sleepy Chicago suburb, and sampled another bite of the marshmallow salad she had insisted I order. "Well, she canceled. But later that evening someone saw her all dressed up, having a fancy dinner in town!" She shot me a steely glance. The implication: mezzo-soprano Evelyn Petros and I were lucky to be engaged, and we'd better not skip out on her.

The fine points of vocal style and expertly crafted pianism didn't count for as much in the heartland as they did in the urban venues. On this circuit it was good to offer music that the audience already knew; it was important to be a showman; it was recommended that a female singer change her gown at intermission, even if the dressing room was a kindergarten classroom with construction paper taped over the window. Our programs were first sent for approval to a central committee, who favored a mix of art song, arias, folk music, and Broadway—crossover rep that was in my comfort zone. They encouraged us to include as much English-language material as we could, and deleted anything they felt was not family-friendly. This was why they censored one of baritone David Holloway's selections, "The Prologue to *The Breasts of Tiresias* by Francis Poulenc." When he resubmitted the program with the title of the same piece in its original language, "The Prologue to *Les mamelles de Tirésias*, by Francis Poulenc," it was allowed. English breasts: no. French breasts: fine.

Some audiences were happy to hear German or French art songs, especially if one of us explained what the poems were about. Others grew restive when they were forced to sit still for Brahms Lieder. There were always surprises. The presenters in Pocatello, Idaho, practically begged Peter Kazaras and me to perform Schubert's dark song cycle *Winterreise*, though we couldn't oblige—they made the request on the car ride from the airport to our motel the day before the concert. At the other end of the spectrum was a venue in Wisconsin where David Holloway and I shared a bathroom with the audience at intermission. From a few urinals down I heard an early review: "I don't know why they sing all that foreign stuff. Don't they know we speak English here?"

Everyone loved arias, especially the most familiar ones. When David sang the "Toreador Song" from *Carmen*, he taught the audience the chorus part and they chimed in at the appropriate moment. During a period when so much of my work was with Martha and Alvin, I was glad to be onstage playing classical music and collaborating with big, operatic voices in no need of microphones.

The artists who hired me for these tours were what you might call the *haute bourgeoisie* of the opera world: singers who had landed important assignments at New York City Opera and regional houses across the country. Some went on to sing leading roles at the Met (Peter Kazaras, Linda Zoghby, Gianna Rolandi); others remained headliners at City Opera (Patricia Brooks, Patricia Wells); some enjoyed successful European careers (Sheri Greenawald); and a few checked all the boxes (David Holloway, Alan Titus, Catherine Malfitano). All of them provided opportunities to experience the mercurial relationship between performers and their listeners.

You needed to be somewhat formal in the big cities, but on the road it was best to break the barrier between stage and auditorium. Those audiences wanted to feel that opera singers were human, down-to-earth. Some artists came by the common touch naturally, while others weren't naturally folksy. I fell in the second category, as I discovered when I gave spoken introductions in places like Temple, Texas, and Fullerton, California. Even I could hear that I sounded impossibly overbred.

THE TRICKIEST branch of my recital career was partnering famous singers as they bid farewell to their glory days. On the face of it, these engagements looked exciting, and their well-known names definitely classed up my bio. Being onstage with them was another story. Having risen to the top of their profession, they were used to a certain kind of pampering. Though their voices were fading, their grandeur was in full bloom.

It was often a challenge to find piano sonority that flattered their frail vocalism. And then there was a strange social challenge. Being a fair amount younger, I wasn't a peer; I was neither a star conductor nor a big-name solo pianist; I wasn't exactly a servant, though I occasionally felt like one. The singers hired me, they wrote the checks. And they could fire me. It was up to me to figure out how to fit in.

Vocalists who are starting to go downhill, or are going through a rough patch hoping to pull it back together, are not a cheerful bunch. And I soon figured out that these partnerships were not true collaborations. By the time I came along their interpretations were set in stone, bearing the imprint of previous pianists and coaches. I was hired to replicate something I could only intuit from their singing, and it wasn't always easy. How can you guess the best way to play an intro before they've sung a note?

One such star was Roberta Peters, a childhood idol of mine. I bought her recording of *The Barber of Seville* when I was eleven and fell in love with her voice. Thirty years after making that recording, she still sang in tune, with a vibrato that retained a decent amount of its former spin. She had saved enough top notes to crank out her old showpieces, minus the super-high ornaments she was known for in the 1950s. But as she approached sixty, the rosiness of her voice was fading into a greyed-out simulacrum.

Accompanying this coloratura star was especially ticklish because she had been coached in her concert repertoire during the 1940s and '50s, decades before we got together in the late 1980s. Those musical choices were frozen, no matter how old-fashioned they seemed forty years later. I understood what Martha must have gone through when she joined the cast of *Fiddler on the Roof*. Like her, I was expected to reproduce someone else's timbre and tempo (but whose?) and make it sound natural.

Some of our rehearsals were at my apartment, which would retain the aroma of her expensive perfume for days. But mostly we worked in her Westchester mansion. It was not easy to find Roberta's musical groove because her rhythm was slightly unpredictable, especially at slow tempos. Her rendition of Handel's "Lascia ch'io pianga," normally a very easy aria, induced panic. The accompaniment is spare, and the piano chords need to line up exactly with the vocal line. Watching her like a hawk, I managed to coordinate the first two quarter notes, but then came an eighth-note rest followed by a sung eighth note to finish the measure. That last note tended to lurch out unpredictably, like a mouse scampering from a hole. I was in Code Red before we'd even gotten past the first bar.

Then there was the matter of dynamics. Roberta wanted the art songs, especially the French songs, played very softly. "Like this?" I asked, trying a hushed *pianissimo*. "Too loud!" I tried again, but her moue of discontent didn't budge. As a joke, I collapsed my sound down to near-inaudibility, with one-fifth of the notes missing, expecting to hear I'd finally gone too far. "Yes. *That's* the style."

At a New Jersey recital I must have edged the dynamics up a bit. After the opening group of songs, she glared at me in the wings and read me the riot act about playing too loud. I obliged with my most colorless timbre and tiptoed through the first half without further incident. After intermission, assuming she wanted all accompaniments on the weenie side that night, I played her Jerome Kern group with the same ghostly sound. The moment we came offstage, her diva smile vanished. "What's the *matter* with you?" she hissed. "*I need suppawt!*" in her best Bronx accent.

No matter how insignificant our concerts looked on paper, any engagement with Roberta was a major event. She filled a basketball arena in Raleigh, North Carolina, with cheering fans; she played to a packed house in Tacoma, Washington. Our fanciest gig was not a public performance, though, but a private concert for J.P. Morgan Chase's investors in Tokyo. The presenters rolled out the red carpet for us, including their best attempt at an American Thanksgiving dinner in our four-star hotel. In those days Roberta didn't usually show me a great deal of warmth—she was businesslike, occasionally imperious. But as I was turning thirty-seven, she took care to arrange a surprise at our dress rehearsal: singing Japanese and American birthday songs, the crew wheeled out a chocolate cake in the shape of a piano, complete with a raised chocolate piano lid. It was the only raised piano lid on the stage—my Yamaha was only open a crack.

The Japanese audience went mad for Roberta, awarding her special ovations for the *Rigoletto* and *Barber of Seville* arias. The tech crew cooked up elaborate lighting effects (including a gaudy "sunrise over the Manhattan skyline" at the end), and our Yamaha concert grand was tuned relentlessly. Roberta was a Metropolitan Opera star, and it was irrelevant how she sang—she was a goddess.

After the performance we had a ridiculous altercation about money in which we were both at fault, and things cooled between us for a bit. I always felt bad about that misstep and assumed we'd never again be onstage together. But in the late 1990s I was persuaded to ask Roberta to give us a couple of songs for the tenth-anniversary celebration of my concert series, New York Festival of Song, and she accepted.

By then she was nearing seventy. At our rehearsal, I encountered quite a different Roberta. While my career was in the ascendant, hers was fading into a series of "special appearances," the province of famous performers and athletes who can still draw a crowd just by showing up. She treated me with a kind of warmth and respect I had not experienced a decade earlier, and my heart opened to her. I finally understood the strength with which she had pursued her dream. Roberta's talent had been spotted early, and she'd been pulled out of high school in her teenage years to devote all her time to opera studies. She was groomed to

With Roberta Peters in 1998 in the Metropolitan Opera Gift Shop, enjoying a surprisingly warm reunion ten years after our Japan concerts. © *Beth Bergman*

sing at the Met, and was rewarded for her diligence. After a spectacular début at age twenty on just a few hours' notice (replacing a singer who had fallen ill), she kept herself in the limelight for nearly five decades.

Having been isolated from her peer group during adolescence and then abruptly thrust into the razzle-dazzle of opera, Roberta had probably skipped some crucial developmental steps in her emotional growth. But she attained what she wanted: she became a celebrity, and always delivered what the audience expected of her. We stayed in touch during her final years, and I think of her with tender, rueful affection.

My relationship with her contemporary, Evelyn Lear, followed a similar pattern, though I first met her in 1975 when she was still a Met headliner. She was in her late forties then, often a perilous moment in a soprano's career. Voices can get a little bashed up after decades of hard use, and Evelyn had spent her resources freely. Her remarkable musicianship, uncanny gift for operatic acting, and enviably thick skin propelled her into a major career. So did her philosophy, "Never say no," which often meant taking on the premieres of difficult modern operas that few others would accept. She became famous for her recordings of Berg's twelve-tone operas *Wozzeck* and *Lulu*, the first ones in stereo.

Evelyn had always struggled with her high notes; her warm, slightly cloudy middle register ascended to an upper extreme that could prove hard and strident at full volume. After her crisis during the run of *Ariadne auf Naxos* at the Met in 1970, it became obvious that she was in need of a vocal overhaul. After reworking her technique with Dan Ferro she made a triumphant appearance four years later as the Marschallin in *Der Rosenkavalier*, launching Dan's career and relaunching her own. But she always had a chip on her shoulder, and her return to grace proved provisional: the next season she stumbled during the opening night of the Met's *Marriage of Figaro*—just three unfortunate high A's at the end of "Dove sono," but it was enough to unnerve her.

It was around this time that Evelyn agreed to sing at a luncheon for the Ladies Auxiliary of the Doctors Orchestra, whom she always referred to as "those LADO ladies." It must have been too insignificant a gig for her to engage her regular accompanist, Martin Katz—a formidable pianist—so on Matthew Epstein's advice she threw it my way.

Saddled with an inexperienced new pianist for a gig she had gotten roped into, she was not in the best mood.

We started our rehearsal with Ives's "Serenity," which I had just learned two days earlier. I was a little tentative. That is not the word I'd use to describe Evelyn. "I thought you played with line. Where's your *line*?" And so it went for the rest of the two hours. Her disappointment filled the room like a bad smell, and I imploded, lacking the ability to analyze her psychological game and take control of it, or the musical confidence to dig in more. After a couple of years spent minimizing my sound to Martha's specifications, I had lost the knack of playing out.

But the concert went decently (I must have found my line), and Evelyn hired me to help her prepare a few opera roles. We didn't perform any more recitals until the mid-1980s, by which point the vocal reconstruction she'd achieved years earlier was coming unglued again. This was to be expected: she was nearing her sixtieth birthday, a time when even the most airtight technique will begin to show cracks. On the operatic stage, Evelyn had been enjoying some late success in mezzo-soprano roles, including Carmen, which she sang for the first time at age fifty-five. Five years later, much of her singing had turned sour and insecure. Yet she still burned with a fierce desire to perform.

I expected her to be even harsher with me than she had been before. But to my surprise, she was kind to the point of docility, treating me like a peer rather than a student. Not that she'd lost her edge: I witnessed her bare her teeth at stage managers and waiters—in a Chinese restaurant, exasperated with her moo shu chicken, she shouted at the poor busboy, "Don't you know who I am? I am a Metropolitan Opera *star*!"

While Evelyn's opera work was theatrically sophisticated, she was prone to overplaying her hand in recitals, alternating exquisite refinement with slightly overdone effects. But even at sixty she was capable of magic, as long as the song sat safely in her middle register. I'll never forget her performance of Jerome Kern's "Bill," the famous ballad from *Showboat*. All her show-biz gimmicks fell away, and she locked into the song's complexity and depth. When she delivered the wonderful last lines, "I love him, because he's... I don't know... because he's just my Bill," she drew us inside her soul. Was that a tear in her eye? She disarmed me again in Tchaikovsky's "At the Ball," which she sang as if she were improvising in front of our eyes—a stunning delivery of a subtle song. With uncharacteristic gentleness, Evelyn had shown me how to phrase the entire song, giving special attention to its short postlude—a lesson I have never forgotten.

Another reason I'm grateful to Evelyn: I received a rave *New York Times* review for our 1986 Town Hall concert with Thomas Stewart, her bass-baritone husband. Over the years I've been called "dapper," "alert," occasionally "fine," as well as receiving some nice ink about programming and speaking from the stage. This time I was given a lengthy paragraph from Will Crutchfield detailing my "care for pianistic finish and character," citing specific moments that had impressed him—including the postlude to "At the Ball." I assumed that Crutchfield's praise would definitively launch my classical music career, and that invitations to play A-list recitals would put the meager resources of my answering machine to the test. But this did not come to pass. I remained where I was: performing with competition winners, Community Concerts, golden-agers.

While it flattered my ego to be around famous opera singers, no matter what stage of their career, I still longed to collaborate with a well-established artist (preferably European) renowned primarily for art song. That was the big kahuna, the Holy Grail. The opportunity finally came when baritone Wolfgang Holzmair was looking for a local pianist to play his American concerts. I had been smitten with Holzmair's singing when I heard him in the mid-1990s at the Met Museum—silky, sinuous, slender vocalism coupled with a poetic approach to phrasing. He had made a number of lovely recordings for the Philips label, and was widely touted as a major exponent of German Lieder. When Matthew Sprizzo, Holzmair's manager, called me, I accepted with joy.

Alas, the Holzmair who showed up in 1999 was not the singer I'd heard a few years earlier. He was prone to hoarseness, and his always-dry lower register was now parched. At first I thought he might be suffering from a temporary cold, but the condition lasted for our entire time together. His artistic persona had undergone a change as well. Wolfgang was now prone to singing like a blustering bully, giving us only occasional glimpses of the ardent troubadour who had conquered me at the Met Museum. His voice may not have been the only source of his anger: he was infuriated by the ascent of Jörg Haider's far-right party in Austria. I once heard him go off on a furious ten-minute tirade in my apartment to a German-speaking colleague, oblivious to the fact that I couldn't understand most of what he was saying.

Wolfgang engaged me for some high-level concerts—Orchestra Hall in Chicago, Herbst Theatre in San Francisco, the National Gallery in Washington. I in turn hired him to sing with New York Festival of Song that season in New York. It seemed like a coup to engage an international star like Wolfgang for NYFOS—until we began working together. Ours was a colossal mismatch.

Though Wolfgang had wanted to work with an American pianist, he was not in any mood for a true collaboration. Our first rehearsal took place two days before the Chicago concert in a downstairs rehearsal room at Orchestra Hall. When I arrived a couple of minutes late for our 10 a.m. meeting, I found Wolfgang standing by the piano looking like a stern high-school math teacher, scowling in a sweater-vest. Even though we were peers, he made it clear that I was to have no autonomy in our music-making. He dictated every nuance of what I was to play before I'd even touched the piano. Normally singers will show you the broad outlines of their interpretation through their singing, chamber-music style. You join them in the dance.

There was to be no dancing this time.

I tried to return his serve by offering to help with his English diction, which was heavily accented. "Giff to me the life I luff," he rasped angrily at the beginning of Vaughan Williams's *Songs of Travel*.

"Wolfgang, there are a couple of things that would make your English a bit more ... idiomatic," I began. "Would you like some help with that?"

"Oh, I von't be needing that," he answered airily. "Venn I sang at Aldeburgh [the Benjamin Britten festival in southern England], they said my English vas PUFFfict." Case closed.

Our Chicago matinée went well enough. I did my best to suppress my musical energy in order to come up with the more sedate pianism Wolfgang was used to, while endeavoring to bring life to the dizzying number of markings in my score from our four hours of rehearsal. The moment the concert was over, we had to board a plane for our next gig, scheduled for the following evening in San Francisco.

I'm sure Wolfgang was nervous that night in the Bay City—back-to-back recitals are difficult even for singers in perfect vocal health. During our warm-up, when we were running through Wolf's "Auf eine Wanderung," I must have forgotten myself at the climax of the song and allowed it to run away a bit. This provoked a harsh tongue-lashing from the singer, and I became enraged. I'd already put up with a fair amount of condescension from him, but he'd crossed a line. In the moment I said nothing more than a few palliative words to defuse the situation; a knock-down drag-out fight is not the best idea before an art song concert, and I didn't trust myself to remain civil.

For the rest of the evening my mouth was locked in a scowling rictus that refused to loosen. I couldn't look at him. The San Francisco paper, noting Wolfgang's tendency to turn Vaughan Williams's gentle *Songs of Travel* into a "daunting tirade," mentioned that I "seemed mostly intent on staying out of the way." If only I could have.

I'm still sad about my time with Wolfgang Holzmair. He was a significant exponent of Schubert, and I had hoped that he'd help me find the path into the German repertoire that had eluded me for so long. But I met him at a bad time. And I learn best through radar, vibrations of sound and psyche that transform into physical, musical impulses. Wolfgang gravitated to a style of coaching I have encountered in other European singers (Elisabeth Schwarzkopf, Michel Sénéchal): a rigid control of the music's surface, with minute directions for executing scads of details. Possibly this was how he was taught, and therefore it was natural for him to draw on those techniques. The top-down approach works for many people, but it makes me feel like an imbecile. When someone else dictates every nuance, they unplug my inner jukebox as I wait to be told what to do. Nothing feels natural.

Still, there was one moment during those grueling rehearsals when Wolfgang dropped his role as Kappellmeister to offer something truly illuminating. We were working on Schubert's "Der Pilgrim" at the end of the second day of rehearsal. It was the one song in the program where I admit I felt clueless; what element of Friedrich von Schiller's ardent poem could have elicited such ... dumpy music?

"The introduction of this song, it is like the music they play in church when people are leaving," he patiently explained. "The ... recessional?" I asked, groping for the word. "Yes, that's it. And the people get up from the pews and walk up the aisles to go home for the Sunday meal. *Pam-pam-pam-pam*," he illustrated. He must have known I was Jewish, and that my experience of Sunday church recessionals would have been limited at best. But in those few moments Wolfgang evoked an image I could turn into music. I don't know if he would have smiled on the complacent, plodding congregation I imagined trudging up the church aisle as I played the opening bars, but he did appreciate the placid, even quarter notes they elicited from my hands.

After our last concert, I never saw Wolfgang again. The question of his tenuous vocal condition—the elephant in the room—had been off-limits the whole time we were together. He had kept our relationship formal, rising just to the level of collegial cordiality. When our business was over, there was no invitation to stay in touch.

Those years were filled with tricky voices and trickier personalities, but among all the exasperating collaborations there was one that proved magical: my partnership with soprano Patricia Brooks.

In her day, Pat lived somewhat in the shadow of the glitzier Beverly Sills, with whom she shared several roles at New York City Opera. But many cognoscenti considered Pat Brooks her equal as a singing actress. She had studied with the greats—Martha Graham, Uta Hagen, and Dan Ferro—and each had left an indelible imprint on her art. She was physically graceful, theatrically daring, and vocally exquisite. I first heard her in a 1965 *Marriage of Figaro* when City Opera still performed at the New York City Center. Her Susanna was a little dangerous—vibrant and sexy, quite unlike the iron-soubrette stereotype of the time.

From then on I tried to hear her in all her City Opera roles. While she was famous for her Violetta in *La traviata* and Mélisande in Debussy's *Pelléas et Mélisande*, for me her crowning glory was Massenet's Manon, fragile and vulnerable without stinting on the character's feckless greed and narcissism. She knew how to give a complex, intimate performance that carried to the very back of the New York State Theater.

Pat was on Matthew Epstein's roster at Columbia Artists, and they were also longtime friends. As a hands-on manager, Matthew offered vocal and musical advice on her new roles, and during my first years after college suggested that I accompany some of their coaching sessions. I was awestruck.

Pat must have had a soft spot for me. She volunteered to come to one of my lessons with Martin Isepp, and she also engaged me for some Community Concert tours, including several duo recitals with Alan Titus (booked by Matthew, of course). Above all, Pat was a free spirit. If she didn't like the bonnets that were part of a costume at City Opera, she would quietly toss them in the trash, later claiming that she had no *idea* what had happened to them. She relished her erotic nature and took full advantage of the sexual revolution of the 1960s and '70s; and she had a risqué, delightfully twisted sense of humor. She was a hippie disguised as a diva.

Yet as the 1970s progressed, it was clear something was going wrong with her voice. At only forty years old, she was losing the clarity of her sound, and beginning to compensate with musical and theatrical exaggerations. I'd later learn that Pat's troubles had a physical source: she was afflicted with multiple sclerosis, and this was the source of her sudden decline. She still had her high notes, and could zip through Strauss's coloratura showpiece "Amor" with every trill tossed off perfectly. But her basic phonation sounded a bit strange, as if she were underwater. Her breath support was gone.

In spite of everything, Pat had booked a recital at Tully Hall in 1977 and asked me to play for her. It was my first concert at Lincoln Center, and her last—one of her final public performances anywhere, in fact. Unbeknownst to me, she had bowed out of future engagements at City Opera.

At Tully Hall that night Pat used every bit of technique and charisma at her disposal to get through the recital. She was motivated by love: her son was going through a troubled adolescence, and, desperate to do something constructive for him, she had earmarked the funds from the concert to benefit his school. It could not have been easy to put herself in front of the New York public when her resources were so plainly diminished. We had to start one song twice, after the first attempt misfired into a squawk. Yet her stage demeanor was as gracious and elegant as in her best days.

Above all, I valued Pat for her kindness as a collaborator. When she gave me musical directions, she would phrase them as a tender question, usually ending with a gesture. "Steve, could the beginning of the second verse be more . . . ?" And then a graceful sweep of the arm, a ballet dancer's third position accompanied by a charming raised eyebrow. I responded both to her body language and her gentleness. I could tell what she wanted, and sometimes I could actually do it.

She saw my talent and my vulnerability, and even at a time when she had almost nothing to spare, she was generous. I wish I had shown her that same generosity when I finally learned that she was ill. But all of our time together had been spent with music, and without that bridge I didn't know how to support her—fundamentally I didn't feel I had anything useful to offer the world besides my skills as an accompanist. At that time I was only semi-aware of my own physical challenges, though they were beginning to manifest themselves bit by bit. Pat had teased me about my "rolling walk," claiming she could pick me out of a crowd a block away. When I witnessed other people's infirmities, I froze. One of the cardinal regrets of my life is that I did not reach out enough to her as a friend in her last years.

Rest in peace, Patricia. I adored you. Your kindness took root within me, and your inspiration has been endless.

The photo that did not get used as the album cover for *Arias and Barcarolles*: at The Dakota on 72nd Street in Leonard Bernstein's apartment, Michael Barrett and the Maestro in his red bathrobe (seated), William Sharp, Judy Kaye, and me (standing)

CHAPTER 7

A New Path Opens

BY 1988 I was starting to get a little frustrated. Young Concert Artists, the Naumburg Competition, and Carnegie Hall had kept me busy on the recital circuit with Bill Sharp and Chris Trakas for a few years, but when our contracts with them ran out we were left high and dry—no more recitals, no more recordings. Bill and Chris had given me my first sustained opportunity to explore the deeper possibilities of song, an oasis after so many years of playing Kurt Weill, opera arias, and classical easy listening. But it was all taxi, no takeoff.

Alas, the more established singers who were calling me for concert work had little interest in learning new repertoire. The more established, the more intransigent. Case in point: Roberta Peters. When she told me she planned to sing Irving Berlin's "White Christmas" for an upcoming concert in 1988 I thought it would be great if she included the song's rarely heard verse, which provides a context for the famous refrain: it's December 24 in sun-drenched Beverly Hills, but despite the gorgeous weather the singer longs for what she remembers from her childhood—a snowy, east-coast Christmas. Since I couldn't put my hands on the sheet music without a trip to a store in those pre-internet days, I wrote out the sixteen bars by hand on a piece of music paper. When I arrived at Roberta's house in Westchester I proudly handed her the page and tried to sell her on including it. I only got a few sentences out before Roberta dismissed the idea. "No one's interested. They just want to hear the part they know." With this, she took my handwritten sheet and while I wouldn't say she threw it on the floor, that is where it landed.

Trivial as the incident was, it was a red flag. I had managed to forge a life in music, yet it seemed oddly uncreative.

As I struggled with this quandary, a life-changing opportunity arrived as if by magic. The deus ex machina was my colleague and friend Michael Barrett, whom I'd met three years earlier in the winter of 1984. We'd found each other through a series of chance connections. A then-housemate of mine was friends with a stage director named Paul Lazarus, who was working on concert at Tully Hall in honor of Marc Blitzstein's eightieth birthday. The late composer was becoming a musical footnote, better known for his grisly 1964 murder in Martinique at the hands of three sailors than for anything he'd written for the stage or the concert hall. His name was kept alive primarily through his 1954 translation of Kurt Weill's *Threepenny Opera*, which remained the standard version for decades, and his opera *Regina*, which sputtered back to life every couple of decades.

Michael was the event's musical director, and was looking someone to share the burden of the piano-accompanied first half, and then play in the orchestra under his baton during the second. Paul Lazarus happened to be over for dinner the night that the reviews came out for Martha and Alvin's latest run of the *Kurt Weill Cabaret*. Hearing that the critics had liked the show, I trotted off to buy the papers. While the *Times* didn't mention my name, not even in the information box that crammed in the names of all the producers and even the stage manager, I'd gotten a nice mention from Clive Barnes in the *Post*: "Steven Blier was the pianist, and he was excellent." That one adjective from a famous critic was enough for Paul Lazarus to recommend me to Michael.

Michael came to hear the Kurt Weill show and afterwards we went out for a drink. I was a bit intimidated by him—I mean, he hobnobbed with Leonard Bernstein, while I was still playing more auditions and voice lessons than actual concerts. Somehow the fact that I was currently the pianist for a successful off-Broadway show did not elevate my status in my own eyes. But after Michael heard me whip through ninety minutes of Kurt Weill songs he took me on as his assistant. The connections between Weill and Blitzstein were familiar to him: Weill had been one of Blitzstein's greatest inspirations, and Blitzstein's *Threepenny* translation turned Weill's 1928 Weimar hit into an off-Broadway sensation that ran for six years.

I never shook the feeling that I played the role of country mouse to Michael's suave city mouse. But I brought something special to the table: I was probably better versed in the music of Marc Blitzstein than any other pianist in town. I first encountered his songs in 1981 when Martha and Alvin attempted a cabaret show based on songs by Bernstein and Blitzstein. Alas, Bernstein's vocal demands taxed them beyond their limits, but the show sparked my fascination with Blitzstein's music. At that time, very few people were familiar with this composer. No wonder—most of his material still remained unpublished in the 1980s, and Xeroxes of the sheet music were passed around like contraband by the few insiders who had access to the archives. Some of it is left-wing agitprop, like his 1937 breakout musical *The Cradle Will Rock*, but he was also capable of a Mahlerian vein of lyricism—just listen to "The Rose Song" from *Reuben, Reuben* (perhaps the most beautiful thing he wrote); even some of his comedy numbers still retain their edge, despite their age ("Modest Maid," "Penny Candy").

Our concert boasted a strong cast, including Patti LuPone who opened the concert with one of Blitzstein's quintessential numbers, "The Nickel Under the Foot." Standing backstage she eyed me suspiciously standing next to Michael. Suspecting I might be an intruder, she blurted out, "Who's he? The page turner?" as if I weren't there.

"No, the second pianist."

She gave me the fisheye and I began to bristle. Then I let it go, realizing that LuPone's disdainful stare might be part of her process as an actress. Maybe she was simply getting into character to play a tough, suspicious broad. The doors to the stage swung open and we all strode out. When LuPone faced the audience she delivered a superb rendition of the song, confronting them with the same wounded fierceness she'd shown me a few minutes earlier.

The first act ended with an appearance by our biggest star, Leonard

Bernstein. He accompanied himself in a comic number Blitzstein had taught him during the 1940s, "The New Suit," better known by its subtitle, "Zipperfly." We cleared the stage for the maestro, who shared reminiscences of his old friend with the audience. Bernstein's career had far outstripped that of Blitzstein, the artist he'd revered when he was a student at Harvard, and his remarks were a fascinating mixture of adoration and condescension. Bernstein then gave a rendition of "Zipperfly" both whiskey-voiced (not a metaphor in this case) and haunting.

The song tells of a preteen's desire for a fancy suit whose new-fangled zipper (instead of the usual buttons) would grab the attention of everyone he passes on the street. The lyrics slyly depict the dream of a kid on the verge of sexual awakening, a world in which everyone is staring longingly at his crotch. I resolved to get my hands on the music for this unpublished song. I knew a good thing: "Zipperfly" brought down the house when Bill Sharp and I offered it at the Carnegie Hall competition two years later. And it became the title song of our Blitzstein CD in 1990.

That night at Tully Hall I played as if I'd been shot out of a cannon. My nervous excitement spurred me on to some electric-eel tempi, including an especially manic rendition of Weill's "Kanonen-Song" from *Threepenny Opera*. But the evening was a success and it cemented my friendship with Michael Barrett.

Our next big collaboration was a return to Tully Hall three years later for a glitzy seventieth-birthday tribute to Leonard Bernstein. It was scheduled for February 29, 1988, just seven weeks after my father's death. I welcomed the Bernstein concert as a glittery way to rejoin the stream of life, but I still felt shaky in the aftermath of my family trauma. For months I'd been up with my dad night after night as he lay on his deathbed, and if I nodded off he'd rouse me with a faint reprimand. Everyone knew of my recent loss and treated me with special kindness, especially Linda Lavin, the Broadway star who achieved national fame as TV's *Alice*.

This time I kept my nerves in check and the evening went extremely well. At the last minute we had an emergency: soprano Julia Migenes, then a name to conjure with after playing Bizet's Carmen in a movie opposite Plácido Domingo, suddenly bowed out. A bit of research revealed that the up-and-coming star Dawn Upshaw was singing the Forest Bird in *Siegfried* that night at the Metropolitan Opera, just across the Plaza. She wouldn't be needed till about 9 p.m., and the Met released her so that she was able to start our show with Bernstein's "I Hate Music!" The minute her last note ended we heard the maestro growl, "GOOD!" from his Tully Hall box seat. Having nailed her song, Dawn skittered off to her Wagner duties at the Met. It was a promising start to a first-rate concert.

A month later I received a phone call from Michael. I heard the guarded enthusiasm in his voice, a signal that there was an opportunity in the offing, just not of the financial sort. He'd spoken to his friend B. C. Vermeersch, who ran the Greenwich House Music School on Barrow Street in the Village. B. C. wanted to raise the profile of his school by programming a few Sunday afternoon recitals in its sweet, petite second-floor concert hall. It housed two onstage Steinway pianos and had room for about one hundred audience members. Michael asked if I was interested. I had nothing special going on in May of 1988, and said, "Sure, sign me up."

I rounded up a couple of singers I loved working with—Christine Seitz, a Valkyrie-in-training with an imposing voice, and Rosemarie Landry, a prominent Canadian soprano with an exquisite gift for French song. Michael chose the mezzo-soprano Lucille Beer. In the scheme of things these Sunday matinées were not major New York events. Yet there was some kind of magic in the air at each concert. The room was intimate, perfect for delicate music-making but big enough for full-throated singing. The windows behind the pianos opened onto the garden and you could hear birdsong during the quiet moments. Out the front windows, of course, we ran the risk of car alarms and boom boxes. But for three Sunday afternoons Barrow Street stayed miraculously quiet. Our miniseries was a gentle success.

B. C. was aware that something unusual had just taken place in his little concert hall, and he invited us back for more. "Sure," I told Michael. "But not for more solo vocal recitals. I think we should do something new—thematic concerts that explore ideas and cultures and poets."

This idea had been germinating within me for three years, ever since

I heard Graham Johnson's Songmakers' Almanac in Israel. I was on tour with Martha and Alvin at the 1985 Jerusalem Festival, and Graham was giving a pair of concerts with his London-based ensemble the same week. He founded his concert series in 1976 as a way to explore repertoire, celebrate anniversaries, and turn the solo recital into a communal effort—a kind of Lieder camerata. The original ensemble included luminaries like Felicity Lott and Anthony Rolfe Johnson before they became international stars. Graham, a superb musician with a scholar's depth of understanding, was the pianist and artistic director. They were able to make their mark in a country that valued art song and by 1985 they had put out four recordings.

Graham had not been able to bring A-list singers to the Jerusalem festival, but that didn't matter. The X factor was Graham himself. With his vast knowledge of history, poetry and music funneled through his quirky stage charisma, he constructed performances that took the listener deep inside the evening's subject matter.

The hall was packed for the second of Graham's two performances in Jerusalem, a light-hearted program called *English Sins and Vices* that included everything from Stephen Foster to Poulenc to Thomas Hardy. But I first met him after his opening show, *From the Hebrew Songs*, a brilliant musical smorgasbord based around Jewish themes. He had not realized that the Israeli audience in 1985 was tired of well-meaning programs about their own heritage, and would be far more excited to hear songs about British lust and murder. For the Jewish concert there were about eleven people in the hall besides me, and it didn't take me long to realize that I was getting what amounted to a command performance. I was dazzled by the mix of repertoire, readings (by an actor), and spoken annotation (by Graham). My fascination with the program was apparently palpable to everyone onstage. I took the van back to the hotel with Graham after the show and we knocked back a bottle of Cabernet in the hotel lobby that night. His fury about the empty hall unleashed a comic rant that blended the free-wheeling lunacy of Eddie Izzard with the patrician wit of Gore Vidal. We bonded as if we'd known each other our whole lives.

We were pretty much inseparable for the three days our stays in

Jerusalem overlapped. Graham was one of the smartest people I'd ever met, and I think he enjoyed having an American acolyte able to keep up with his multilingual repartee. His depth of experience on the concert stage, combined with his extremely salty sense of humor, was pure catnip for me.

Our friendship didn't survive the return to our regular lives in England and the States. Intense bromances like ours thrive best in foreign locales, and there was no way to fan that kind of flame with an ocean between us. As I gradually went from being Graham's kid brother in the musical pantheon to his peer, the camaraderie forged in the Holy Land faded away.

Nevertheless, Graham's genius for song showed me my own path.

Graham provided one of the inspirations for the new concert series I had in mind; Joan Morris and William Bolcom provided the other. Bill is a musical polymath. He has composed Pulitzer Prize–winning, atonal piano etudes as well as four books of cabaret songs. The Chicago Lyric and the Met produced his operas, while his musicals premiered at the Yale Rep and the Actors Studio. Concert audiences dig his gnarly twelve-tone pieces, while pianists delight in his graceful piano rags. Bill also has enjoyed a side career as accompanist to his wife Joan Morris, whose repertoire spans the entire range of American popular song from its earliest days to the present. I started buying their records in the early 1970s and was totally starstruck when Martha and Alvin introduced me to them after their Tully Hall concert on March 4, 1977. (Bill had been the pianist for their Kurt Weill show before I got the job.)

That concert at Tully Hall traversed a century of American popular song from the Civil War era to the 1970s. I remember being flabbergasted by the fact that they knew the date of every song they offered, and had a pithy anecdote at the ready about the composer or the singer who introduced the song. At age twenty-five I had only the most piecemeal connection to the history of the pieces I played. It didn't occur to me that I needed to know anything but the basics. I'd been at Yale when New Criticism was all the rage, a theory that promoted close reading and all but jettisoned historical context. We were encouraged to see each work as a self-contained entity ready for the modern scalpel. I brought that same approach to my music, bouncing from the printed score straight into my imagination without worrying about the details.

So when Joan told her audience, "That song premiered in 1924—no, wait 1923—yeah, '23," that small correction set off an explosion in my brain. How amazing to know such a fact! And for one year to matter! In a single flash I realized that everything you can find out about a song matters. Each one—whether a Schubert Lied or a vaudeville strut—has a story that leads you to the heart of the song.

Even more amazing was Joan and Bill's ability to honor the original intent of their songs without resorting to camp or mimicry. When Joan sang a song from the jazz age I felt like a denizen of the Roaring Twenties, hip to all the cultural assumptions woven into the words and music. At the very same moment, though, I was keenly aware of my historical remove from that time—a dizzying sensation of knowing what the song was when it was new, what it was in the present moment, and what it would always be. This had a lot to do with Bill Bolcom's ability to sprinkle early jazz harmony like saffron into Richard Rodgers's "Little Girl Blue," or morph into a virtuoso parlor pianist for a turn-of-the-century piece like "Wait Till the Sun Shines, Nellie." Bill used the sheet music as a catapult for his dapper, stylish arrangements, and provided me with a lifetime of inspiration.

No doubt my previous musical experiences, from Beethoven to Brel, from Verdi to Weill, had made me a prime candidate for an artistic awakening. But those three concerts—the Bolcoms' at Lincoln Center in 1977 and Graham Johnson's in Jerusalem in 1985—were my Revelation. Graham showed me how European art song could address the modern world with unapologetic vitality, while Joan and Bill's respect for American popular music was the key to a limitless treasure chest.

Everything coalesced the moment B. C. Vermeersch offered Michael Barrett and me the use of his performance space on Barrow Street. As if by magic, Michael received a spontaneous grant of $1,000 from the musicologist Joseph Machlis, with the instructions, "Do something interesting with it." Here was something very interesting indeed: a new home for song in an intimate setting. I didn't know anything about running an arts organization—Michael, thankfully, had more of a head for administrative matters and did some serious homework about running a not-for-profit arts organization. Meanwhile I was exploding with ideas for programs I could at last bring to life.

I had no idea that this project, begun so humbly, would become my life's obsession, that it would allow me to explore all my musical interests and discover new ones, drive me to explore new frontiers as a pianist, and introduce me to a raft of beautiful musicians I would otherwise never have met. In effect I was building the only music school I would ever want to attend, and these concerts were my endless postdoctoral thesis.

Michael decided our new concert organization should have a fall season and a spring season—three concerts in each, scheduled just two weeks apart to build momentum. We also planned a seventh show around Christmastime, a concert reading of Rodgers and Hart's 1937 musical *The Boys from Syracuse*.

Having spent the first fifteen years of my career waiting to be hired, I suddenly found myself engaging musicians to work for me. It was fascinating to see who was willing to take a chance on a new venture in a small hall. The renowned actress Blythe Danner gracefully accepted an invitation to be on our opening concert, while several less starry performers literally hung up on me when they heard the modest fees we were offering. And we had no idea what to call the series—my idea of what we were offering was so exalted that no name could capture its magnificence.

That answer emerged, as so much about our venture did, out of an odd series of coincidences. I'd been unsuccessfully wooing a guy on my block, the most recent in a long series of men who liked-me-but-not-in-that-way. He had a part-time job with a graphic designer named Gerald Lynas and recommended his boss to Michael and me. We took our materials over—his studio was in a brownstone two blocks from my house—and discovered a confident designer with a breezy, professional manner. We still had no idea what to call our concert series until Gerry announced, "You're going to be the New York Festival of Song." He stated it as a fact, not a discussion point. He then designed a logo and seized on the acronym NYFOS. He knew nothing of our music and never attended a concert. But he christened us and gave us an elegant send-off: a gorgeous brochure and a name that has stood the test of time.

We opened with a far-ranging Shakespeare program. It ran the gamut from the tried-and-true (iconic songs by Roger Quilter and Ralph Vaughan Williams) to the recherché (rare settings of Shakespeare sonnets in Russian by Dimitri Kabalevsky) to the snazzy (numbers by jazz icons Dick Hyman and John Dankworth). I had never in my life produced anything more elaborate than a house concert. While Greenwich House took care of the basics—printing programs, running the box office, setting out the chairs, tuning the pianos—it fell to me to supply everything else—the playlist, the notes, the texts, the artists, and the butts in the seats. Our publicity in those pre-internet days was rudimentary: Xeroxed note cards to which we affixed address labels and postage stamps by hand.

I cast my friends Brenda and Braden Harris to sing the Shakespeare concert. It made sense that their first names were anagrams of each other—they seemed to function as a perfectly balanced unit. Brenda was on the verge of a significant career in opera that would blossom into leading-lady roles over the next thirty years. Braden, a less showy stage personality, was primarily a voice teacher whose students included his very gifted wife. Observing them as they worked on their duets, I learned a lot about ensemble singing: how to place final consonants so the line concluded with a satisfying pop, when to plan dynamics and when to leave them to the inspiration of the moment. For star power we had Blythe Danner. She had recently done some Kurt Weill songs with Alvin Epstein and me, in an attempt to replace the irreplaceable Martha Schlamme. That experiment didn't pan out—Blythe was a bit too patrician for Brecht—but she was a godsend for Shakespeare sonnets and monologues.

The small offstage area for the artists did double duty as a children's art studio, and one of the early prerequisites for singing with NYFOS was an ability to inhale acrylic paint fumes just before singing a concert. It wasn't the formaldehyde that made me a little dizzy when I started the show that day. It was the unprecedented amount of non-piano details I had been handling up until curtain time. I was so distracted that I momentarily got lost in the second piece, Finzi's "It was a lover and his lass," which I was playing a tone lower for Braden. I didn't write out the transposition but the key change had never posed a problem in rehearsal. That afternoon I momentarily skidded off course. It's unnerving to make an unexpected blunder onstage, and it served as a reminder to stop worrying about late seating and typos in the program, and pay attention to the music. There were no more accidents that day.

The house was about three-quarters full but once again there was a feeling of electricity in the hall. Among the listeners were Paul, my old flame from the NYU gig, along with his wife Nancy. In the thirteen intervening years since he'd left town and broken my heart, our friendship managed to find a stable footing. I adored Nancy, a choreographer whose feisty New York energy complemented Paul's ethereal New Age vibe. They took me out to dinner after the show to celebrate the new venture. A wave of exhaustion hit me during dessert and I almost keeled over into a bowl of tiramisu.

So many of the NYFOS trademarks that have sustained us for over three decades spontaneously emerged during our very first season. Michael and I didn't have any sense that we were putting long-term artistic policy in place. We were just following our instincts and exploring all the concert ideas that had been tantalizingly out of reach since we started our professional lives. We were like two kids left to run free in FAO Schwarz after closing time, playing with every toy in the store. We mixed genres freely. We always filled the stage with singers—and sometimes instrumentalists and actors. I discovered my passion for Latin music and did the first of many programs devoted to South American song.

Speaking from the stage was not part of my plan. Sure, I knew from my tours that sharing a few thoughts could put the audience at ease. And Greenwich House was so informal that it was easy to lean over the piano and give the listeners a leg up on what they were about to hear. I also wanted each of our concerts to explore lesser-known repertoire, not just "the part they know" (à la Roberta Peters). And it became clear that audiences were more excited to hear something unfamiliar if they knew what to listen for.

But I did not want the chat to upstage the music. I still had one eye on succeeding in the old-time, austere concert world where the big stars never said a word until they stammered the name of their encore (and the pianist was mute all night). I also wanted each of our concerts to have a different feel—"No two alike!" was one of our mottos. With those things in mind I decided not to say a word at our second concert, *Americans on America* with Bill Sharp and soprano Karen Holvik. It was a beautiful afternoon—and the last one with no verbal component. Sharing music without sharing thoughts suddenly seemed like thin gruel.

I found out in those early years that my interstitial patter was like a drug for the audience and, at times, for me too. A new, Jewish-vaudevillian Steve was emerging from the shadows. I became punch-drunk on my ability to get a laugh when I was introducing the most obscure, arty material. Even after a program I considered serious and high-minded, people would come backstage and say, "Oh, that was so much fun!" I had mixed feelings, though, when I began to get the compliment, "Oh, we love it when you *talk*!" The less musically inclined would tactlessly add, "Oh, we'd rather hear you talk than play!" I was caught between my urge to entertain and my urge to be taken seriously. Could I have it both ways?

Our concerts that first season were scheduled close to one another in an attempt to keep our audience coming back for more. I was at the helm of four out of seven, and sharing pianist/music-director duties for two others. I felt as if I were in the spin cycle of a washing machine for most of the year. Our programs were far more research-intensive affairs than I had anticipated, each requiring weeks of work and coordination.

The most difficult was also the dearest to my heart, a South American song program called *From Rio to Buenos Aires*. Through a stroke of luck I met the Argentinian-Slovenian mezzo-soprano Bernarda Fink in the summer of 1988, and engaged her for a show in our 1989 spring season. She was in New York with her husband Valentin Inzko, who had a high-level gig at the United Nations. Bernarda was just at the beginning of a career that skyrocketed when she returned to Europe in 1990—by now she's made thirty-five major recordings and sung at festivals all over the world. Bernarda brought me my first stash of Argentinean songs—

music that was not to be found in the States at that time. I became insanely attached to *From Rio to Buenos Aires* and practically went into withdrawal the day after the concert. I brought it back the next season and have continued to program music from Spain and Latin America practically every year. My love for it remains a kind of fever—the best kind of fever.

IN EARLY June 1989, after our first season had ended, Michael called me with an interesting piece of news: the Chamber Music Society of Lincoln Center, who had commissioned a piece called *Arias and Barcarolles* from Leonard Bernstein several years earlier, had decided not to premiere it. A new work by an American icon was just dangling in the breeze, and (pending Bernstein's approval) we might have the opportunity to grab it for NYFOS. Obviously we had to go for it. I just hoped it was a decent piece, fearing that the Chamber Music Society had passed on the premiere because it was not. But Michael believed in *Arias and Barcarolles,* and with good reason: he'd been around Bernstein when he was writing it. He'd sight-read it with the maestro from the manuscript and knew it was quirky but worthy. Michael went to Lenny to ask for the premiere, and we got his blessing. Now we just needed to prepare the music.

As and Bs, as it is commonly known, derives its title from an encounter Bernstein once had with Dwight D. Eisenhower, who complimented the maestro after a performance at the White House in 1960. The president had especially enjoyed *Rhapsody in Blue,* saying, "You know, I liked that last piece you played: it's got a theme. I like music with a theme, not all them arias and barcarolles." While the lyrics of *As and Bs* do revolve around a central theme, marriage and the family, the musical material and narrative style of its eight movements are all over the map, from Broadway soft-shoe to twelve-tone row. By turns clangy and sweet, tuneful and disjointed, open-hearted and occluded, it can be a puzzling work to encounter for the first time. Eisenhower might have flinched.

With great patience Michael taught me every note of *Arias and Barcarolles*. The piece had not yet been engraved and I had to learn it from the composer's handwritten manuscript, more legible than some composers but still a daily challenge. This was Bernstein's final composition, and he wrote about delicate personal matters: the uneasy truce between his gay nature and his traditional marriage, his unruly sexuality, his love for his mother, and his urge to confess versus his need to use coded language to speak about such intimacies. It took some time for the piece to make sense, but Michael seemed to have the music in his bones. Eventually I could traverse the *As and Bs* moonscape without incident.

We offered the premiere to Judy Kaye, still riding high from her 1988 Tony Award for *Phantom of the Opera*; her partner would be Bill Sharp, who'd made his Carnegie Hall début with me that past winter. I made the mistake of trying to ingratiate myself with Judy by baking muffins for her at her first rehearsal. No dice. For this project she was all business, punctual to arrive and out the door briskly when the call was over. The muffins went untouched. But she and Bill began to take possession of the piece as we prepared for a premiere in early September at Merkin Hall.

A Leonard Bernstein premiere is a gift you receive only once in your career. We wanted to get the performance right, but we also wanted to make the most of the opportunity by recording it as well. There was no use contacting prestigious labels like RCA Victor and Deutsche Grammophon, who would have wanted to record it with the star singers and pianists on their roster. (Seven years later DG did precisely that, using the orchestrated version and superstars Thomas Hampson and Frederica von Stade.) Instead, I contacted four of the era's best smaller record companies: Pro Arte, Arabesque, Nonesuch, and Vanguard. The last of these, I thought, was a shoo-in, since it was run by our longtime family friend, Seymour Solomon.

Cold calls turned out to be a singularly ineffective way to approach record companies. "We have no interest in it," sniffed one. "We don't accept any unsolicited projects," bristled another. The third said they might consider it if we laid out the money ourselves, rented a studio, hired an engineer, and brought them a finished master for their consideration. We didn't have the means to do that, and it struck me as insulting.

My hopes now rested with Seymour, the only one who had not

turned it down outright. We invited him to a house concert Michael and I arranged to prepare for our Merkin Hall date. Our friend Hillary Brown, one of NYFOS's earliest advocates and a charter member of our board of directors, had a loft on Park Avenue South, a decent Steinway, and a gift for throwing elegant musicales. This one was no exception.

Alas, through no fault of Hillary's the evening didn't go especially well. Bill Sharp hit bad traffic and arrived late, which delayed our start. The audience was getting restive as tension gathered in the room. At one point Judy's husband exploded in a rage, which didn't make things any calmer. When we finally did the performance, we found that the piece was almost ready—but not yet completely smooth. I wasn't troubled by this. *Arias and Barcarolles* is a minefield of rhythmic challenges and now we knew what we needed to polish for opening night. We'd pummel it into shape.

Seymour didn't see it that way. "I don't want it," he said flatly. "A second-drawer Bernstein piece cast with unknowns."

"Judy Kaye?" I spluttered.

"Who is she? No one's ever heard of her."

"Um, no one except a zillion Broadway-goers and the Tony Awards Committee..."

"I'd only do it if you got von Stade, and paired it with songs from *West Side Story*."

I stopped myself from saying something I'd later regret, and muttered something like, "Well, maybe next time."

Though it now seems inconceivable that no one would want the premiere recording of *Arias and Barcarolles*, there was a widespread perception in the late '80s that Bernstein was no longer at the top of his game. The bon vivant who'd created tuneful, upbeat classics like *On the Town* and *Chichester Psalms* had given way to a composer of craggy complexity with a penchant for the didactic. Bernstein's fall from grace began in 1971, when the premiere of his now-popular *Mass* stumbled at the opening of the Kennedy Center in Washington, DC. His bicentennial musical *1600 Pennsylvania Avenue* had been one of Broadway's most resounding flops, leaving Bernstein so embittered that he refused to sanction an original cast album. And his opera, *A Quiet Place*, had a troubled birth in 1983, still a recent memory when we were shopping *As and Bs* around.

At this point we didn't know where to turn. Then we had one more amazing stroke of luck: I got a phone message from a record producer named Michael Fine. It seems that he had just received a call from Michael Koch, the head of a large record distribution company eponymously named Koch International. Koch was interested in having his own in-house label, would Michael Fine like to be at the helm? At first Fine was reluctant—new CD labels were flooding the market already. Then he heard from Michael Barrett's manager at the time, Sheldon Soffer, who had a juicy bit of gossip: Seymour Solomon had just turned down *Arias and Barcarolles*. I naïvely had no idea that this was public knowledge, nor that his rejection would have interested anyone in the music business. As far as I could tell, everyone treated *As and Bs* like radioactive fallout. But Michael Fine thought differently. It might just be a reason to start a new record label after all.

I couldn't quite tell what to make of this sudden influx of Michaels in my orbit—Koch, Fine, Barrett. (Around this time Michael Barrett took official ownership of my nickname for him, Mikey, probably to distinguish himself from all the others.) But Michael Fine was a familiar—and comfortable—type: a combination of slouchy confidence and go-getter energy, the quintessential New York mix of the blasé and the driven. One thing was certain: he seemed serious about the recording. And he was the only person who wanted it. We said yes.

We paired the Bernstein premiere at Merkin Hall with Brahms's *Liebeslieder Waltzes*, a classic piece for four hands and four voices. The pairing worked like a dream: Brahms's comfortable bourgeois opulence set the stage perfectly for Bernstein's chaotic psychodrama. We gave it our all and had a success. A year earlier we'd ventured out as neophytes. Suddenly NYFOS was in the limelight, with critics from the *New York Times* and *The New Yorker* spilling a good bit of ink on us.

Then came the recording studio.

I was still new to the sweet torture of making CDs. When you're practicing for a concert you fantasize about how much easier it would be to have the luxury of repeated takes to nail the difficult technical spots.

The reality is that the studio is far more unforgiving. In a live concert you can motor through the tricky spots with a liberal infusion of pedal and panache, and if you screw up you just move on, no one's perfect. But in front of the microphone you do have to play everything perfectly at least once, preferably at a moment when your colleagues are also delivering the goods. It's stressful enough to make you fantasize about looking for work in a sleepy upstate children's library.

Michael Fine had a budget of $18,000 for the recording, and he opted for the industry's latest innovation, digital tape. He was almost done editing when the money ran out. It was 3 a.m. and there were still a couple of important things to fix, including a spot where the singing was heavenly but one of us—probably me—was playing the piano line in the wrong octave. Record producers have a standard monologue for moments like that—stories about glorious recordings that also have audible bloopers, usually involving legends like Segovia or Heifetz. The message is clear: we didn't have the money to airbrush all your blemishes, it's beautiful anyway, get used to being human.

It would have to do.

There were a few hurdles left. First, we had to take the recording over to Bernstein's apartment for his blessing. Michael Barrett's confidence bolstered me and I was able to remain relatively calm. Leonard Bernstein, I admit, did make me uncomfortable. In his later years his temperament was mercurial, and his reactions to me had ranged from effusive enthusiasm (a fawning monologue about my playing) to cool indifference (the aloofness of a displeased headmaster). I had given up on trying to predict how he'd receive me, but I thought the CD would pass muster. Michael Fine, on the other hand, was quietly terrified about the errant piano octave. There was no way he could explain that he'd simply run out of the funds for that crucial piece of editing. He copied the recording onto a cassette and met us at Bernstein's apartment in the Dakota.

When we arrived we also found a reporter from the *Gramophone*, England's most prestigious magazine for record reviews. I knew that this meant that the maestro would be putting on a show for him, giving him the kind of drama and pull quote that would make for a good article. It started from the very first beat of the CD, where I had revoiced a couple of chords in "Some Other Time" in an effort to recreate the sound of Bill Evans, one of my favorite jazz pianists. This gave Bernstein a chance for a short, copy-ready monologue about how proud he'd been when he'd written those harmonies forty years earlier—with the implication that he was unhappy with my changes. And he reacted with mock horror that we recorded his song "Dream with Me" in an arrangement that included several modulations—the only available edition of that as-yet unpublished song. "Oh, Maestro, I love that version," I offered. "Well, I *don't*! And *that's* what counts!" he snapped. Maybe our performance changed his mind about that arrangement; not long afterwards he asked for it to be sung at an important AIDS benefit.

Things started to improve, though, and soon Bernstein was clearly finding lots to enjoy. Every time he heard something he liked in the piano, he'd ask which of us was playing that passage. Often enough it was me, and he'd tilt his head with a Mona Lisa half-smile, a quizzical expression of approval.

We finally got to the dreaded wrong octave passage in *Arias and Barcarolles*, and I fooled myself into thinking he wouldn't notice. No such luck. Bernstein's bushy eyebrows went up—had he heard right? We feared the verdict.

Bernstein remonstrated with Michael Fine, who remonstrated back at the maestro. No, there was no way we could go back in the studio. Apologies, but the recording had been finalized. So sorry, but this was the best vocal take and it had been a judgment call. What went unspoken was that Michael Fine was leaving the next day for New Zealand, and there wasn't a dime left in the budget for cab fare, not to mention two hours of studio time.

Bernstein held the moment for a beat, and then said, "The whole thing is so damned good I'll let you get away with it."

The drama was not quite over. We wanted to get a photo for the album cover with him surrounded by the cast and pianists. He was scheduled to conduct the New York Philharmonic in October, and we managed to wedge ourselves in for a half-hour session at his apartment. We were on notice that the maestro was on a strict timetable that evening: he was due at Lincoln Center at 7:30. We arrived at 6. No sign of Bernstein. His assistant was in a nearby office alcove and went off in search of him. Around 6:12 Bernstein finally showed up, dressed in a red bathrobe. Not a fancy dressing gown, an actual bathrobe.

"Are you... going to get dressed?" asked our photographer, Peter Schaaf.

"I thought I could just wear this," said Bernstein. Awkward pause.

We snapped a few pictures around the piano before Schaaf got the nerve to speak up.

"Maestro, I wonder if you could perhaps... get dressed."

"Well, I need to get into my tails for the concert, and I don't want to do that until just before I leave the house..." The assistant swept in. "Come with me."

A docile Bernstein disappeared, and soon came back clad in a pair of elegant dark blue silk pajamas.

In the twelve remaining minutes Peter Schaaf made haste to snap the official shot that we used on the cover. But the photo I like best is from the bathrobe series—everyone at their ease, Lenny looking at me as I crack up laughing. For one brief moment Lenny and I finally relaxed with one another, and Peter Schaaf caught it on film.

Koch International released the CD in the winter of 1990, and it garnered international attention. In the summer of that year Michael Barrett and I ventured up to Tanglewood to hear Bernstein conduct what turned out to be his final performance. I had not realized how much his health had declined in the past ten months. With a mixture of fierceness and frailty he led the orchestra in works by Britten and Beethoven, using a red handkerchief to conceal the blood he periodically coughed up. I had always been somewhat frightened by Bernstein's chaotic vitality—a libidinous, uninhibited, febrile genius for music that led him to excesses, some delirious magic carpet rides, some nine-car pileups. That afternoon I watched Bernstein's inner Eros and Thanatos duke it out on the podium. Eros—his life force—prevailed at Tanglewood. Two months later Thanatos, the death force, had the final word. Bernstein died on October 14, 1990, and the world mourned him.

At the turn of the new year, I heard that our recording was nominated for a Grammy. I remained blasé. I attached little to the award, which I assumed was a popularity contest won by record companies with the biggest publicity machines. I associated the ceremony with pop stars wearing spangly gowns. True, our CD was doing well—we were number seven on *Variety*'s crossover charts. But why nourish hope when we were sure to lose to some glitzier CD from Nonesuch or RCA? At best the nomination seemed like a lovely memorial to one of America's greatest musicians. As for winning, I told myself, "Be happy—how many snowballs even *get* to hell?"

The night of the awards I was busy assembling some bookcases I'd bought at Ikea. It took all my concentration to chase down errant braces, hunt for a missing Allen wrench, and avoid getting bonked in the head by a misaligned shelf. I was in a black mood, stewing over my latest romantic snafu. I didn't even bother to put the television on. Around 10 p.m. I got a call from Cayce Blanchard, a college friend I hadn't heard from in several years.

"Oh Stevie! Wow! Congratulations!"

"On . . . what?" I said as I spotted an itinerant screw on the floor.

"What do you mean? ON THE GRAMMY! Of course, Plácido Domingo didn't pronounce your name right, but your CD won!"

It takes me a while to process information like that, and I continued to downplay the Grammy's importance for weeks when anyone brought it up in conversation. Taking an airy tone of moral superiority, I insisted that our ongoing work was the important thing, not the tinselly prize. Still, there was no denying that something had changed. NYFOS wasn't just a cool, scrappy, underdog concert series. It was now a Grammy-winning cool, scrappy, underdog concert series. Our rocket had launched.

A few days later I heard from Seymour Solomon, who called to congratulate me on the award.

"It's so wonderful. Your father would have been so proud."

"Yes, Seymour, thanks, I'm sure he's smiling, wherever he is."

He let a short pause go by before continuing. "You know, I made a big mistake when I turned that project down. And I'm sorry. You were right. I should have done it."

It was my turn to leave space before responding. Years earlier my parents had enlisted Seymour's help to talk me out of a career in music. He had been a beloved family friend since I was five years old, but he'd misguided me at two crucial moments in my life.

I could hear my father's voice saying, "Always be a gentleman." I made a stab at it.

"Oh, Seymour, it all turned out OK. Maybe next time."

There never was a next time, and in a few years the entire recording industry would implode as the internet made it increasingly easy to acquire recordings without paying for them. For now, it was my job to comfort Seymour. And I reflected that adversity had been one of my best teachers all along. It was a lesson I'd need in the years that followed.

Jim Russell and me at Mt. Sinai, summer of 2010: me in my new wheels, Jim in the dowdy old scooter, before our race through Central Park. (I won.)

CHAPTER 8

The History of My Legs

As I was going through the drama of getting my career off the ground, there was a parallel drama in my life: my increasingly contentious relationship with my body. In the early years I was only dimly aware of how those two stories connected. But as time went by I began to understand that they were virtually the same.

I've always had an *entente* not-so-*cordiale* with my legs. From the beginning they seemed to have a single M.O.: to make trouble for the rest of me. My earliest memory is of waking up in the middle of the night crying because of leg cramps. And without a dependable foundation, the rest of my body had difficulty locating a trustworthy Command Central. Seated at a desk or piano, I was fine. But once I was standing or walking my legs betrayed me whenever they got the chance. By my twenties, my body was like Europe after World War II, a tangle of conflicting factions and occupied areas. My legs were East Germany, compromised in movement and short on nourishment. My arms were more like Italy—mostly weak and impoverished except for my hands, which were as powerful as the Vatican.

My gait was pretty normal as a kid, though I was somewhat bandy-legged. By adolescence I couldn't run far without getting winded, though I was still capable of walking quickly and tirelessly. At no point was I ever athletic, nor did I feel a shred of interest in watching sports. I collected baseball cards just to keep up with the other boys, secretly preferring the bubble gum and the players' tight striped pants to the stats. As for prowess on the playing field, I had none. Having been hit in the head by a tennis ball as a child, an accident caused entirely by my own ineptness, I developed a terror of anything that flew at me. Naturally I panicked in junior high softball when I was at bat. As the ball sailed toward me, I swung out randomly like a blind man defending himself from a mugger, longing for the safety of strike three. The coach assigned me a place deep in right field where I could do the least damage. The one time someone managed to slug a ball into my domain, I let it come to a safe stop on the ground before tossing it to the more adept boy further infield. Baseballs, footballs, basketballs—they all might as well have been bombs.

My one area of prepubescent physical expertise was the dance floor. My mother enrolled my brother and me in after-school lessons, where a patient middle-aged couple taught a gaggle of eleven-year-olds ballroom dancing. Classes were held at Christ Church, a deliciously incongruous place for a bunch of Jewish kids to learn to boogie, especially under the tutelage of Mr. and Mrs. Uhl (pronounced, appropriately, "Yule"). The Uhls dressed for the occasion—suit and tie for him, tea-length cocktail dress for her—and so did we: white gloves for girls, blazers and ties for boys. Although this was the early 1960s, the Twist era, we were learning the old-fashioned stuff: waltz, cha-cha, fox-trot, polka. They even taught the Lindy Hop, a dance from the 1940s that I loved—tap-and-step, tap-and-step, march-march. We kids didn't have the context or vocabulary to label the enterprise "retro." Our teachers did make one concession to modern times when they taught us the merengue, a Dominican dance whose eely sinuousness had made its way to North American shores. I felt both liberated and appalled by its lascivious hip movements. Was it really okay to move your pelvis like this in public?

Since I was a graceful dancer, I would occasionally get summoned to the middle of the room to demonstrate a step for the class, in tandem with a girl who was to become a lifelong friend, Ellen Kirschner. And at a bar mitzvah a few years later, the bandleader cleared the floor for another girl from the class and me to dance a schottische—a kind of Moravian hoedown, a line dance that needs a bit of space. Jaws dropped as we cut across the floor: one-two-three-hop, one-two-three-hop, step-hop-step-hop-step-hop-step-hop.

That was my terpsichorean victory lap. After my bar mitzvah, I abruptly gave up dancing forever. The deck was stacking up the wrong way: bad at sports, good at dancing; hated the Rolling Stones, loved Renata Tebaldi; friends with girls, uncomfortable in all-male dens like Hebrew school; bad at shop class, good in Home Ec. I played the piano, liked romantic novels and advice columns, spoke French with a gorgeous accent, and ran in terror from baseballs. Once, during a tumbling session in gym class, a running somersault went awry and knocked me out cold. I awoke cradled in the brawny arms of the instructor, my only pleasurable memory of Phys Ed.

My older brother, who was signed up for the later session of the dance class, tacitly sent me the message: real men didn't do this sort of thing. He hated it so much that after he arrived at Christ Church, he would immediately turn around and saunter home on foot, timing it so that he got back at precisely the hour the return bus would have dropped him off. And he's managed to live a successful life without knowing how to dance the polka.

After my bar mitzvah I suddenly became too self-conscious to do the Mashed Potatoes or the Freddie, to say nothing of the schottische and the meringue. On November 15, 1964, I relegated myself to the sidelines, where I have remained ever since.

Since I was the youngest in my grade at school by some distance, I didn't expect to be as strong and developed as my classmates. I'd skipped third grade and was already the baby of my second-grade class, with the result that some of the boys I went to school with were almost two years older than I. In the locker room we surreptitiously scanned one another to see who was growing pubic hair, an unexpected adolescent status symbol. I was the last. I was also the weakest and least coordinated. Assuming I'd eventually catch up, I allowed myself to ignore all the warning signals of what was actually happening to my body.

When I was fifteen I had an alarming encounter with my dad. Catching sight of my unclothed back one day, he yanked me over to the hall mirror, where he inspected me for some time. He then exploded in anger: "Look at your back!" I twisted my neck to look over my shoulder. "You have a curvature in your spine," glaring at me as if I had willfully neglected the upkeep of my skeleton. "You need to get stronger!" I then expected one of his boilerplate tirades—either "I should have enrolled you in military school" or "I'm buying you a set of weights." This time was different. He became quiet, too disturbed to go into his usual spiel. Soon he sent me to an orthopedist for X-rays, to document the condition and to begin assembling records in case I was drafted. In fact, those X-rays came in mighty handy five years later when I drew a low number—11—in the national lottery and was accorded a 1-A draft status after graduating college. I slouched my way through an Army physical, and managed to avoid being sent off to Vietnam.

Although I knew my father was wrong to blame me for the state of my back, I still harbored an irrational guilt that I was at fault. Soon my willowy scoliosis intertwined in my teenage mind with all the other ways I was different and cemented my self-image as an outsider. Still, I tried to reassure myself that I'd grow into normality one day. My curvy back would get straight. And so would I.

Of course, none of this came to pass. My gait grew more and more distinctive, half Popeye, half Teletubby. Like every other guy in Manhattan, I joined a gym after college. At my first encounter with the Nautilus machines, the health club's lissome instructor set the weights at their wimpiest numbers, yet I still struggled to move the handles. In hindsight, he must have sensed that there was something off-kilter about my body and was afraid I'd get injured on his watch, since I was unable to maintain proper form even on the idiot-proof machines. Something was always flipping out of line, shoulders rising, shoulder-blades popping, neck straining.

Three times a week, for several years, I doggedly pumped iron, but the juicy biceps and pecs and delts never materialized. My six-pack was more like a juice box. My one area of semi-competence was the swimming pool, where I could replicate most of the traditional strokes in a manner one might describe as well-intentioned but graceless. When I was on tour in Jerusalem in 1985, a handsome Sabra lifeguard swaggered up to me as my testosterone took a delicious little spike. "Was that you swimming in the pool yesterday?" he asked. "I think it might have been," I purred. "Well, you swim *terrible*." Having delivered his verdict, he about-faced, according me the final view of a backside I would clearly never possess.

I lived in a self-willed fog, vaguely (though increasingly) aware that something was wrong while keeping myself too busy to investigate the problem. The evidence was all around me: my mother had problems walking, and so did her two sisters. They struggled with staircases, tired quickly, dreaded low-slung chairs, and avoided appliances that involved bending down. But so did a lot of other people in my family, including non-blood relatives. It was easy for me to conclude that all Jews over a certain age were destined to wear clunky orthopedic clodhoppers, walk with a cane, and plop onto a sofa as soon as they entered a living room. Evidently I belonged to the Lost Tribe of Gimp.

The source of my blindness was my father, who had always served as my doctor. His love for me, which was immense, had made him overprotective ever since the day I was born. I was a premature baby, and Dad never stopped seeing me as someone who needed to be shielded and controlled. He didn't encourage me to trust my instincts—he knew best. And when it came to medical matters I never questioned him.

When I was in my early twenties, my mother went away to get some tests done at Johns Hopkins. Her mobility problems were increasing, her muscular strength was waning. I was told almost nothing about this at the time, nor did anyone share the results when she came home. But a few weeks later, my father took me aside. "What your mother has is nongenetic. It doesn't pass down through the generations."

"What about Aunt Jannie and Aunt Florence? They have problems too. Like, really similar problems."

"Well, they have two different conditions. Also nongenetic. They may have picked up some virus, well, some *viruses*, in their teenage years. But you don't have to worry about having any of that." It wasn't the truth, but I believed it.

As my condition grew more eccentric, I conveniently blamed everything on my scoliosis. It's actually a very minor curvature of the spine, but I let it bear the brunt of the increasingly eerie problems I was experiencing. Once, in a department store changing room trying on a polo shirt, I got a gander at my back in the three-way mirror for the first time in years. I was horrified. It looked as if someone had taken a sledgehammer to my lumbar area. There also appeared to be a couple of claw marks just under my shoulder blades. I was swaybacked, with what looked like only the thinnest layer of musculature over my rib cage. Having at last glimpsed the unnervingly frail, crooked structure John Kirkpatrick and my father had observed, I freaked out. My bed-partners never brought it up, although my physical frailty had certainly kept that number fairly low. Gay culture is muscle culture, and I didn't have much to bring to the table. It was one of the main reasons I stayed so long with Alvin, who accepted me just as I was.

On my way home from the department store, I took a bad fall in the middle of the street. I had no idea what I had tripped over, but I managed to hoist myself back up and keep moving. That was the first of many falls to come. I'd be walking up the street whistling a virtuoso rendition of "Una voce poco fa," and just as I was revving up for the cadenza, boom—I was splattered on the pavement, always landing on my left knee, which often sustained a bleeding gash. After a tumble, I would glower at the sidewalk: Could it have been that slightly raised crack, or maybe that tiny pebble? Was the city putting up invisible barbed wire? Worse than the wound, though, was the rip in my trousers. Cheap jeans or dress slacks, I wrecked them all in a matter of seconds. So I became a regular client of the French American Reweaving Company, a tailor on Fifty-Seventh Street that specialized in making perfect insets for torn garments. With kindness and tact, they repaired practically all my suits. "Left knee again, Mr. Blier? We'll need a bigger patch because of the bloodstain, let's see if there's enough material in the bottom hem..."

After my father's death in 1988, I received a phone call from my sister-in-law Vicki, who had been badgering me for some time to take better care of myself. We all knew my father had brought on his own decline by ignoring early symptoms of prostate cancer, and Vicki was determined that no one else in the family should follow him down that path. At that point, I didn't even have a primary care physician; my general health had been good enough for me to coast for well over a decade. But Vicki was aware that my shambling way of moving around had slid from charming to alarming, and that even my way of lifting a book or fork was beginning to look strange.

"Every syndrome has a diagnosis, Ste," she said, using my family name. "Doctors love to see their names attached to medical conditions—trust me, nothing goes unidentified. You need to find out what's going on. Maybe you should see a specialist, like a physiatrist." By coincidence, I had just spoken to a pianist colleague who was also having some physical issues, and she told me that she had "found the most amazing doctor, Dr. Fazzari. He's a physiatrist! He saved my life!"

"Fazzari the physiatrist?"

"Don't laugh, call him."

Dr. Fazzari's office was at Columbus Circle. I took a seat in the long corridor outside his examining room, where I was surrounded by a cluster of athletic-looking men and women. Most were in their thirties—tennis players with bursitis, baseball players with rotator cuff problems, shiny, healthy people who had taxed their toned physiques past what they could bear. Some had even brought along their gym bags. Looking at my fellow patients, I pined for a nice, simple case of groin pull that could potentially be solved with some massage therapy.

After a short wait I was ushered into the doctor's office. I realized I didn't know how to answer his "What seems to be the problem?" This visit hadn't been my idea and I didn't have a prepared statement. "Well, I got your name from a friend," I ventured, as if this would explain everything.

"Ah," he said sympathetically. "And?"

"I guess she wanted me to get some help with—" I stopped again. "I have a little trouble on my feet sometimes."

"Let's have a look."

His examination was quick; he felt my neck and shoulders, touched my back, had me walk around a bit. Then he abruptly walked back to his chair and gestured for me to sit. "I can't help you," he said. "You need to make an appointment with a neurologist, and if I were you I wouldn't wait." He tried to hide his emotion with a veneer of Hippocratic blandness, but I could see something had upset him.

"There's nothing you can do for me here?"

"This is a place for sports injuries. And what you have is definitely not a sports injury." Then, as he showed me to the door, "Good luck, Steven."

Dr. Fazzari had regressed from cordial to curt in such a short space of time, barely five minutes, that I experienced a kind of vertigo. My first reaction was the predictably deep sense of relief at leaving a doctor's office, a sugar-high of escape. I gulped down lungfuls of New York City air as though emerging from a deep-sea dive. But soon I remembered the doctor's dark mood, and understood that he had palmed a painful diagnosis onto another doctor.

By 1990 I had become an old hand at watching middle-aged men lose it when they examined my spine: my father, John Kirkpatrick, now Dr. F., to say nothing of the entire piano faculty of the Yale School of Music who had focused their disapproval on my torso and wrists. Each time, I felt like an innocent defendant in a court case facing a hostile trial lawyer. I'd done nothing wrong. Why were all these angry guys treating me like a criminal?

My father was no longer around to recommend a neurologist, but my mother gave me the number of an East Side doctor she occasionally saw. It had never occurred to me to ask exactly why she went to a neurologist at all. Her increasing disability had been shrouded in silence, and my brother and I had come to accept it as the new normal. In typical Blier fashion, my mother in turn asked me no questions when I told her that Dr. Fazzari had referred me to a neurologist. Her tone was neutral: "Go see Dr. X. He's a nice man."

A week later I hied myself off to his office. I defused my sense of foreboding in a cocoon of spaced-out detachment, an emotional technique I had developed to help me through other panic-inducing situations. I rang the buzzer and took a seat in the waiting area, where there was not a soul to be seen. Suddenly from the back rooms of the office I heard a man screaming at the top of his lungs. "You've screwed up AGAIN, you made a total MESS out of this like you ALWAYS do! That chart goes in THIS file, you're a total IDIOT! I don't know why I haven't FIRED you!! You're HOPELESS!!" It was the aria of a rageaholic at full tilt, Wagnerian in volume and as malevolent as Titus Andronicus. Though it seemed her offense had been minor, he berated his receptionist as if she had mistakenly administered a hydrochloric acid enema. What hellhole had I ventured into?

Eventually the tongue-lashing came to an end, and Dr. X strode into the room wearing a bland smile. "Steven, how nice to see you." Had we ever met, I wondered? "How's your mother doing?"

"Okay, under the circumstances."

"Oh yes, of course. My condolences to you and your family. Your father was a fine man." Then, "So what brings you here today?"

I recounted the story of Fazzari the physiatrist. Dr. X listened, performed the most cursory examination possible, and then observed casually, "Oh sure, you've got what your mother's got."

I stared. "And what is that?"

"Well, muscular dystrophy, of course."

My face must have fallen, and he paused, perhaps registering the fact that I had never been told her diagnosis. To buck me up, he added, "But don't worry. You have a few years of normal function left!" He rose and extended his hand. The meeting was over, with no more information provided than those two sentences. I was unable to think straight, and far too disoriented to formulate a question. "Send my regards to your mother, Steven!" he chimed as I left the office.

Dizzy from Dr. X's unbridled screaming, the brittle falseness of his bedside manner, and the unexpected diagnosis, I sank into a dull state of dread. What lay in store for me when those few years of normal function reached their sell-by date? Trudging across East Eighty-Sixth Street, I fixated on what my father had told me. Surely he must have suspected the truth the moment he caught sight of my back twenty-two years earlier. But fearing that a prediction of muscular dystrophy would send me into a tailspin, he thought it would be best to evade the issue altogether. His instinct was to protect me, a decision I once resented but have come to understand. Would I have been less neurotic if I'd known the truth about my body earlier in my life? Probably not, but who can tell?

Hustling across Park Avenue on a yellow light, I took a calamitous fall right in the middle of the street. This time I landed on my hands and knees. To the oncoming cars roaring up the wide avenue, the crosswalk must have looked like an impromptu yoga studio, with me practicing the cow asana. Traffic slowed, horns blared, and I pulled myself to the center island with only a scraped hand, a bloodied knee, and yet another pair of torn trousers.

It was finally time to talk everything over with my mother, whose strength and energy had taken a downward turn in the months after my father's death. She was beginning to spend more time lying on her bed, although with assistance and a walker she could still get out of the house. While she was also able to cook, bending down to lift a pan out of the oven took a Herculean effort. When I worked up my nerve to relate my experience with Dr. X, she seemed unsurprised by his temper tantrum, merely lifting her eyebrows as if to say, "What do you expect from neurologists? They're all big divas." Then I brought up his diagnoses—of me, and also of her.

"Mom, you never told me you had muscular dystrophy."

"I didn't?"

"No, and neither did dad. Why did you keep this information from me and Mal?"

She stared into the middle ground. "Well, it's obviously something *dystrophic*," she said, taking uncharacteristic refuge in medicalese. The implication was that only an idiot would need to have it spelled out.

Nothing could have been further from the truth. A family friend had once told me my mom had Lou Gehrig's disease. A breathtakingly tactless man in Steamboat Springs, Colorado, once complimented me on playing so well in spite of my cerebral palsy. To this day I receive admiring arm squeezes of support from people who murmur, "You're so brave, the way you cope with your multiple sclerosis." My visit with Dr. X, unhappy as it was, did at least dispel a multitude of lingering bogeymen. Given those alternatives, I'd grab muscular dystrophy in a heartbeat.

Another person might have sought out every available piece of information about facioscapulohumeral dystrophy—better known by its acronym, FSHD—but true to form, I kept my blinders on. My motto was always "What you don't know can't hurt you," never "Knowledge is power." And I was out of my mind with work. Michael and I were in the second season of the New York Festival of Song, and I hadn't any concept of how much time it would take to present six annual concerts in a 110-seat hall. I was confronted with an avalanche of obligations I'd never shouldered as a mere pianist-for-hire playing concerts, auditions, and voice lessons. And during the 1990s, my career began to burgeon into the major leagues as a recital pianist, squiring Cecilia Bartoli, Lorraine Hunt, Renée Fleming, June Anderson, and Susan Graham to gigs at Carnegie Hall, Lincoln Center, Wigmore Hall, and La Scala. I walked a little funny, but played just fine.

The sudden whirlwind of my career made it convenient to ignore sporadic falls. Occasionally there was even a touch of black comedy. On the way to a post-recital reception with June Anderson in Edmonton, Alberta, the concert producer ostentatiously grabbed the singer's fur-coated arm as we climbed out of the car. The city was in a deep freeze and the driveway was a sheet of ice. "Now, we wouldn't want our *star* to fall down, would we?" he cooed. Right on cue, splat, I fell flat on my face. They practically walked over me, narrowly avoiding my splayed-out arm, completely unaware that I'd taken a tumble. Still on the ground, I muttered to myself, "Ah well, too bad about your pianist, Ms. Anderson, but you can always find another. I wonder where he went?"

I told this story to my co-teacher at SUNY Purchase (where I taught art song once a week), Dennis Helmrich, who listened with glassy, impassive eyes. By chance, my next fall happened only a week later, on the way to pick up a rental car to drive to school. It was a particularly bad fall on a steep, oil-soaked garage ramp, and was certainly going to prompt yet another visit to French American Reweaving. I arrived late at Purchase, having stopped at home to change out of my blood-soaked trousers. When I explained to Dennis what had happened, I could see the gears in his head spinning.

"Didn't you also fall a week ago in Edmonton?"

"Oh yes, but that was on the ice."

"Mm-hmm. Well. Your class is waiting." He gave me one more searching look, and then disappeared into his studio.

I could see that Dennis had put two and two together, and I was suddenly having trouble denying that they made four, whether you added or multiplied. I had to face the fact that muscular dystrophy was the cause of my physical instability, and indeed of the rather strange way I walked—which my cousin Sue casually observed at a family gathering.

"Oh, you have foot drop."

"Foot drop?"

"It's when the muscle that flexes the foot upward loses strength. That's why you fall. You're tripping over your own foot."

By this point I had upgraded my health insurance and acquired a primary care physician. My father's frightening, at-home death from cancer had put the fear of God in me, and I had decided to keep tabs on my PSA levels and blood pressure like every other guy my age. Finding help for muscular dystrophy, however, was elusive. There was no medicine to prescribe, and a series of neurologists (including another really crazy one) had little to dispense besides "Come see me in six months, and we'll measure your decline." Some offered warm encouragement, for which I was thankful. But when it came to practical advice, I seemed to be on my own.

I shared my cousin's diagnosis of foot drop with my doctor. "Yes, your cousin is right."

"So what do I do?"

"You need orthotics."

"Huh?"

"Orthotics, plastic inserts in your shoe that keep your foot elevated. There are over-the-counter ones, but you'll really need to get them fitted for you." That process involved sticking my feet in a trough of plaster of Paris, which seemed like a fitting punishment for all the damage they'd done to my wardrobe.

The orthotics saved me from falling down all the time, but as I reached my early fifties, it was becoming exhausting to walk. By this time I had seen FSHD confine my beloved mother to her apartment in Riverdale, though she retained her wry wit and her compassionate insight into people until the very end. Since she didn't go out very much, certain modern conveniences had eluded her: she had never used an ATM, and she was dumbfounded by the sight of text scrolling on a computer screen. Yet until her final days she was a shrewd observer of the world, always ready with a salty comment as she watched the evening news—"Unsavory character," she would mutter as she saw some slimeball politician lie through his teeth, and for the truly despicable, a scathing "Oh, you are such an ass," a phrase given extra tang by her Boston accent. She was also startlingly perceptive about the people she knew, and unfailingly kindhearted. She would have made a great therapist. One of the great satisfactions of my life is that she met my husband Jim and had a couple of precious years to get to know him—and embrace him as a son.

Her death in the year 2000, after a nine-month bout with cancer, hit me very hard. And as I mourned her, my body took a rapid turn for the worse that I assumed was temporary but was not. I would be standing in my living room talking to a friend, and without warning my knees would buckle—as though the rug had literally been pulled out from under me, a physical representation of my grieving soul. After staggering, I would right myself, hoping no one had noticed. But I'll never forget the way my cousin Ned looked at me when he witnessed one of these abrupt lurches. Ned is not a subtle man, and I could tell he was troubled.

In a fugue state of mourning, I tried to work on the fall NYFOS programs, both of which were in trouble. But first I had to play at Carnegie Hall. Evelyn Lear had been invited to sing at a benefit to raise funds for breast cancer research. The survivor of a double mastectomy, she accepted, and engaged me to accompany her. The concert took place only three weeks after my mom died, and I was still feeling shaky; but Evelyn was singing only one song—Sondheim's "I'm Still Here"—and I thought I could manage it. She'd decided to include a monologue in the middle of the song in which she told the story of her diagnosis and recovery, and it ended up being one of the emotional highlights of the evening. But there was one lyric she always messed up: she would sing "I've been through all of last year" instead of "I got through all of last year."

"What's the difference?" she asked.

"Well, everyone in the audience has *been* through all of last year. You *got* through it in spite of huge obstacles."

"Oh, I see."

Despite our discussion she still sang the wrong lyric that night—another one of those indelible beet stains—but she brought down the house. Evelyn had the force of personality to command Carnegie Hall whether the words were right or not. After the song, I stood up from the piano and she took my hand in what I think of as "the diva-clutch," no doubt a move perfected to control overweening tenors at the Met. Squeezing my knuckles together with the force of a pair of pliers, she pulled me down in a joint bow. There I was, eyeballing the floor of Carnegie Hall with a seventy-four-year-old soprano at my side and no idea how I would get my body back to a standing position. Frantic, I lurched my head backward, and my cranium managed to jerk my torso upright. No one knew how frightened I had been.

But the worst was still to come. At the end of the concert, all the performers filed onstage for a final bow, joining Mandy Patinkin, the evening's MC. I figured I'd be okay as long as I didn't allow anyone to grab my hand. But then Patinkin decided to cap the evening with an impromptu a cappella rendition of "Over the Rainbow." I realized that I might not be stable enough to remain standing unassisted for the duration of the song, and hadn't positioned myself close enough to the piano to hang on for support. I felt my knees quavering as he crooned, in his famously vibrato-laden falsetto, "Where troubles mellllt like lllllemondrops." I moved one foot slowly in front of the other to broaden my stance and create a bit more support. "That's wheeeeeere youuuuu'll fiiiiiiiiind meeeee." I practiced deep breathing and began to wonder how bad it would really be if I just keeled over. By sheer force of will I made it to the double bar as he warbled, "Why oh why can't I?"—a lyric that all at once took on a new, grim meaning.

As I mourned my mother in the ensuing weeks, life grew perilous in a whole new way. One day I reached for a piece of music on the shelf and without warning collapsed in a heap on the floor. The slant of a steep curb could throw me off my balance. I'd grab a student's arm just to navigate the carpeted hallways of Juilliard. I took cabs everywhere, even the ten blocks to and from the pool, where the ladder was also becoming impossible to manage. And I couldn't climb out of a taxi without assistance from the driver. I acquired a series of canes, eventually graduating to an arm crutch, a tall pole with a cuff in the middle that looked like a cup holder.

My death grip on the crutch's handle brought on a class-A case of tendinitis. It was agony to spread my left hand open. Still, I kept concertizing through it all. I probably hit bottom in 2005 during a NYFOS program called *Teatros españoles*, doped up on Advil and obsessively murmuring positive, New Age-y mantras in the wings. Having audaciously programmed a famous Granados aria with an ornate piano part—"La maja y el ruiseñor"—I struggled through it on sheer will power. Amazingly, I must have done more than just squeak by. In the *New York Times,* Anne Midgette, after dismissing the soprano with a lukewarm write-off, wrote: "That piece, like most of the evening, belonged to Mr. Blier, whose lovely playing of the nightingale's liquid trills drew a touched smile from the singer and warm applause."

Though my hands were capable of trills, my legs were still bent on spills. Rising from a chair was a risky proposition, and I couldn't be sure I'd land on the pavement safely when descending from a bus. As a result, I became more and more conservative about leaving home without a persuasive reason. I live on a very windy corner, where a stiff breeze could blow me to the ground. I was so busy adapting to my new limitations that I didn't perceive how restricted my life had become. Once again it was a friend, not a doctor, who came to my aid: Eric Schwartz, who noticed I was turning down more and more invitations to meet up in the neighborhood. I couldn't be sure my legs were up to the three-block walk to his house.

A few days after one of my polite demurrals, Eric gave me a call. "Steve, I'm coming to see you on Sunday."

"Oh, how nice . . ."

"No, listen to me. I found this guy who sells mobility scooters. And you're going to love it."

"Mobility scooters?"

"Yeah, it's time. You don't go out except to Juilliard, you're always exhausted, and you keep falling on your ass."

"If only! Usually it's my knees."

"Whatever. This guy doesn't have a store. He brings the scooter to you. And—get this—he makes sure it's the right machine for you, and then he leaves. Poof. You get to drive around in your new wheels for a week, see if you like it. It's like he left his toy in your apartment and you get to play with it for seven days."

"And then?"

"And then, you either buy it or give it back. No commitments." I wasn't comfortable with the idea of driving around in a contraption I associated with the elderly and infirm. But if it was just another kid's go-cart I could use until the next weekend... well, that might be fun.

The first few days were rough. Ramps felt like roller coasters, and it took me a while to master the techniques of getting on a bus and shopping for groceries. During that first week, I knocked over a wire rack holding twenty-four packages of pita bread at Balducci's, and smashed into the electric eye on a Juilliard elevator. But a gym buddy named Alan insisted on accompanying me the first day I took the scooter for a spin. He patiently showed me how to park the thing on a bus, and he retrieved all the flying pita bread. Neither Alan nor Eric was a close friend, but they both ministered to me when I was at my most vulnerable. I can never thank them enough.

I loved riding my motorized tricycle around town. After years of being hauled bodily in and out of taxis, hobbling with terror from the curb to the first grab bar I could find, and praying that my knees wouldn't fold into one of their unpredictable collapses, I was drunk on my sudden speed and freedom. I drove like an aggressive New Yorker, leaning on the horn—a tiny squeak I dubbed the "mouse orgasm." In nice weather I drove the forty blocks south to Juilliard, then sped down the halls at full throttle. Sold.

After a few years of relative contentment, I began to feel the limitations of my new wheels. Sure, I could now outrun my husband Jim, but I couldn't stay put in the scooter at the dinner table, or at the piano, or at the theater. And those transfers were becoming a little fraught, with muscles beginning to atrophy from disuse. The price of motorized liberation was the accelerated decline of my ability to stand on my own two feet.

Everything came to a head at a NYFOS benefit in 2010. By then our subscription audiences had attended enough concerts to be familiar with my uncertain journey from scooter to piano chair. But the high rollers who paid a thousand bucks to attend the galas saw me less often and were also less indulgent of my physical frailties. One man came up to congratulate me after the concert. "Wow, great show. And man, we were *all* holding our breath when you went from your tricycle to the piano bench. Scary! We weren't sure you were going to make it!" Tactless, yes. But this patron's rudeness-with-a-smile made me aware that my physical struggles were not escaping scrutiny and in fact might be starting to damage my career in a way I had not anticipated.

It fell to another patron to bail me out: a warm-hearted man named Chris Kinney. Like many of the Samaritans who intervened to help me out in those years, Chris was not someone I knew very well. He sat on the board of NYFOS for a couple of years and took his duties seriously—one of which, evidently, was to upgrade my wheels. Later that evening at the gala, he mentioned that he was friends with Chuck Close. "Would you like to meet him? He said he could give you some advice about mobility stuff."

I jumped—metaphorically—at the chance. Close, an American artist revered for his huge, intricate photorealist paintings, had suffered a spinal artery collapse in 1988 that left him unable to walk, and with only limited use of his hands. Yet he persevered and continued his creative life, and along the way became an expert on devices for the handicapped.

Chuck Close was not a warm and fuzzy personality, but he was generous with his time and attention. When I rolled in on my blue scooter, his first words were "Well, the first thing we need to do is get you out of that piece of shit."

I adjusted to the tenor of the conversation. "And into . . . ?"

"You need a wheelchair."

"I've heard about this new type that goes up and down stairs . . ."

"The iBOT. Yeah, I got one of those. It's great if you want to take a chunk out of all your furniture and destroy your walls. And it doesn't go up all staircases—or down some of them. No, you want this type."

"This type" was a Permobil, made in Sweden, apparently the Rolls-Royce of mobility devices. It looked like the Centre Pompidou, festooned with pipes and wiring. Chuck connected me to his vendor, and soon after, all the insurance hurdles cleared, I was whizzing home from Mount Sinai Hospital where I had gotten my brand-new wheels. Jim struggled to keep up with me, driving the now-obsolete scooter through Central Park. It took some months to learn to drive the Permobil—for the first time, I wished I'd played video games as a kid so that I'd have some idea how to handle a joystick. I crashed into every corner in our place, scraped tables, smashed my toes.

But Chuck was right: scooters are toys, wheelchairs are freedom. After long years of hobbling around, fearing sudden gusts of wind, and falling on my keister, I was king of the road. And I've never looked back.

June Anderson and me onstage at Carnegie Hall in 1991. © *Steve J. Sherman*

CHAPTER 9

Halfway Up Mount Rushmore

THE YEAR WAS 1991, NYFOS was planning its fourth season, I was about to turn forty, I was teaching one day a week at SUNY Purchase, and I was still trotting around on my own two legs, though not without the occasional face-plant onto the sidewalk. As successful as NYFOS was, I had never let go of my other dream: to become a major player in the upper echelons of the classical music world, while somehow retaining my status as a scruffy countercultural upstart in America's grass-roots concert scene. It seemed unrealistic, until I got a phone call at the end of the summer. It was from superstar soprano June Anderson.

"I've been asked to sing a recital at Carnegie Hall," June began, then, hedging, "I'm not sure I'm going to say yes, but if I do, would you *in principle* be interested in playing for me?" I would indeed be interested, in principle. We had already done some work together—Michael Barrett had steered her in my direction to prepare the role of Cunegonde when Leonard Bernstein cast her in his valedictory performances of *Candide*. The soprano's star had risen quickly: in the 1980s she made her mark at New York City Opera, capping her bel canto successes there with a thrilling turn as Lucia di Lammermoor, as well as a brilliant performance of Rossini's *Semiramide* at Carnegie Hall. Shortly after singing *Candide* with Bernstein, she made her Met début in *Rigoletto*. She was known for her virtuosity, intelligence, and Garbo-esque aloofness.

Still, her uncertainty about a Carnegie Hall recital début was understandable. June had become close to Bernstein in his final years—she had also been his soprano soloist in Beethoven's "Ode to Joy" when the maestro conducted it after the fall of the Berlin Wall—and his recent death had affected her deeply. And she still mourned another beloved mentor: her voice teacher, Robert Leonard, who died just three days before Bernstein.

Finally she decided to go ahead with the concert, but her resistance to recital work didn't end there. For one thing, much of the traditional song repertoire did not appeal to her. "I can't sing about trout!" she exclaimed in our first conversation, alluding to Schubert's done-to-death Lied "Die Forelle." I gently assured her that she would not have to sing about anything that swam if she didn't want to. And after my experience at Juilliard with Beverley Johnson fifteen years earlier, I didn't want to go anywhere near "Die Forelle" either.

Since June had been a French major at Yale, she had an unusually refined understanding of poetry. I hoped that would endear French *mélodie* to her, but her Ivy League education only seemed to make her more critical. "I love the poem, but the music just isn't very good," she groused in response to an iconic song by Henri Duparc, esteemed by many as a pinnacle of the genre.

Since her artistic nature was not geared to gentle confessions or meditations on nature, building a program became a challenge. June thrived on costumes, lights, high drama, virtuoso coloratura and—more than anything—physical distance from her audience. Born for the grandeur of opera, she relished the safety of an orchestra pit gaping between herself and her listeners. Supported only by a piano and with Row A right under her nose, she seemed to feel vulnerable.

But the most pressing issue was something I could not bring up for fear of rupturing our working relationship. It was becoming obvious that her voice was in transition, taking on greater weight and size in her middle register. In the process, she was losing some of the silvery evenness that had first lifted her to fame. This was to be expected as she neared forty. Healthy voices naturally acquire more mass and color over time, but these growth spurts need to be managed carefully. At this point the upper part of her voice hadn't quite found a way to match what was happening an octave lower. June could still excite audiences with breathtaking rapid-fire passagework, she retained her magisterial command of those super-high notes that decorated the ends of bel canto arias, and her years on Italian stages had taught her to confront her audience with the boldness of a gladiator. But I began to feel the absence of her late voice teacher Robert, who would have been able to help her even out the registers and negotiate the changes in her voice.

Still, June was the only big-name singer who ever asked for my help in choosing repertoire. We finally settled on songs by Franz Liszt, which suited her, Joaquín Turina, which suited me, and a trio of American composers—Rorem, Bernstein, and Barber—which suited us both. It wasn't hard to make music together, except that no matter what tempo I chose, she would slow it down. It finally dawned on me that I must be starting all of her songs too fast. The next time, I tried to begin at the tempo she would be taking at her vocal entrance. I guessed wrong: after my spacious four-bar intro she came in even slower, practically running out of breath.

"What are you trying to do, kill me?" she shot across the piano.

"No, but what a fabulous idea," I thought as I bowed my head in mute apology. I grew accustomed to playing the piano intros at a normal clip and instantly downshifting when she started to sing.

June's Carnegie recital was a decent success, and the prelude to six more concerts, including performances at the Kennedy Center and La Scala in Milan. The more we were together, the more it became clear that she harbored a deep antipathy to the concert platform. Offstage after the first group of songs at our Kennedy Center recital, she pressed up against the wall looking as if she wanted to sprout wings and fly away. "June, it's going so well, and the audience is loving it!" I gushed by way of encouragement. She looked at me with the sadness of a woman mourning a deceased pet. I might as well have told her that her puppy was happier in puppy heaven.

June was always cordial to me, and I admired her strength and razor-sharp mind. But it was hard to break through her aloofness, and our partnership never flowered into a friendship. It was becoming obvious that I walked with a bit of difficulty, and most people slowed their pace to match mine when we were together. June seemed not to notice. In Paris to rehearse for the La Scala concert, she strode briskly through the streets, blond curls flying in the breeze, unaware that I was three paces behind her, struggling to keep up.

No, it was not a love match. But working with June did take me to the grandest stage I'd yet seen: La Scala. To prepare for that concert, her manager, Jack Mastroianni, booked a tryout in Modena, where I was puzzled to see that all the posters, programs, and even my dressing room tag listed my name as "Ivan Steven Blier." It took me a few days to piece the story together: June's manager had told the auspices that June's pianist was called Steven. When they didn't recognize the name, he must have made the joke, "Steven—you know, like, 'Even Steven'!" Which they heard. *all'italiano*, as "Ivan Steven." The nickname stuck to me for quite a few years afterwards.

The night of the La Scala concert I was given the dressing room that had once housed Maria Callas, or so they told me. The audience, polite for the European art songs if somewhat nonplussed by the American pieces by Rorem and Bernstein, went mad for the Italian songs and arias. June knew her crowd and whipped them into a frenzy. As always, I felt free and easy about the encores, and when she sang "The Last Rose of Summer," I played my own reharmonized arrangement of the Irish folk tune, not the version from Flotow's opera *Martha* that most opera singers use. The artistic directors of La Scala practically had a stroke in the wings—what was I doing? Where did these chords come from? And when I strode onstage without a score to play "Ah! non giunge," from *La sonnambula*—I didn't need the music, she wanted to sing it, no big deal—they practically needed a fainting couch and smelling salts.

My brother Malcolm and my sister-in-law Vicki had flown in for my La Scala début, and I finally spotted them in the Royal Box just before the last encore. I was overjoyed they were with me on this special night. If they hadn't come, I would have been completely alone after scaling the Everest of a La Scala début. I lost sight of June in the mêlée afterwards when a crowd of autograph seekers descended on her, and I never saw her again that evening. I was hurt that I hadn't been included in whatever after-party had been planned, but I had a better one to go to. Mal, Vicki, and I found a nearby trattoria, split a bottle of wine, and ordered a *cotoletta alla Milanese*.

Halfway Up Mount Rushmore | 139

Groovin' with Cecilia Bartoli at Carnegie in 1998. © *Steve J. Sherman*

BY THE early 1990s I had acquired a reputation for knowing my way around both Italian opera and American popular song. That's when I got a call from June's manager Jack Mastroianni, who was scooping up some of the hottest talents in the classical world. Hottest among them was the young mezzo-soprano Cecilia Bartoli, who was about to give a highly anticipated New York recital at Tully Hall—and she had just fired her pianist after a quarrel. Jack was pushing Cecilia to include an American song as an encore, and he had his heart set on "Summertime." Now, who could play both Rossini and Gershwin? Answer: me.

Since this was to be an arranged marriage, I had to present myself for inspection at Jack's place. Initially Cecilia was polite but somewhat reserved, held back by both the awkwardness of the situation and her limited English. I privately thanked the Almighty that I had ignored the earnest advice of the Dean at Yale, who counseled me to take an 8 a.m. physics class instead of what he referred to patronizingly as "Italian lessons." I'd recently supplemented those two semesters of Italian 101 with some private study, so I was able to hold up my end of a slightly stiff conversation. At Jack's invitation we drank some wine, and then a little more, until Cecilia proclaimed, "*Son ubriaca*" (I'm drunk). I caught Jack's eye and nodded to the piano, and he confirmed my impulse: What better moment to see if she and I were compatible as musicians?

"Want to do a few songs, Cecilia? *Vuoi cantare un po'?*"

"*Sì!*" she exclaimed.

For once, my loosey-goosey, non-conservatory way of making music worked in my favor. Cecilia was a born improviser, and music poured out of her freely, unpremeditated. We sailed through a Mozart song, and her zest for singing signaled me to let go and follow her fantasy. She seemed happy, and decided she wanted sing a famous Rossini aria. When she started to hunt for a score and I stopped her with "Oh, don't bother, *lo so a memoria, non ho bisogno di una partitura*," her eyes lit up. No score necessary? Visions of sugarplums danced in her head—here was a pianist who would be able toss off encores at her whim, surprising the audience by walking onstage with no music.

There were two concerts on offer—in Kentucky and at Alice Tully Hall—but the first one conflicted with a date at Weill Hall I'd promised to baritone Kurt Ollmann, and I wasn't about to leave him in the lurch. I worried that that would be the coup de grâce for my relationship with Cecilia, but miraculously she kept me on for just the Tully concert. Although she had appeared in New York only a few times, her recordings had made her the toast of the town. This was her second New York recital after a three-year absence, and it quickly sold out the thousand-seat hall. In a rare move, Tully added four rows of stage seats, which meant that throughout the evening I could receive reassurance from my childhood friend Karen Brudney, seated in my line of vision. Cecilia offered "Summertime" that night as her third encore, and (as far as I know) she never sang it again. Gershwin had done his job: he got me through the door.

We proceeded to give recitals across the States and in Canada, Scotland, and Brazil. Making music with Cecilia was easy. She didn't like to rehearse, and she knew how to guide me into her phrasing without having to explain much verbally. Listening intently to my sound, she turned every song into an intimate duet, unlike any of the big leaguers I'd worked with before. When necessary, she could fix any problems that cropped up with just a few words. I once began the second section of Rossini's aria "Bel raggio" (from *Semiramide*) with quick vigor, the way I'd played it for June Anderson. In the process I also tripped over the sixteenth notes at the end of the intro. Cecilia leaned over the Steinway and gazed into my eyes. "*No, Stefano. Meno forte, più lento.*" I was confused—softer and slower? Wasn't this the brilliant virtuoso cabaletta to the piece? She raised her eyebrows; it was so obvious. "*Ma—it should be a dolce momento!*" Of course—a sweet moment! Those are the opening lyrics of the cabaletta—but who ever took them to heart? I responded with my rosiest, most amorous sound, like musical foreplay. Needless to say, when the fireworks began eight bars later, they erupted like a meteor shower.

Cecilia's mother Silvana, herself a former singer and her daughter's first teacher, traveled with us on several of our tours. Since she spoke almost no English, she was grateful for my somewhat antiquated, operatic Italian. Silvana and I were both from big cities (Rome in her case) and similarly chauvinistic about our hometowns, two classic urban provincials. But she was not fond of North America and found some of the restaurant meals inedible. At an Asian-Italian fusion place in Edmonton, she took one bite of her noodles and laid down her fork in disgust: "*Non è pastasciutta.*" It's not pasta, it's not even food. "Come to Rome," she advised me in Italian. "The only pasta worth eating is made from the wheat they grow near our house."

Silvana always came to our dress rehearsals, where she found my pedaling too wet for her taste. After every song I'd hear "*Troppo forte, troppo pedale.*" Having been through this before with Martha Schlamme and Roberta Peters, I had some experience shrinking my sound down to size AAAA. But making my piano playing dry enough for her was more difficult. Playing eighteenth-century music without pedal was hard enough, but I had to knead the piano like bread dough to create legato in the Ravel songs. As a result, I occasionally received unflattering reviews that chastised me for my timidity as a musician. Fond as I was of Silvana, I began to mentally dub these concerts the "Throw Momma from the Train" tour.

Cecilia was soon aware that she could throw me pretty much any song or aria she liked, breeze through it once, and sing it confidently to a crowd of 2,500 listeners without a second thought. I remember standing backstage with her before a concert at Hill Auditorium in Ann Arbor, Michigan. We were beginning with some Schubert songs set to Italian texts. I'd never played them before, and we'd only touched on them lightly just before the show. Not only was the 4,000-seat hall full, the concert was being taped for broadcast. But when I sat down at the piano to start the concert, I could not for the life of me remember the tempo of the first song—was it a saunter, a trot, a sashay? I took a breath. "She trusts you, that's why she doesn't rehearse," I told myself. As I plowed into the first measures, Cecilia turned to me with a megawatt smile. To the audience it probably looked like an expression of joy. But I saw the real message in her eyes: "Too fast, don't worry, I'll fix it when I come in." I threw in an arty bit of rubato that would allow for a new tempo, and relaxed into her phrase when she entered.

Cecilia was the most dazzling virtuoso I'd ever encountered. No one could match the brilliance and accuracy of her rapid passagework. She was also a mistress of long-lined melody, to which she brought a surprising emotional depth and sense of wonder. Luckily, I wasn't required to match her virtuosity in kind. The piano parts were not technically difficult: the fast ones played easily into my sense of rhythm, and I seemed to have a knack for matching her delicacy, nuance for nuance, in those slow, spun-out arias. Fearless and vocally consistent, she exuded a joy onstage that helped me shed some of the self-doubt that had dogged me as a performer. And when Silvana was not around, I discovered I could edge the volume up a notch or two without repercussions.

Onstage we may have looked like a pair of lovebirds, but offstage it became evident that I was never going to be part of her inner circle. I was neither a star musician nor Italian, categories that might have propelled me from dependable colleague to trusted friend. I remember only one long private conversation in our four years together. We were in a limousine returning to New York after a concert at Caramoor (in Katonah), and we were the only people still awake in the car. With no one else to talk to, Cecilia shared some personal thoughts about the evening and about the music world. I remember her frank avowal about making a career: *"Lo sai, Stefano, tutto è pubblicità."* Everything is about publicity.

It was a disarming late-night confession: you can be the greatest artist in the world, but without the right press agent you could still end up singing for change in the subways.

With Cecilia I got a taste of the high life, wined and dined in the best restaurants before being swept back to a first-class hotel in a limo. She seemed to accept me as an equal partner in her art, affirming my musical instincts, allowing me to trust what I heard in my imagination, in my soul. At the same time, I was also learning that even superhuman virtuosity can cloy when witnessed too many times. I felt guilty as I began to weary of her musical genius—the miraculous, lightning-fast coloratura and artfully molded phrases—and also of the narrow scope of the repertoire. Ultimately the job came with a glass ceiling. I was constantly in second place to Jean-Yves Thibaudet, a world-famous French pianist who, like Cecilia, was under a multidisc contract with Decca. It suited the company to record them together and then pair them up onstage. As Jean-Yves became increasingly capricious about his concert dates, I found myself holding ten-day slots open for tours while we waited to see whether he was going to cancel, which happened with some frequency. No real complaints from me—it was how I got to play at Carnegie Hall with Cecilia Bartoli. Bridesmaid or bride, you still earn your fee.

In spite of the long odds, I proposed a recording project to her: an album of South American song. I made a binder with six or seven of the best numbers, bought a box of the ritziest pastries in Manhattan, and invited Cecilia (and her mother, who was in town) over to pitch the idea. Though we had spent much time in one another's company, it was rare for the three of us to be alone together. I presented my idea and played some of the songs, while they made a dent in the petit fours.

"South American songs," mused Cecilia, "isn't that what José Cura did?" referring to a well-known tenor who had released an album of Argentinean music about a year earlier.

"Well, sort of. This rep is different—I don't think there would have to be any songs in common."

After I'd shown her some beautiful music by Guastavino and López-Buchardo, she turned to her mother. *"Mamma—che pensi, è originale, no?"* Silvana didn't need to say whether she found the songs fresh and novel. Her wincing eyes and pursed lips sent the message: "We are not amused." Some days later I heard from Jack, Cecilia's manager, thanking me for the idea. But the singer's musical passions, it seemed, were leading her toward an exploration of the Baroque era. She'd also be inching away from piano-and-voice solo recitals and gravitating to original-instrument orchestras.

Meanwhile Cecilia's love affair with America was starting to go south. In February 1996 we landed an appearance on the David Letterman show, and were kept waiting until the last five minutes of the program. Dave got carried away horsing around with Kathie Lee Gifford, who was starting a new line of cosmetics. In one gag, he ate two of her "lipsticks," filled with something edible made to look like the real thing. Cecilia, cooling her heels backstage, grew about as angry as I ever saw her. When we were finally ushered onstage during a commercial break, I warmed up while the band blared some crazy jazz fusion improv. I had to get my hands moving—the studio was kept at about fifty-five degrees and my fingers were turning into icicles. Cecilia came on and we zipped through the fast section of the *Cenerentola* aria, leaving time for her to answer just one lame question from Dave, along the lines of "How do you learn all those notes?" Then the show was over.

Not long after, Cecilia (ever the scholar) sang the rare Act IV alternative aria Mozart had written for the Vienna production of *The Marriage of Figaro* in half the performances, while offering the beloved, familiar "*Deh, vieni, non tardar*" in the others. Some members of the New York audience were outraged not to hear the aria they had been waiting for all evening, and she received a harsh scolding in a *New York Times* opinion piece. No one from the Met defended her decision. Her revenge was swift and to the point: she canceled her next appearance, a production of Ravel's *L'heure espagnole*. She has not sung at the Met since.

I saw Cecilia one more time: at a Carnegie Hall concert in 2002 where she was singing Vivaldi with one of those early music vegetarian orchestras. After a rehearsal for a NYFOS show, I arrived just in time for the second half. When she spotted me in Row H, her face lit up with a radiant smile. I blew her a kiss, she returned the gesture, and I bathed once again in the glow of Cecilia's irresistible warmth.

A sweet moment with Jessye Norman backstage at Weill Hall in 2014, when she served as host for the NYFOS gala there. She was on her very best behavior that night.

IT WAS easy to form a tight musical bond with Cecilia, whose tempo and phrasing seemed so natural as to be inevitable. With Jessye Norman . . . not so much. My brief partnership with her began (and ended) in 1999 when her regular recital pianist, Mark Markham—a classy musician with a patrician technique—was living in France. It made no sense for him to fly back for a single college recital Jessye had in the middle of the season. As she investigated various options, our mutual friend Steven Cole threw my name into the hat. And he can be very persuasive.

My initial interview couldn't have been more civilized: tea with Jessye and Steven at the Carlyle, an elegant East Side hotel whose famous cabaret space was home to luminaries like Bobby Short and Woody Allen. When I approached her table, Jessye looked up at me and smiled. Although I'd first heard her in concert as far back as 1970 and attended her performances for decades, I was still bowled over by her glamour when we met face to face. As we shook hands, I spontaneously blurted, "Oh my, you are so beautiful!" With an even wider smile, she murmured, "Honey, you got the job."

It was no mere pleasantry. She had a couple of gigs coming up where she could safely try out a new collaborator: that lone recital, at Washington and Jefferson College just outside of Pittsburgh, and a one-song appearance on a morning TV show. We sealed the deal.

Our work together began promisingly. Booked on *Good Morning America* to promote her new CD of songs by Michel Legrand, she chose not to sing "The Windmills of Your Mind" or "What Are You Doing the Rest of Your Life" but instead a song by Duke Ellington, "Come Sunday." Even at 7:40 a.m. Jessye could tap into that rich vein of nobility that had mesmerized audiences for decades. I kept my arrangement simple, taking care to track every twist and turn of her phrasing. Jessye must have liked what I did—when she surfaced from her Ellington-induced trance, she turned to me and mouthed, "Thank you." My mother, watching at home, caught that moment and wept with pride.

Jessye then scheduled three rehearsals to prepare the upcoming recital, two at her place and one at mine. I soon learned that there were several Jessyes, a chiaroscuro of chilly hauteur, sophisticated wit, and disarming warmth. At all times I was aware of her charm and intelligence. And at all times I was equally aware that she had extremely firm boundaries.

I wish I'd been able to work with her ten or fifteen years earlier. By the time we met, her voice was no longer in its prime. She had been an oracular singer, building her songs and arias into Gothic cathedrals of sound. And when we rehearsed I did hear moments of that enveloping Mother Earth sonority, but they emerged intermittently between patches of foggier singing. I wondered if she was marking—singing lightly to preserve her voice—and only taking certain phrases in full voice. Or were these swerving dynamics her new normal?

I quickly got the measure of how capricious her music-making had become. At our first rehearsal I struggled to figure out the tempi of her Strauss and Poulenc, but could not discern a steady pulse. In truth, there was no pulse. Everything was what you could charitably call "free tempo" or, less charitably, "tempo di diva." This situation presented a dilemma. I wanted to be ready for our concert, but I couldn't figure out how to practice. When you woodshed a piece by yourself, you imagine a predictable musical flow. And in the process you develop habits—what some people call an "interpretation." But it was impossible to prepare for Jessye's wild alternation of gas pedal and brakes. Familiar songs began to feel like a moonwalk, as I picked my way through each measure trying vainly to line up with her, syllable by syllable.

I knew she must be disappointed. I bobbed and weaved with as much grace as possible, though I couldn't play with any freedom for fear of wrecking our ensemble. Through it all, Jessye remained cordial, a *semifreddo* of majestic reserve and spontaneous warmth. Finally the day of the concert arrived. A friend of the singer's had recommended a hotel spa not far from the college, so she'd built an extra day of pampered rest into our travel schedule. Alas, the scheme went awry. Before she traveled, Jessye always sent detailed instructions to the upcoming hotels and concert halls. The spa apparently screwed up on several counts, and she had a bad time of it. When we met in the car to the concert hall, she was not in a good mood.

I had heard stories about how difficult Jessye Norman could be backstage and thought that would prepare me for any displays of bad temper. Still, experienced up close, her outbursts were frightening. She only snapped at me once, since I quickly realized that I should keep my distance. She was at her most imperious with the lighting guy, who had focused his instruments perfectly—until she asked to have the piano moved back four feet. "You seem to have chosen to light my feet," she intoned with disdain from her new position on the stage, "whereas I think people might want to see my face." Onstage I did my best to inch my way through the music. I thought of Mark Markham with renewed awe—he had surely made more sense of the singer's phrasing than I could manage that night. Every beat arrived unpredictably, like turtles being flung at random from a fifth-story window. The concert was so stressful that when I came offstage at intermission, I made a beeline for the backstage mirror, fully expecting that my hair would have suddenly gone white, like a terrorized character in a sci-fi movie.

The second half included Chausson's "Chanson perpetuelle," which ends with a juicy, romantic climax that wells up first in the piano, sweeping the voice to the highest notes in the piece. Because the music was originally written for string quartet and piano, it's an especially unwieldy score to play on your own; the solo reduction takes in the original piano part plus all the notes of the string parts. As we rounded into the last thirty seconds of the seven-minute song, I made an executive decision: the windup to the climax, with its jumping tremolos and leaping bass notes, would only work if I took over the reins. This was going to be *my* orgasm.

Well, it was mine, but not hers. I got done first, and as I began the postlude I heard Jessye swoop up to her high G-sharp, about two and a half beats behind me. An unwritten law of collaborative pianists: *never* lose your singer. I had broken the law—a minor infraction, but with a major player.

We still had a couple of spirituals to go. In that rep I tend to use the published arrangements more as blueprints than holy writ, serving suggestions as opposed to recipes. While I didn't diverge wildly from the printed scores that night, I did play them with more of a blues feeling than she was used to. Jessye clearly appreciated the added swing and occasional jazz harmony, and for the first time all night we were really cooking together. After the concert she was wreathed in smiles. "For those spirituals, you get an honorary backwards baseball cap. And a pair of those sagger jeans."

In the wake of our two-car pileup in the "Chanson perpetuelle" I was pretty sure Jessye would not offer me more concerts. She delivered the expected verdict to Steven Cole: "Mr. Blier is a lovely man, but he plays in the modern way, and I need someone who understands the old-fashioned style." I was sorry that I wouldn't be hanging out with Jessye any more, but relieved that my trial recital was over. With Cecilia, I barely needed a run-through of a new piece to feel musically grounded. With Jessye, I feared that I would never stop skidding and lurching. As Mark Markham returned to his post, I echoed Jessye's rueful comment on that Pennsylvania spa: "Ah, *une expérience de plus*." Well, one more experience. And for all its problems, one I will cherish forever.

With Susan Graham at Matthew Epstein's fiftieth birthday concert, after she (and I) aced a notoriously difficult Handel aria.
© *Steve J. Sherman*

IF SCAMPERING after late-career Jessye Norman on a college recital series was a disappointment during my life as a pianist-for-hire, my concerts with mezzo-soprano Susan Graham and soprano Renée Fleming were the glory. Both singers were at the top of their game when I worked with them, two American Beauty roses in full flower. I enjoyed their repertoire, an appealing smorgasbord of French art song, German Lieder, and American music. And for women with their kind of cover-girl renown, they were remarkably down-to-earth. Smart and articulate, they wielded voices of great beauty and amazingly high function. Nothing seemed to disrupt the easy flow of their sound, nor did there seem to be any technical challenge they couldn't overcome. Both artists sang with joy and dedication.

When I met Susan in 1991, she was just starting out. She asked me to play her audition for the stage director Stephen Wadsworth, who was directing a production of Mozart's *La clemenza di Tito* in Houston. Stephen was running late, and as we waited, it was evident from the way

Susan paced abstractedly around the room that she was quite nervous. She wanted the role of Sesto badly, though I was pretty sure that Stephen was aiming to cast Lorraine Hunt. By age thirty-nine I had learned when to keep my mouth shut, so did not share this intel with Susan—nor that Stephen felt he'd been railroaded by her manager into holding the audition at all. When he finally hobbled into the session, he had to lie down on the floor to listen to us. His back had gone out earlier in the day.

In spite of her nerves, Susan sang impeccably. Stephen then threw her a curve ball: he asked her to perform the aria to my piano accompaniment without singing it. She turned upstage, looked at me cross-eyed, and then proceeded to do her best Marcel Marceau impression. The result was what I expected: the role went to Lorraine, who possessed a kind of fervor and mystery Susan hadn't yet tapped into. But she and Stephen did merge their artistry sixteen years later, in a beautiful production of Gluck's *Iphigénie en Tauride* at the Met—well worth the wait.

My own reunion with Susan happened when she offered me a recital tour in January 1997. In the half decade since our first meeting, her voice still had the bloom of youth, but her musicianship had deepened, and her beauty queen poise had ripened into chic sophistication. She was now a citizen of the world with a home in Europe. You could hear the patina of authenticity in her Mozart and Strauss.

Our tour took us to Fort Worth, Atlanta, Greenville (South Carolina), Washington, DC, and Tully Hall; the last of these was to be her New York recital début, and a highlight of the concert season. I had just begun dating the guy who would eventually become my husband, James Russell, and was feeling the glow of an auspicious new relationship. I met him after a half year of self-imposed monasticism brought on by a pair of egregiously botched attempts at romance in the summer of 1996—the nadir of my dating life. The cure must have worked: when I saw Jim across a crowded room, I knew we were meant for one another. And Susan's whisking me away only turned up the heat on our budding courtship. After she and I returned to New York for the Tully concert, I introduced them; as Susan pulled him in for an embrace, she caught my eye over his shoulder and broadly mouthed, "HE'S GORGEOUS!," her eyebrows almost touching the ceiling.

On our travels, Susan and I often had dinner together, conversation flowed freely, and it felt as if we were building an intimate friendship. Rehearsals were relaxed, and we shared a sense of humor. Since this recital program was relatively new to her, we built the songs as a team. I've met few vocalists who could sing with Susan's ease. Her tone spun so effortlessly and consistently that occasionally I longed for a little more sinew, a little less cream. Still, it was hard to argue with that kind of purling beauty. If her Mahler songs were more of a purée than a hearty stew, the Reynaldo Hahn songs were the last word in perfumed delicacy.

Our tour had its share of unexpected dramas. One took place at the after-party in Washington, when I briefly lost my temper with my longtime friend Matthew Epstein. By that point I had become comfortable speaking with an audience, and with that audience in particular—it was my fourth annual concert with Vocal Arts DC. Onstage that night, I compared Richard Strauss's high-handed wife, the soprano for whom he wrote many of his songs, with the notoriously willful soprano Kathleen Battle. It hadn't occurred to me that Kathy (along with Susan) was one of Matthew's clients, and that he would be highly protective of her. "*Vergogna*," he snarled at the party, the classic Italian phrase for "Shame on you." And for the only time in our six decades of friendship, I raised my voice back. No one was more shocked than I, but it was clear that something new was shaking loose in me.

The week before, when Susan and I had arrived in Greenville, I realized I was only seventy minutes from Asheville, North Carolina, where my cousin Joanna had gone to care for another cousin, Jonnie, who was dying of cancer. Early on the day of the concert, I hired a car to drive me to the hospital where Jonnie was passing his final days. Barely conscious, he gave a sign that he knew I was there. He was the only other person in my family who'd tried to make a career in music, though his folk-rock band had not established much of a footing.

Joanna was a tower of strength in a highly emotional moment. She had learned how to communicate with him, and seeing that I was freaked out by the shadow of Death in the room, she helped me make the best of my moments with our cousin. I knew that Jonnie had always felt he'd lived in my shadow. That afternoon I was blessed with the chance to tell him I loved him, had always respected and admired his devotion to music. At one point Joanna took my arm and positioned it above his body about four inches, guiding me from his neck down to his ankles. I felt something I had never experienced before: an energy field of startling power. Jonnie's spirit seemed to be leaving his body. I had always taken it on faith that each person possesses a soul, but that day I knew it for certain as I felt my cousin's rising out of his body like an electrical charge. At a cue from Joanna, I bid him farewell and made my way back to Greenville. Three hours later he was dead. "You freed him to leave this earth," Joanna later told me.

Susan was a sweet, sensible companion during all the dramas of love, death, and fury. In return I gave her every ounce of musical support I could muster. Our New York concert was a triumph and received a glowing *Times* review, which cited me as an equal partner in the afternoon's musical pleasures. Since then, we've stayed friends and collaborated on sporadic musical projects, but never again on a solo concert. If our hot musical romance in 1997 proved to be a fling rather than a marriage, it was certainly a fling to remember.

RENÉE FLEMING'S fast track to stardom ran parallel to Susan's, beginning in 1988 when they were both winners of the Metropolitan Opera National Council Awards. Renée always claimed that Susan seemed to have emerged from the womb with a perfect vocal technique, while she herself had dealt with every problem a singer can confront. If that's true, her achievement is all the more remarkable. The singer built one of the most sensuously beautiful voices the world has ever heard, and lavished it on the full spectrum of opera from baroque to contemporary.

We met when I was assisting the conductor James Conlon for the 1993 Richard Tucker Gala, an annual benefit for the foundation named after the great American tenor. I helped her prepare her music and even landed a spot in the program, partnering her in Duke Ellington's "Prelude to a Kiss." Four years later we were both on the bill for another gala concert: Matthew Epstein's by-invitation-only fiftieth birthday bash at Weill Hall, where I was accompanying Susan and a few others. After the concert Renée sought me out: "Your playing really touched me. I heard a bunch of good pianists today, but your music spoke to me."

It had been a stressful afternoon for all of us—minimal preparation for maximum risk, with an audience made up exclusively of top-level singers, conductors, coaches, and managers. Matthew had made everyone learn something new for the show, including Marilyn Horne (at age sixty-three) and Thomas Stewart (at age sixty-nine), and there were a few meltdowns along the way. (Catherine Malfitano, driven around the bend by Renata Scotto's looming presence in Row B, went into an aggressive series of bumps and grinds after singing "Io son l'umile ancella," from *Adriana Lecouvreur*, a Scotto showpiece.) Although I didn't think I'd acquitted myself especially well, apparently some reservoir of musicianship had seen me through. My reward was a series of recitals with Renée that scaled the heights of Carnegie Hall, La Scala, and the Kennedy Center, with major dates in Vienna, Boston, and Chicago and lower-profile ones in places like West Palm Beach and Escondido, California.

Although Renée dresses the part of the soignée star, the Valentino and Issey Miyake gowns are a costume. In essence, she is the eternal student, burrowing insatiably through cultural history, languages, and obscure repertoire. For one series of concerts, she based the first half on Goethe's female archetypes, unearthing rare songs by Liszt and Glinka that I'd never seen before. Whether in the great classical music capitals or venues where concertgoing was more of a social event, she always delivered high art. Yet for all her serious scholarship, there is nothing cerebral about her vocal style, which has been known to lend a touch of Streisand's bluesiness to Strauss and Handel. She is an unusual cocktail, a combination of nerd and voluptuary.

It was fascinating to experience the wide range of audience response as we journeyed across the Western hemisphere. The Viennese public glared at us like a hostile jury receiving a dose of musical castor oil, and I was sure they would take exception to my nontraditional approach to Wolf and Schubert. All afternoon their hard stares held out no comfort. What a relief to hear the ovation at the end—a verdict of not guilty—but I never felt a moment of musical communion with those listeners.

By contrast, red-blooded Latin drama reigned at La Scala, where

Renée had recently been booed by a malevolent cabal at the premiere of a production of Donizetti's *Lucrezia Borgia*. Her altercation with a notoriously difficult conductor had transformed the opera house into a bullring and made headlines. Many of her fans and professional associates thought she would—and should—cancel our concert. Instead, she faced the La Scala public with assurance and a touch of steel, wielding her voice like a sorceress. At one point I imagined there might have been an attempt in the top balcony to start a rumble, but it came to nothing. It's not easy for Italians to get exercised about Schubert. The concert was a howling success.

After the final number, the still-nervous artistic staff hovered over us in the wings, desperately trying to take control of her encore selections. Her program had been entirely in German and French, and they were determined to prevent her from singing an Italian aria for fear of another anti-Renée demonstration. "You will sing 'Summertime,' then you will sing 'Depuis le jour,'" they shouted with the manic energy of a Rossini finale. Renée smiled and nodded. She had a secret weapon: an accompanist who didn't need music for the Italian arias, so that she was able to waft onstage and announce, "'Chi il bel sogno di Doretta,' from *La rondine*. Di Giacomo Puccini." A collective gasp was followed by dead silence as I rippled through the piano intro. Renée then delivered an almost insolently voluptuous rendition of the aria. It was as though she had filled the entire theater with a Valrhona chocolate fondue, unleashing a pandemonium of "Bravas" from the Milanese crowd. The singer had slain the dragon.

We experienced the other end of the spectrum at a concert in West Palm Beach, Florida. Although the presenters had assiduously denied me a single comp ticket, claiming that the recital was sold out to the walls, the hall was only 70 percent full. Once onstage, I saw why: it was the oldest audience I had ever played for, and it wasn't hard to picture the reasons a subscription-holder might not be in attendance. The West Palm public responded with placid appreciation, along with a few unintentional call-and-response moments. Debussy's "La chevelure" ends with a piano postlude that normally goes, "Tweedle, pause, tweedle, pause, tweedle, pause, left-hand D-flat, pause, chord." That afternoon it was more like:

ME: Tweedle—
Audience member: [loud cough]
ME: Tweedle—-
Another audience member: [loud yawn]
ME: Tweedle—-
Another audience member: [soft cry of "oy vey"]
ME: Left-hand Db—
Another audience member: [the unmistakable sound of a fart]
ME: Final chord.

Renée and I formed a comfortable musical partnership. She sang with romance and sensuality, but I always knew how to shape the phrases with her. Even when she stretched out her lines like a languorous cat, her musical impulses remained clear. In rehearsal she mostly let me find my own way, but there were certain gestures she depended on, and she was not shy about correcting me if I zigged when I should have zagged. And she zeroed in on one of my bad habits: doubling the melody in songs by Gershwin and Ellington. It was a security blanket I didn't need, and removing it forced me to find more creative ways to improvise with my right hand. In some ways she and I were made for each other. We both had deep roots in American popular music, we loved unearthing beautiful, forgotten art songs and building strong thematic programs. We shared a strong streak of musical hedonism, as well as a tendency to overinflect our phrases—bending the line as we explored the nooks and crannies between notes.

I was on board for some of Renée's swankiest gigs, including a "Live from Lincoln Center" telecast in 2001 and a concert in Barcelona's Palau de la Música Catalana. That *modernista* hall was the most beautiful performance space I have ever seen. During my warm-up, I gradually acclimatized myself to the mild gazes of the eighteen tile-and-terracotta muses festooning the back wall. But when I noticed the winged horses suspended in the upper balcony during the concert, I nearly lost my place—the only time in my life that architecture distracted me from the task at hand.

Two problems cropped up during our collaboration. One of them was predictable: for all the high-level concerts I played with Renée, it became clear I would never be her partner in the recording studio. For those projects she had her pick of the world's greatest pianists—Christoph Eschenbach and Jean-Yves Thibaudet for Lieder, Brad Mehldau and Fred Hersch for jazz. Given the stature of Renée's other collaborators, I was honored to be in their company at all. But our lovely hajj was not going to arrive at the Mecca of a CD contract, and this mattered to me more and more as I reached my half-century birthday.

The other issue was more subtle, and not crystal clear to me at the time. Though she had studied with Jan DeGaetani and Arleen Augér, two singers known for their scrupulously clean, somewhat angular vocalism, Renée's style was swirling and ogival. Her Mozart and Schubert could sound luxuriantly sexy or inappropriately bluesy, depending on whom you asked. I was prone to similar tendencies; one piano teacher I worked with gently suggested that my Brahms Lieder might sound better without a backbeat. I instinctively felt that my playing needed to balance Renée's soft elasticity with something firmer and squarer. If I gave in to what some saw as her excesses, the music might die on the vine. The result was that I never felt I could fully release my musical essence—until the encores, when I cast aside all inhibitions and went commando (musically).

At one concert, however, I gave in to Renée's freewheeling spirit. We were doing a Sunday matinée at Symphony Hall in Boston, and both of us were still tired out from the Carnegie concert a few nights before. Too exhausted to boot up my inner Kapellmeister, I decided to adopt the singer's impulsive approach to Wolf's *Mignon Lieder*, using more rubato and more extreme colors than usual. I knew this might be a risky choice, especially in Boston, where musical tastes tended to be conservative. Sure enough, the critic in the *Boston Globe* wrote that the final Wolf song suffered from my "tendency to sectionalize pieces rather than keeping the momentum going," though elsewhere in the review he showered me with sweet adjectives: expert, experienced, stylish, dapper, superb. I never repeated the experiment.

On February 3, 2004, I had the great pleasure of accompanying Susan and Renée in a duo recital, part of a French music festival at the

With Renée Fleming at Carnegie Hall, shocked by the ovation I received for the Duke Ellington song. © *Steve J. Sherman*

Kennedy Center. I hadn't seen Susan in seven years and welcomed the invitation. The concert was to be followed by a series of master classes with the two singers, along with the stage director Frank Corsaro, French language coach Denise Massé, and me. For us, it was Old Home Week, but for the student singers it must have been daunting to be critiqued by a panel of five experts.

Renée, of course, had done her usual research, so the program was loaded with oddball songs and duets—all three of us had to learn new pieces by Franck, Fauré, Debussy, and Messager. To accommodate her schedule, the rehearsals got crammed into a couple of three-hour sessions just before the performance. Relying on experience and musicianship, and using scores and music stands onstage, we sailed through the recital with only one derailment, in the Fauré "Pavane." I still don't know who skidded, but our lily pad capsized for about ten seconds before righting itself. Listening to the recording of the performance, I am struck by the plush assurance of the singing and the sure-footedness of my piano playing. The French repertoire agreed with all of us, and we enjoyed what amounted to a first-class public jam session as we careened through the material.

It would be my swan song with Renée, and I wouldn't make music with Susan for another seven years. There were a few good reasons why this part of my career ended: NYFOS concerts were claiming more and more of my time, and I was also teaching ten hours a week at Juilliard. And soon my mobility issues would knock me out of the pianist-for-hire game forever. No one was going to engage a pianist who walked with a cane, let alone one who entered the stage in a motorized wheelchair. But subtler issues were at play as well. I'd always felt like an outsider in the world of opera stars. As a pianist, I had the goods. But I was growing increasingly uncomfortable about the power relationship between singer and hired accompanists. I was not good at coddling divas, though I always did my best to be warm and supportive. And I often struggled to make contact with my inner muse, fearing that if I allowed myself to play from my gut I would lose the job.

When interviewers ask who controls the ensemble, singer or pianist, the standard answer is, "Of course it's a duet, and each person plays an equal part in the artistic process." Sure, that's the Platonic ideal, but the real answer is more Marxist: the person who writes the checks has the last word. At NYFOS I was in charge of the payroll and the casting. As a result, I felt musically generous, released, and confident. I couldn't be fired. This didn't mean that I ran roughshod over my colleagues. On the contrary: I felt that much freer to enter each singer's unique musical universe with tranquility and become one with them. As I began to grow used to a more equal relationship with my musical partners, it became difficult to take orders from other people—even the world's greatest artists.

At our Carnegie Hall concert, Renée sang eight encores. One of them was Duke Ellington's "It Don't Mean a Thing (If It Ain't Got That Swing)," complete with scat singing. I'd never worked out a good way to play this tune, which seemed to require horns and percussion to make its true effect. To compensate, I threw myself at the music in a frenzy, dredging up every high-energy jazz riff I could think of. I was somewhat ashamed by the way I faked my way through it; at a jazz club I would most likely have been dismissed as an over-caffeinated wannabe. Nevertheless, the song brought down the house, and Renée graciously gestured for me to take a bow. When I rose from the piano, I received a huge ovation, a roar so abrupt and so loud it almost knocked me over.

Receiving applause like that at Carnegie Hall was a glorious arrival point. But I knew deep in my heart that it might also signal a departure. Renée Fleming had flown me to the top of the mountain, but the vista was not what I was expecting. My true Promised Land lay elsewhere.

Lorraine in Moab, 1995, consulting with her inner voices.

CHAPTER 10

Lorraine

I FIRST HEARD LORRAINE Hunt (as she was known before she married Peter Lieberson) in 1987 at SUNY Purchase, when she was singing Donna Elvira in Peter Sellars's production of Mozart's *Don Giovanni*. His chaotic, épater-le-bourgeois staging presented the cast with hurdle after hurdle. Don Giovanni and Donna Anna shot drugs before singing their fast-tempo arias, while Don Ottavio put a pistol to his head during his sweetest one. Everyone onstage gave their all to the crazy business they were asked to execute, but only one performer made it truly convincing: Lorraine.

In just a few years, Lorraine would be hovering on the outskirts of superstardom, with a worshiping cadre of fans all over the world. Critics would be comparing her to Callas. But that night, Lorraine—then age thirty-four—was still vacillating between battling it out as a soprano or downshifting to the relative comfort of life as a mezzo-soprano. She always had a troubled relationship with her upper register, and at Purchase she was clearly struggling to sing Donna Elvira. The role's constant, darting ascents to high A and high B-flat seemed to press her to her limits. Yet she managed to turn her vocal distress into theatrical gold. As she rifled madly through her purse to find her keys during her aria "Ah, fuggi il traditor," the coloratura climax became a wild cry of triumph. And in Elvira's most demanding piece, "Mi tradì quell'alma ingrata," she rolled around the stage like a crazed bumper car. She didn't camouflage her battle with Mozart's music. She used it to create artistic magic.

I went backstage to congratulate her, but I didn't begin my friendship with her until she did her first concert with NYFOS in 1990. My friend Kurt Ollmann, who had played Don Giovanni in that production, was her advocate and pressed us to hire her. She made her début in a program called *Music, Marriage, and Madness* which featured songs by Johannes Brahms and his mentors, Robert and Clara Schumann. Michael Barrett was at the keyboard, Kurt was her co-star. The performance was on October 21, 1990, not long after Leonard Bernstein's death, and Michael programmed Lenny's wordless vocalise "Nachspiel" as the encore. As Lorraine hummed her descant to the slow waltz in the piano, tears rolled down her face.

While she was in town working on the Brahms/Schumann concert, she and Mikey came over to my place for dinner. After we ate, the three of us went over to the piano for a jam session—Mahler, Fauré, zarzuela, a musical feast. At any given moment at least one of us was sight-reading, but you wouldn't have known it—all of us were soaring. Even at her most unguarded Lorraine's command of phrasing was patrician. When she sang, you felt there was no better way—no *other* way—that music could possibly go.

As the evening began to wind down, I looked at Lorraine and impulsively said, "A lifetime isn't enough to make music with you." I was overcome by the supersaturated eloquence of her singing. None of us had any idea how prophetic my words would be.

Between that Schumann concert in 1990 and her final appearance with NYFOS in 2004, Lorraine sang fourteen concerts with us, starting at our tiny home base at the Greenwich House Music School and moving on to the 92nd Street Y, London's Wigmore Hall, Weill Hall at Carnegie, and the Spanish Courtyard at Caramoor. I also got to appear with her in solo recitals four times, bringing the total to eighteen concerts with Lorraine. No, it wasn't enough.

In those early days NYFOS couldn't afford hotels for our out-of-town cast members, so my home office became the de facto Holiday Inn for visiting singers. When Lorraine returned the next season to do *Spanish*

Love Songs with us, she agreed to bunk down at my place. In retrospect I realize how out of character this was. Normally Lorraine required a lot of privacy. When I went to work with her in Brookline where she rented space in a large house, she adamantly refused to let me anywhere near her room. Yet she trusted me enough to stay in my place, where we fell into each other's company like compatible college dorm mates. We had pet names for one another—"Stevester" and "The Rainstress."

Both of us were night owls, so we ate late, rehearsed late, and watched movies till 2 a.m. The night before our 1991 Spanish concert I rented *Matador,* Pedro Almodóvar's surrealist drama of love and murder. The film seems to take place in a haunted fugue state, and its mysterious atmosphere acted like a hallucinogen on the two of us. When we performed our Granados and Turina songs the next day we were still under the spell of Almodóvar's brew of blood and obsession.

Lorraine's artistic persona dwelt somewhere between flower child and high priestess—a hippie-oracle. She spun out her music in a timbre that managed to blend the best qualities of Janet Baker and Joan Baez. In her everyday life, Lorraine also presented a double persona: the slightly raucous Lorraine who camped out in my apartment, and the lofty artist whose singing made me dizzy with delight. Offstage, Lorraine was earthy and mercurial, with an abrupt horse laugh that could silence a subway platform. At one moment she could be suspending a Massenet song with that unearthly, warm purity, and at the next she might make a joke that you could charitably call "down-to-earth." Her halo came and went.

Lorraine had the surest musical instincts of anyone I have ever worked with. While she did not seem especially intellectual about music, she burrowed into the essence of everything she sang. Her musical roots went back to the rigorous—and not always joyous—training imposed on her by her father, followed by years of playing viola in a series of orchestras. Being the alto line of a string section seemed to imbue her with a talent for hearing music's inner voices—and her own inner voice as well. In our initial concerts, all I needed to do was listen to Lorraine and let her guide me. She took me to heaven.

In the early 1990s Lorraine might have been a favorite of cognoscenti, but to the general public she was still known as "that New England Bach singer," or as the protégée of Peter Sellars, bad-boy director of that *Don Giovanni* at Purchase. Since Boston was her home base, our little downtown hall at the Greenwich House School of Music offered Lorraine the possibility of making intimate, high-quality music in the Big Apple. In those early concerts Lorraine treated our tiny audience of 110 to some of the most sophisticated singing they would hear in their lifetime.

Her genius was not confined to the patrician elegance of her phrasing. Lorraine also knew how to structure the entire arc of a song, building to its climax and caressing the final phrases in a gentle afterglow. In her hands a parlor piece like Paladilhe's "Psyché" turned into the outcry of a troubled soul, unforgettable in its emotional weight. She was deeply grounded physically while remaining in touch with the vaulting space around her. Her stillness was sibylline, but she was capable of moving onstage with astounding energy and control. Who could forget the trancelike calisthenics Peter Sellars asked of her in his staging of Bach's "Ich habe genug"? How could anyone else honor that sublime music while doing sit ups?

After her début in Michael's Brahms/Schumann show in 1990, he shared Lorraine with me at NYFOS. She was a headliner with us every season until 1997. Her gift for musical style gave her the kind of versatility our programs required. Lorraine was equally comfortable with a new work like "Song to a Second Child" by Robert Convery (a piece she adored) as with a Ladino folk song by Mario Castelnuovo-Tedesco. She never fretted about stylistic authenticity. Music and words spoke to her with such immediacy that she seemed to intuit their exact weight, color, and spacing at first glance. I have no doubt that this musical security was the product of hours of practice and study. But that part of her work, like her living quarters in Brookline, was off-limits, and I never got to see her in her artistic laboratory. Only when she came to me to coach the role of Carmen did I get even a glimpse of her process, and by that time she had already done the lion's share of the work on her own.

The honeymoon lasted a few years.

Somehow I had acquired entrée with the Queen of Song, and more than with any other artist in my career I felt privileged to be welcomed into her musical world. Knowing how self-protective she was, I did my best to respect her boundaries. However, this did not stop her from overstepping mine. She could be mocking, and she was not averse to harsh practical jokes. Once, when I had made a date with a guy I met through a personal ad, she called me on the phone from the other room using my fax line, impersonating him by lowering her voice and sweet-talking me. The call didn't make too much sense to me, so I remained hesitant in my responses. Very cautiously, I kept the conversation going until I heard that familiar horse laugh both on the phone and barreling out of the office. She had me—but she hurt me. My rickety romantic life was my greatest area of vulnerability, a sensitivity we shared. Even knowing that, Lorraine's jokes didn't stop there, and I soon began to feel somewhat unsafe around her.

By the mid-1990s Lorraine was making the transition from cult figure to diva, transcending her old status as "that amazingly gifted singer from Boston." Her performances had taken on the kind of depth, nobility, and musical class that earned her star status. In 1994, her Carmen with Boston Lyric Opera was the best I ever saw—earthy, dangerous, and musically sinuous, without a hint of sexpot cliché. Stephen Wadsworth's 1997 production of *Xerxes* provided her definitive breakthrough; Lorraine brought a startling, Shakespearian fierceness to Handel's baroque formality, half caged tiger, half ecstatic siren.

Things between us began to change around 1996, and I wasn't quick enough to understand how to handle Lorraine as she evolved. As pals, confidants, and jam session buddies, our music used to flow from a similar well of spontaneous inspiration. Those days started to wane.

Lorraine would no longer stay in my apartment when she came to New York for concerts. And she took complete control of our rehearsals—tempo, dynamics, the precise timing of every nuance. I rapidly learned I might be taunted for following my own musical impulses.

It would be easy to blame this change on Lorraine's ascent to stardom, but the causes were more complex. I think the shift began years earlier, after a concert in July of 1993. She was singing Mozart's "Ch'io mi scordi di te" at Caramoor, with André Previn both at the podium and playing the aria's elaborate piano obbligato. Leading the orchestra while dashing off Mozart's filigree kept Previn busy, and he seemed indifferent to Lorraine's vocal needs. She would have required a very sensitive conductor to help her negotiate the volley of high notes at the end of the aria, and Previn was in no mood to collaborate.

At the performance, his tempi made it impossible for Lorraine to get the breaths she needed. Reverting to emergency mode, she rewrote the ending to avoid singing its three high B-flats. Previn was angry. So was Lorraine.

Afterwards she rode back with me for a weekend at the summer house I was renting with friends. On the drive home she said, "That was my worst concert of the year."

I offered a pro forma rebuttal. "Oh, no, Lorraine, really, you did a lot of beautiful stuff...."

"No, it was the worst. And I made a decision tonight, I am not going to do anything onstage that isn't comfortable for me. I am not struggling any more. I am only going to sing things that are perfect for me."

It was the dawn of a change that would lead to her greatest successes, but it also brought out a side of Lorraine that we'd seen little of before. Hippie-Lorraine remained her public persona, but in the rehearsal room we would soon have to get used to Imperious Lorraine.

The big rift between us came during her love affair with the renowned composer Peter Lieberson. Lorraine and I both found our life partners the same year, 1997, but our newfound domestic bliss had the paradoxical effect of driving a wedge between us. Though Peter seemed well disposed to me, Lorraine began to exude a strange haughtiness to her old friends. We were all thrilled to see her so deeply in love with a man of spiritual and intellectual depth. But we weren't prepared to lose our friendship with her in the process.

My second-to-last concert with Lorraine was in November of 1997—a NYFOS program called *Heaven on Earth* with soprano Dominique Labelle, one of Lorraine's most intimate friends during her Boston years. Despite the ethereal subject matter, Lorraine was especially harsh with both Dominique and me, occasionally scathing in her mockery when she didn't like our musical choices. After one especially torturous rehearsal, Dominique sat at my kitchen table, put her head in her hands, and wept. "Please don't make me work with her again," she murmured.

The *Heaven* program was ambitious and lengthy—twenty-four songs ranging from Handel and Mahler to John Musto and John Duke, plus an encore. I indulged Lorraine by shoehorning a new song by Peter into the program—I learned it so quickly that I have no recollection of the music, but I now realize that I was premiering one of Peter's *Rilke Songs*, soon to become a signature piece for both Peter and Lorraine.

To my relief, *Heaven* was a tremendous success—Dominique and Lorraine sang with exquisite sensuality and refinement, delighting the ear, nourishing the soul. Still, the abrasive atmosphere of the recent days had left me feeling somewhat off-balance, and every note I played for Lorraine seemed to have a question mark attached to it—"Is this what you wanted? Am I doing this right?"

I remember one particular moment—the end of Mahler's "Urlicht," where the singer holds the penultimate note for four beats while the pianist has eight moving notes in a slow arpeggio under her. The bar is marked "ritardando"—getting slower—so like it or not, I had control of the tempo. Moments like these are always a judgment call: How much breath does the singer have? Did her note land in a strong placement that will be efficient with air, or was it a near-miss with a bit of air escaping into the tone? I knew Lorraine wanted a broad slowdown under her sustained note, but I also didn't want to hang her out to dry with a *ritard* that she couldn't handle. With great care I ventured slowly up the piano with my left-hand arpeggio and arrived at the next downbeat, where her vocal line was to cadence with me. I played the resolution of the harmony . . . no Lorraine. Despite my best efforts, it seemed that my *ritardando* hadn't passed muster. She cadenced a split second later, like a private rebuke.

After the concert we went to the Trattoria Dell'Arte across the street from Carnegie Hall for a celebration. We left room at the table for Lorraine and her guests, who said they would show up a little later. But when they arrived they didn't join us, going directly to their own table. She was with her new friends—her fiancé Peter and his buddies, violinist Joshua Bell and cellist Fred Sherry—and she sat down facing the other direction, literally turning her back on Dominique, me, and the whole NYFOS crowd. The body language couldn't have been clearer.

In the wake of everything we'd just been through, I took it disproportionately hard. By now the sting has faded, and I understand why Peter and Lorraine broke off to make their own party. They preferred a private reunion where Lorraine could bond with her fiancé's friends, rather than a gathering with people they didn't know. In the moment, though, the optics were very bad—a bunch of famous musicians who disdained sitting with the likes of us. I grabbed Jim and swept out of the restaurant in a huff.

And then Lorraine swept out of my life. It seemed that she had indeed been sending us a signal at the Trattoria Dell'Arte. Not long after that evening, she and Peter left the East Coast and relocated in Santa Fe. Lorraine found other pianists for her concerts. I was jealous of them, but I have to admit she chose the best—Robert Tweten in the States, Roger Vignoles and Julius Drake in London, sensational artists all. I knew I'd made mistakes with Lorraine—I allowed myself to be too vulnerable to her, and I'd put her on a pedestal. We had a stupid quarrel about money that got blown out of proportion and drove a further wedge between us, and there was no way to walk it back. Forgiveness did not come easily to Lorraine.

I didn't care about the money. What I wanted was my partnership with her. My mistake was wanting it too much.

I wasn't alone in feeling abandoned: after that concert Dominique never again saw Lorraine. The singers at Emmanuel Church in Boston where Lorraine had famously sung Bach in her earlier days lost touch with her. And she even separated herself from conductor Nic McGegan, with whom she made some spectacular early recordings.

I was luckier than those colleagues: I managed to have one more concert with Lorraine. Soon after Michael Barrett took over the reins as general director of the Caramoor Festival, he invited Lorraine to sing a recital with the two of us in the Spanish Courtyard, a beautiful outdoor space. Michael always enjoyed a less contentious relationship with Lorraine, and she had appeared as a guest artist at his other festival in Moab, Utah. I knew that we would do well to revive an old program rather than ask her to learn something new, so we offered *Spanish Love Songs*, which she'd last performed in 1996. Then, it had featured baritone Christopher Trakas as her co-star; this time, it would be tenor Joseph Kaiser. It is one of our most durable playlists: French and German pieces on Iberian themes in the first half, a big mix of Spanish songs and arias in the second, and a clever encore: "Barcelona," from Stephen Sondheim's *Company*.

Lorraine accepted.

By 2004 I had learned a thing or two about how to maintain professional boundaries in my musical collaborations. I also knew that Lorraine had been through a health crisis that had forced her to cancel a number of important engagements, but she'd kept the details vague even to her friends. Michael intimated that her claims of "back pain" were in fact bouts of cancer. In one of our extremely rare phone calls a few years earlier, Lorraine excitedly told me that she'd been to see a shaman on a mountaintop in South America for help—a treatment appropriate to her otherworldly nature. She was leery of Western medicine.

Before our first rehearsal I had no idea what to expect from Lorraine after a seven-year interval. I was pleasantly surprised to find that we were able to collaborate with the ease of our earlier days in almost all the songs we shared. We'd always had a telepathic kinship in Latin music, and my ability to transpose at sight came in handy when a few of the songs now taxed her upper register. Lorraine was fifty years old. The amber of her voice had taken on a mahogany hue, and some phrases sounded a bit grainier, a bit more effortful. But her eloquence was greater than ever, as was her exquisite sense of detail. I felt my old joy making music with her.

Only when we worked on the German material did I get a dose of Lorraine's old penchant for micromanaging. I was her pianist for Wolf's "Komm, O Tod von Nacht umgeben," a dark plea for death to relieve the unbearable pain of love. Wolf's music is like a post-Freudian mini-*Liebestod*, harmonically dense and twisted. Lorraine flooded me with directions: "On the second page at the '*poco rit.*' [slight slowing down], start it on the second half of the second beat, and then the last eighth note is almost like a fermata, and then start to get back to the original tempo on the second half of the second beat in the next measure..."

It has always been hard for me to do microsurgery on musical gestures and make them sound natural. I began to bristle, but I caught myself just in time. My inner voice of wisdom spoke loud and clear: "Steven, you are the artistic director of this concert. You have hired this woman to sing, and she has a short top and a short breath span. And she is a sorceress, a genius musical magician. She casts a spell, but her spell only works *one way*. So if she says 'eye of newt,' give her eye of newt. Don't say, 'How about toe of frog?' Check your ego at the door and just *do what she says*."

Wolf's "Komm, O Tod" remained a fraught experience for me, particularly that gnarly spot on page 2. Years later I stumbled upon our performance when it was broadcast on WNYC, prior to its release as a live recording on Bridge Records. I happened to tune in just as they were playing this song, and after a couple of seconds—even before I consciously realized what (and whom) I was hearing—I started to gasp for air. I haven't touched "Komm, O Tod" since.

I saw Lorraine just one more time: at Carnegie Hall in the autumn of 2005, when she sang Peter Lieberson's *Neruda Songs* with James Levine and the Boston Philharmonic. I was seated at the front of the Parquet section very close to the stage, and when Lorraine walked out she spotted me, smiled, and winked. That unexpected flash of intimacy lifted my soul just as much as her performance of Peter's songs was soon to do. His music is, in equal parts, a love song to Lorraine and a portrait of her in all her complexity. Peter may have taken Lorraine away from her old circle, but in these songs he restored her to us and to the whole world—forever.

I went backstage to see her at intermission and she welcomed me with tenderness. When the bell rang for the second half of the concert, she said, "Why don't you hang out with us in the green room instead of going back?"

Her invitation threw me into a dilemma. I desperately wanted to stay, but I was the guest that night of Judy Evnin, who chaired Caramoor's board of directors. Having already deserted her at intermission to greet Lorraine, it would have been an unpardonable rudeness to disappear for the rest of the concert.

After a pause, I said, "Oh, I am so sorry, but I really have to go back downstairs to rejoin Judy."

Lorraine's face fell a bit.

"Might you be somewhere later on I can join you?"

"No, we're celebrating here, and then we have to split."

An awkward silence.

"God, I wish I could stay. But I hope I'll see you one day soon..."

I never did. Eight months later she died.

My most precious memory of Lorraine is her performance of a late Fauré cycle called *Le jardin clos*—"The Walled Garden." The piece is rarely performed, perhaps because the music has so few recurring phrases that it can seem formless on first hearing. The poems tell a story in two time frames, which can baffle listeners used to the orderly progress of a Schubert song cycle. But I loved *Le jardin clos* and wanted to program it to close the first half of my 1993 NYFOS concert, *Romance in the Belle Époque*.

Kurt Ollmann, who partnered Lorraine in this project, had first introduced me to the cycle, and he also had a brilliant idea for presenting it. He proposed that we divide the cycle between himself and Lorraine: he would take the four songs in which a male narrator speaks about a woman who appears to be his fiancée, while Lorraine would sing the other four songs written in the voice of the bride-to-be. This gave the work a gentle dramatic arc as well as two familiar characters, the ardent young lover and the joyous, frail fiancée.

We didn't stage *Jardin clos*. It was enough to position Lorraine a few feet closer to the audience, lost in her own world of love, while Kurt stood slightly behind and to her left. He could see her from a slight remove, while she remained isolated in her walled garden.

Lorraine had the penultimate song, a gently ecstatic salute to the god of love with allusions to an engulfing river of fire and kisses. It is just before the wedding, and all the joys of life await her. After the song she stood motionless, gazing out expectantly, as Kurt finished the cycle with the eighth song, a slow, gentle eulogy:

All of her, with her dress and her flowers,
She, here, became dust again,
And her soul carried elsewhere
Was born again in song of light.

But a light, fragile link
Gently broken in death,
Encircled her frail temples
With everlasting diamonds.

As a sign of her, in this place,
Alone amid the pale, yellow sand
The eternal rocks still trace
The image of her brow.

Though Lorraine still had another decade with us on earth, Gabriel Fauré and his poet Charles van Lerberghe were preparing us for her departure. Yet her essence remains. Lorraine is constantly reborn in a song of light, an artistic beacon for me to this very day.

The cast of *Schubert / Beatles* at the Moab Music Festival, August 2016; *top row:* Sari Gruber, Charles Yang, Michael Barrett, Andrew Owens; *bottom row:* me and Theo Hoffman.

CHAPTER 11

How the Sausage Gets Made

I WAS A LITTLE too young and lot too shy to join the hippie movement during the '60s. I spent one soggy afternoon at Woodstock with a bunch of friends who sweet-talked me into a road trip, telling me we'd "decide in the car" where were going. "I want to go to Tanglewood!" I exclaimed. "Yeah, cool idea..." they said evasively. Once on the road I was instantly outvoted, and we headed up to the now-legendary rock festival. After many muddy hours I insisted on driving back to the city. Woodstock held no attraction for me. Yet something of the '60s counterculture seemed to have lodged itself in my psyche. I could never get comfortable with the high-gloss glamor of classical music's upper echelons, always preferring intimate, down-to-earth venues—and down-to-earth colleagues.

NYFOS's first six seasons were gloriously unglamorous, and the funky charm of our Barrow Street home was the ideal clubhouse for our musical parties. But when audiences regularly exceeded the hall's modest fire limits, we had to find a new home. This turned out to be two homes: half our concerts would be in Carnegie's elegant recital space, Weill Hall, which has room for 265 people. The others would be in Kaufmann Hall, the 900-seat theater at the 92nd Street Y on Manhattan's Upper East Side, where Michael Barrett had taken over as general manager. This two-hall arrangement lasted for ten seasons—the 624-seat Sylvia and Danny Kaye Playhouse replacing the Y in 1998—until we finally settled into a single home in 2003, the medium-sized, acoustically friendly Merkin Hall on the Upper West Side.

The Y was an especially daunting proposition. In one jump we were replacing our snug hideaway with a space eight times its size. The Y boasted a long tradition of hosting legendary musicians—I'd heard Victoria de los Ángeles and Hermann Prey sing there. How would our grassroots operation fare in the chill of Lexington Avenue?

We opened with a concert called *American Dreams*, exploring both the metaphorical and literal meaning of the title. With a cast of six singers and two guest artists (Joan Morris and Bill Bolcom), we concocted an ambitious program that ranged through Griffes, Rorem, Bernstein, Irving Berlin, Stephen Foster, and an Appalachian folk tune—art song, theater music, American songbook, and Americana in one beautiful salad.

Seeking something modern, I programmed "Tumbling" by Aaron Kernis, a prestigious young composer who would soon win a Pulitzer Prize for Music. For this piece Aaroon used a kind of quaalude-laced minimalism, creating the weightless effect of a soap bubble. Despite its placid effect, though, "Tumbling" is a snarl of rhythmic challenges. It is also a very long piece with almost no place for the singer to rest. To make "Tumbling" easier to perform, I thought it might be a good idea to reformat it as a duet for the evening's two sopranos, Amy Burton and Lauren Flanigan. Unfortunately, Lauren learned Amy's part, and in the aftermath every single rehearsal ended in a train wreck. We were having the same problem with Sondheim's "Country House," a tricky, acerbic duet from the London production of *Follies* that knocked Bill Sharp off his perch on a daily basis.

But there are nights when everyone is in a state of grace, and *American Dreams* at the 92nd Street Y was such a night. Amy and Lauren nailed "Tumbling" for the first and only time, and Bill performed the same miracle with "Country House." Unfortunately, his duet partner Kim Barber and I weren't quite ready for him to get every entrance right after seven days of short circuits, so we were the ones who fumbled a bit at the performance while Bill sailed through with magisterial poise.

American Dreams played to a full house and the response was overwhelming. The sound of 850 people applauding in a live acoustic was an unanticipated benefit of leaving the confines of Greenwich House. Another pleasure awaited as we left the hall, when an usher stopped Michael and me. "I just wanted you to know that several people told me that was the best concert they'd ever heard in their lives," he said. "I think so too."

The elements that contributed to our success that night were the same ones we'd developed downtown, and they have continued to sustain NYFOS throughout its existence. The most obvious one is that each concert has a theme and a title. Nowadays thematic recitals have become commonplace, even from star singers who don't require an additional hook to sell tickets. A few decades ago, though, it was still unusual to think of a concert as needing a through line. After so many years of smorgasbord programs I became obsessed with the different ways songs could turn into a kind of lyric architecture. As the structure begins to reveal itself, songs start to form a kind of narrative, and if all goes well every piece speaks to every other piece in ways that often surprise me as much as they do the audience.

I absorbed much of this during my dozen years with Martha Schlamme, and have come to realize that the art of programming is best transmitted the way I learned it—by example. Over the years I have been asked to give a lecture or a short course to grad students on programming, and so far I have not been able to turn my knowledge into a concise how-to manual. A song might sound trivial or banal in one setting, and earth-shatteringly meaningful in another. Another song may be a soufflé in the hands of one performer, and a leaden matzo ball in the hands of another. You learn by doing, and sometimes you learn the most by screwing up. And how do you teach taste, that most intangible gift?

Having a clever idea is a good start, but there are no shortcuts for turning it into an actual program with a cast and a playlist. Months before that comes to fruition, though, the concert has to look like something marketable for the season announcement, and I've learned that the title is crucial. You might come up with the most exquisite concert of your life, but if the title doesn't have curb appeal you'll cut your audience in half. After several decades, I finally realized that it's best to steer clear of poetry and tricky wordplay. These days, ticket buyers just want to know what they're going to hear, not what they're going to feel.

At the beginning, people seemed more willing to take a chance on us no matter what the concert was called. But even back then a vague title could keep the public away. One of our early shows was comprised of chamber music with narration, including a fantastic piece by James Sellars called *Beulah in Chicago,* with the basso Spiro Malas reading poems by Frank O'Hara over Sellars's irresistible honky-tonk underscoring. I called the concert *Words Without Songs,* which I thought both clever and clear. Clever, yes; clear, no. Few people understood what those three words signified, and we played to a small crowd. Who wants to come to a song concert without songs? Still, the concert proved to be dazzling both musically and theatrically, and all thirty-eight audience members agreed.

No, it pays to be direct. For Ned Rorem's ninetieth birthday tribute, the working title was *Ned Is Ninety.* In the absence of a better idea the in-your-face name stuck, and the box office line outside the theater snaked all the way down Sixty-Seventh Street. It's true that all of our Ned celebrations have played to full houses—his name has been a big draw in New York. But our title implied a quiet urgency, and the public responded as if they'd received an engraved invitation to his home. They got what they came for—Ned was in the hall that night, and for many people it would be the last time they would ever see him.

Dreaming up the theme and naming the project are only the first hurdles. The heftiest challenge is finding the structure of the program, a way to tell a story I may not have completely figured out. It's an elusive process, like making a painting based on a hallucination, or recreating a dish without the benefit of a recipe. To get the ball rolling, I make a list of songs that got me fired up in the first place, plus a few that I know I won't use, just to give myself the impression of *abbondanza.* Then I put a few crucial numbers in place: the opening song, the first-act ender (if there is an intermission), the eleven o'clock number (right before the finale), and the last song. The eleven o'clock number is crucial because that moment coalesces everything that went before; it's a good spot for a slow, sustained song or a brilliant, emotional tour de force. Once those are in place, it's time to chart the intervening journey.

No matter how many decades I've been doing this, I always start with the same fear: "Where's this one going to come from? Do I have the material to make this work?" My dread is not born out of pure neurosis. A few times I have run into a wall as I realize too late in the game that I am tilling rocky soil—either there really is no compelling narrative lurking behind the idea, or the repertoire I assumed I would find doesn't turn up, or it does but I realize too late that it richly deserves its obscurity. I have a mantra for those queasy early stages: The grit creates the pearl. Self-doubt makes up half of the grit, and bullheaded chutzpah takes up the slack.

Ned Is Ninety was, in fact, one of the most difficult concerts to structure. I knew Ned was going to attend, and that he would prefer a program that included only his music. But after listening to six or seven all-Rorem CDs, I began to sense that his prevailingly soft-hued palette would not provide enough variety to sustain a full evening. We'd need some side dishes. I was sure that would present Ned in the best possible light, yet I feared offending him.

After a fruitless week of grit-but-no-pearl, I found the hook. Ned was a prolific memoirist, with a catalog of over fourteen books of essays. We would intersperse his music with songs composed by his friends and mentors, each of them introduced by a short anecdote from one of Ned's books. The unique character of Ned's music would shimmer in the company of composers like Virgil Thompson, Francis Poulenc, Aaron Copland, and Leonard Bernstein. It wasn't surprising that all his intimates turned out to be gay men—Ned was out and proud decades before Gay Pride was a thing. This added another dimension to the concert, which became a portrait not just of the composer, but of a vital enclave of New York's musical culture.

To find the quotes, I borrowed seven Rorem memoirs from the library (to add to the four already on my shelf). After a rehearsal I fed dinner and adult beverages to Michael and the two singers, Andrew Garland and Kate Lindsey. We then divvied up all the non-Ned composers I'd programmed and dove into the memoirs in search of stories about them. With the clock ticking and my dining room table strewn with books, we looked like a bunch of college students cramming for an exam. At intervals someone would yell, "Got it!" and regale the rest of us with a quote—salty, clear-eyed, aphoristic, quintessential Ned. About Poulenc: "[At his villa at Noizay] he wrote the greatest vocal music of our century, all of it technically impeccable, and truly vulgar." About his own music: "My predispositions are French. People sometimes show surprise that I, being a songster, show no affinity for Schubert. His *Lieder* leave me absolutely cold." And quoting Bernstein: "The trouble with you and me, Ned, is that we want everyone in the world to personally love us, and of course that's impossible: you just don't *meet* everyone in the world." Now Ned's songs existed in a musical context, shedding light on all the other material in the program. The playlist had settled into its arc, and I slept well for the first time in a month.

Some concerts reveal their dramatic shape early, while others lie around for weeks like drugged-out sloths unable to rouse themselves. It takes the faith of a true believer to wait until the path announces itself. But it always does. Well, almost always.

One of my most puzzling projects was a concert we took on at the request of the New York Philharmonic. They were mounting a Tchaikovsky festival and asked us to do a song program in tandem with their orchestral series. Who can say no to the New York Phil—or Tchaikovsky? I spent that summer reading biographies of Tchaikovsky and devouring a six-CD album of his songs. The more I read, the more I came to understand that every writer viewed this composer through his own lens. He was ambitious; he was depressed; he was lonely; he was promiscuous; he was closeted; he was flamboyant; he craved fame; he craved privacy. I soon began to envision my own version of Tchaikovsky, simultaneously driven and terrified by the power of his gay libido. As for the songs, I liked almost all 103 of them—a sea of A–/B+ material, lots of decent choices. But only a few stood out as sine qua nons.

A few months before the concert, I began to get nervous. How was I going to capture this mercurial, fascinating man in a song program? The answer came to me in the middle of the night. I woke up at four in the morning from a dream in which I saw emblazoned five words in gold against a red background: **family, men, teachers, women, death.** My REM sleep had provided me with a guide to the pillars of Tchaikovsky's emotional and creative life. Now I knew what to look for: songs that told the story of his relationship with his family; the men he desired; his teachers and colleagues; his entanglements with four women; and his mysterious early death. While I held no illusions that Tchaikovsky's songs were explicitly autobiographical, I began to see how clearly they captured his furtive loves, his musically gifted siblings, and the premonitions that haunted his final days. In his last song, "Again, as Before, I Am Alone," the composer practically wrote his own obit. It ended his career as a songwriter, and of course it ended our show too.

Now that I knew the arc of the concert, Tchaikovsky's 103 songs snapped into sharp focus. No longer a collection of generic romantic effusions, they began to reveal his secrets, hidden in plain sight. Still, I'd painted myself into one tricky corner: I had to evoke the story of the composer's ill-fated, unconsummated marriage to Antonina Miliukova in one four-minute song. Tchaikovsky's wedding, intended to silence the rumors about his gayness, backfired disastrously, leading to decades of extortion and hush money. Nothing in his songs suggested the repugnance he felt for Antonina.

I ultimately turned to an aria from Tchaikovsky's most famous opera, *Eugene Onegin*, which he wrote during the uncomfortable interval between his proposal and the wedding. In Act I, the title character receives an effusive love letter from a young woman, just as Tchaikovsky had from Antonina; but unlike the composer, Onegin coldly refuses her. He tells her that their marriage would be a torture, and that he could only love her like a brother. In the context of the opera, this seems like an act of gratuitous cruelty. Tchaikovsky's luxuriant music for the heroine, Tatyana, has already won the audience's sympathy, and Onegin comes across as a heel.

Everyone imagines that Tchaikovsky identified with Tatyana, the way that people tend to assume that gay writers see themselves in their female characters. Of course there is some truth to this: Tchaikovsky knew very well what it meant to pine for an unattainable man. But I detected something else lurking in Onegin's famous aria: the composer's desire, perhaps unconscious, to have written a similar dismissal to his fiancée, an act of courage that might have saved both of them decades of anguish. Onegin does precisely what the composer didn't allow himself to do: refuse the emotional entreaty of an unwanted female lover.

Every program brings a similar hunt for a needle in a haystack. Everything is in place, except I still need one last piece—let's say, a medium-tempo song for bass-baritone in French on the subject of foreign travel, no longer than three minutes, not too sad, nothing above a D-sharp. In the old days I might go to the library and pull fifteen books off the shelf, and then another fifteen, until I had what I needed. These days libraries are of limited use, since I can only reach the lower shelves and the aisles are sometimes too narrow for a wheelchair. But the internet has obligingly filled in the gap, at least as a starting point. Without leaving my desk I can dredge up recordings and trawl through repertoire, examine concert programs from decades past, and access the complete song output of an amazing number of composers.

I also consult with colleagues. Among the beauties of a long career is the ability to connect with scholars and historians in a wide variety of subjects. Over the years I have received invaluable help from an army of specialists—there's my Lorca expert (Jonathan Mayhew), my Dvořák maven (Michael Beckerman), my Catalan guy (Albert Carbonell), my French gurus (Bénédicte Jourdois and Rosemarie Landry), my early jazz and blues genius (Elliott Hurwitt, the inspiration behind some of NYFOS's best concerts), and three Spanish-language aces (Dorothy Potter Snyder, Pablo Zinger, and my brother Malcolm). Dorothy has guided me through the thickets of Cuban street slang, penetrated the mysteries of Lope de Vega's poetry, and revealed unsuspected layers of meaning in a single Argentinean word. It ain't over until Dorothy says it's right.

Ultimately, no one can find the missing song but me, since it is almost impossible to describe exactly what I'm looking for—it just has to pass the smell test. I am blessed with a preternaturally good memory for all the vocal pieces I have ever heard. I may forget people's names, or historical facts, but songs: never. This mental library is one of my best resources, and I find myself in my private internal stacks at odd moments. Sometimes when I am at my most spaced-out—in the pool, or when I am staring at a blinking "Don't Walk" sign trying to decide if

I can make it across the street before the light changes—my mental fog clears, and there's the song I need.

One reliable joy of programming is choosing the encore. Sometimes it will be one of the first things I'm sure of. For *Art Song on the Couch*, an exploration of Lieder in Freud's Vienna, I knew from day one we'd do Tom Lehrer's "Alma," a comic tribute to Mahler's libidinous wife. For a program of Scandinavian songs, it would be the buoyant quartet that opens Act II of Sondheim's *A Little Night Music*—a musical set in Sweden. And for *Ned Is Ninety*, we planted a corps of students around the hall who strolled down the aisles, joining the cast onstage to serenade Ned with one of his earliest successes, "Early in the Morning."

But when it came time to pick an encore for *Obsession à la Russe*, a program about the artistic connection between Paris and Moscow, I hit a wall. The problem was that I'd already planned what I considered a devilishly clever final song, Vernon Duke's "April in Paris" sung in a Russian translation. Duke, *né* Dukelsky, was Russian-born, and the program listed the song only in its Russian transliteration so that the audience would be surprised to hear the familiar tune in Russian. How could you top that?

Once again the answer came to me at 4 a.m., when I woke from a deep sleep and sat bolt upright in bed: I remembered a song from Cole Porter's *Silk Stockings*, called "Siberia." It's a comic number sung by a trio of Russian agents in Paris who have failed at their mission. They sing a hangdog foxtrot as they ironically extol the virtues of the exile that surely awaits them when they go home—they'll never lack for ice cubes, there will be no unemployment, and so on. The song had three verses, one for each member of the cast—triumph!

Ah, but there was a difficulty I had not foreseen. American musical comedy style is something I take for granted, especially Golden Age musicals like *Silk Stockings* (a hit in 1955). The tenor for the concert was American-born Nicholas Phan, who knew exactly how to play the dry irony of Porter's jokes. But the other two singers, Anton Belov and Dina Kuznetsova, were born in Russia. Although they had spent most of their lives in America, they were unable to see the humor of being sent to Siberia. I did my best to explain the style, even singing it to them à la

Bobby Short, but still they delivered this soft-shoe number like the last act of *The Cherry Orchard*. I prayed that their Chekhovian melancholy would read as funny in context. And perhaps it did.

NYFOS has tended to favor off-the-beaten-track repertoire, mainly to avoid the recital warhorses that everyone programs with numbing frequency. When we do present familiar songs, we want people to hear them with fresh ears. One way to do this is to interleaf two classic works, making a kind of musical Dagwood sandwich. In *Dvořák and the American Soul*, an exploration of the Czech composer's years in New York at the end of the nineteenth century, I wanted to recreate the now-legendary moment when Dvořák heard a Black student, Harry T. Burleigh, humming spirituals in the hallway near his office. The two men inspired each other: for Dvořák, their friendship led to the glories of the *New World* Symphony and the *American* String Quartet; for Burleigh, a groundbreaking career as the first Black composer of art song. Still, I wasn't prepared for the emotional effect of hearing Dvořák's somber *Biblical Songs* interspersed with Burleigh's settings of spirituals. The modal stateliness of "Don't Be Weary Traveler" previewed those same qualities in Dvořák's setting of "Oh, my shepherd is my lord," and it seemed as if the two songs were made to be heard together. For twenty-five minutes we experienced a transatlantic ecumenical council, a cross-cultural meditation on life and death, adversity and triumph.

Our biggest, craziest Dagwood was the brainchild of my then-student Theo Hoffman and NYFOS's then-publicist Aleba Gartner, who cornered me after a concert with conspiratorial grins. "We think NYFOS should do a concert of Schubert and Beatles songs," Theo began. After noticing a flash of terror invade my face, he hurried on. "No, really! Think about it for a second! It's a great pairing." Even though I desperately needed one more program idea to finish the 2015–16 season, I balked. For one thing, I'd tiptoed over this territory in the past: out of town I'd paired Schubert with Jerome Kern, a safer proposition. And in New York we'd done an all-Beatles program called *Ticket to Ride* in 1990—wouldn't everyone remember that one twenty-five years later? (Answer: no. Theo hadn't even been born yet.) But most daunting of all: putting Schubert, the holy of holies, with the Fab Four, the oldie of oldies?

The more I mulled the idea over, the more I saw its potential. There were hidden parallels between Schubert and the Beatles, beginning with a strain of folk music that runs through their compositions. Both had short careers; Schubert's was truncated by his tragic death at age thirty-one, while the meteoric flame of the Beatles' burned out in a tangle of discord and exhaustion after seven years of superstardom. Yet in those few years, both created art that captured their Zeitgeist for all time—the bittersweet elegance of the early Romantic era, and the swinging, psychedelic '60s. More than anything, both explore young adulthood with vividness and depth: the confusions of early romances, first betrayals and breakups, the sense of yearning for something unnamable and just out of reach. Under Schubert's sweetness and the Beatles' swagger lies a melancholy that reminded me powerfully of my own young adulthood, so filled with indefinable heartache. Michael was gung-ho for the pairing, and I signed on.

In the twenty-five years since *Ticket to Ride*, my resources for programming and arranging had developed. My circle of colleagues had also widened, and I was able to assemble a cast who could sing both Schubert and Beatles with total authority. I also possessed a secret weapon: my violinist friend Charles Yang, the Paganini of nontraditional genres and the very definition of hipness. When Marsha Hunter and Brian Johnson and I performed *Ticket to Ride* in 1990, it always took the audience six or seven songs to get used to hearing the material in piano-and-voice arrangements. We tried changing the order, leading off with songs that brought the house down when placed later in the show, but nothing worked. Wonderful as they were, there seemed to be no way to hit the ground running. Now, especially with Charles Yang on board, I thought we might grab the public from the first note.

My original plan was to play it safe and follow an all-Schubert first half with a group of Beatles songs on the same themes after the intermission, so that when you perused your program after the concert you would be struck with how well-planned it had all been: "Oh, I get it, *that* song echoed the one we heard before the break!" But everyone in the cast—Sari Gruber, Andrew Garland, Paul Appleby, Theo, Charles, and most of all Michael—insisted that we interweave the two composers:

"An Schwager Kronos," in D minor, would lead directly into "Taxman" in D minor—a short treatise on death and taxes. "Im Frühling" (in G) would segue to "Yesterday" (in G)—two beautiful meditations on lost love; "Du liebst mich nicht" would introduce "For No One"—a pair of devastating breakup songs. To end the concert, I dovetailed Schubert's very last song, "Die Taubenpost," and "In My Life," with the Beatles song beginning on the last chord of the Schubert.

I feared the heavens would rain thunderbolts on us—and on me in particular—for our audacity. Experience had taught me that Schubert lovers can be militant, while Beatles fans feel they are the temple guardians of everything the Fab Four wrote. But my six colleagues felt nothing but enthusiasm and joy, and *Schubert/Beatles* remains one of my sweetest NYFOS memories. Michael took on Schubert duties, while I covered the Beatles tunes. Most of my arrangements came out of spontaneous reactions to both the Lennon-McCartney song and the Schubert song that preceded it. While I wasn't worried about the ballads, which unwind gently and don't depend on percussion, the rock 'n' roll songs were a bigger stretch. For pieces like "The Word" and "Taxman" I simply threw my hands into the keyboard, latching onto a rhythmic pattern to see where it led me. Once the music was churning, I shared the steering wheel with the singers and the band—not just Charles but also Theo on (acoustic) guitar, each musician building the groove. This kind of free improvisation worked for everyone except Paul Appleby, who came into rehearsal with some specific ideas about how he wanted to do his solos, "Julia" and "For No One." His concepts were detailed and ingenious, closer to art song than jazz and a nice break from the looseness of the other arrangements.

As concert day approached, I couldn't shake my qualms that pairing Schubert and the Beatles might be like serving an order of Wiener schnitzel with a side dish of cotton candy. But the opposite proved to be true: the Beatles songs stepped up to the plate, glowing with a complexity to rival any classical composer. In return, the Schubert pieces, freed from their usual formal presentation, took on a kind of immediacy that is hard to achieve in traditional recitals.

It was baritone Andrew Garland who supplied the encore: a hilarious arrangement of "When I'm Sixty-Four" incorporating motifs from Schubert's Greatest Hits. I had long known that this song would end the show—I had just celebrated my sixty-fourth birthday. Andy, a first-class pianist and a nimble musician, offered to take the helm and serenade me at the show. But I wanted to spring it on the audience as a surprise—a real one for them, a fake one for me. So after the program-ender, "In My Life," I began to stammer an apology, "I'm so sorry, but this time we don't have an encore because we have just been too busy rehearsing...." when Andy interrupted me. "AC-tually, Steve," he interrupted with baritonal authority, "we *did* prepare something." I feigned amazement, open-mouthed and touching metaphorical pearls, as Andy sat down at the piano and ripped into his P.D.Q. Bach–style pastiche. I proceeded to laugh at all the musical jokes so convincingly that most people actually believed I was hearing it all for the first time. I'm proud to say I managed those phony theatrics at every subsequent performance.

The group spirit that drove that show has remained a hallmark of our success for decades. Each project is a complex endeavor, and we have somewhere between five and nine days to find its atmosphere, its shape, its soul. I present the architectural plan, the singers and sidemen build the musical house. It works best when the cast becomes a family; then the creative work can take on a heady joy unlike anything else I've experienced as a musician. Mostly they have been very happy families. But I have occasionally been seduced by a beautiful voice, only to discover that the singer is actually an inert gas, not a spritz of Chanel No. 5. They learn their songs, they plant their feet and deliver them to the top balcony, they collect their check, they go home. In rehearsal, they read *Harry Potter* or play games on their phones when other people are singing. For me, this is like trying to bake a cake with flour, sugar, eggs, and a lead pipe. Then there is the opposite extreme: occasionally an artist will twist my invitation to collaborate into an excuse to wrest control of the project, effectively hijacking the rehearsals. Colleagues who fall into those categories don't get a chance to make their mistake twice.

All through the process I am aware that our intimate creative team is at the service of a larger, ongoing community: the audience. In the early days of NYFOS I was bowled over that people gave us their time and attention (not to mention their money), and after three decades I have never lost my youthful, missionary zeal to reward them for turning out to hear us. The audience is our honored guest, and our hospitality must be at the highest level. Exalted as it sounds, I feel a sacred obligation to them. I know that there will be a wide range of listeners: experts and neophytes, song mavens and song laymen. A quote from the scientist C. P. Snow has served as a guiding principle onstage—"Never overestimate your audience's knowledge, but never underestimate their intelligence."

Writing the program notes and translations for each concert is a sweet torture each time, akin to solving a difficult crossword puzzle. My ostensible purpose is to offer the audience some background material underpinning the show they're about to hear. But in truth I am really writing for myself, organizing what I've learned putting the concert together. Nowadays we post them online a few days before the performance, but in the past most of the listeners would not have read the notes before the show—who has time for a 3,000-word essay before an 8 p.m. curtain? (If it's less than 2,000 words, someone will let me know I underperformed, as if I were a cow giving thin milk.) But I don't mind supplying post-concert subway or bubble-bath reading. I've also learned that I can't afford to make mistakes, for fear of being called on the carpet by a scholar or a family member of the composer. And if we get a review, I am often amused to see the critics helping themselves to large hunks of my writing.

I always pretend to be burdened by the task of doing NYFOS's translations, but I have to come clean: cracking the mysteries of a foreign language is one of life's greatest delights, whether it's the Franco-Iberian allure of Catalan, Lorca's Andalusian wordplay, or Jacques Brel's mid-century colloquial French. Sometimes it can take years to learn what a single word means. I first programmed the "Poema valseado" from Astor Piazzolla's *Maria de Buenos Aires* during NYFOS's opening season in 1989. The librettist Horacio Ferrer writes of a "bandoneón que huele a sombra de macroses." Okay, I got this, the bandoneon, right, the Argentinean accordion, which smells like the shadow of...*macroses*? That word wasn't in any dictionary. None of my usual sources had ever heard it either. *Lunfardo*, the patois of Buenos Aires, resists dictionaries and earnest Manhattan pianists. Every time I returned to the song over the years, I simply made up a translation—"the bandoneon that smells of the shadow of the trees." While no one ever questioned me, I knew perfectly well I was faking it.

Help arrived when I programmed the "Poema valseado" twenty years later at Wolf Trap, where Stephanie van Reigersberg was on staff to coach the Spanish diction. Knowing how she loves a challenge, I told her that I had been unable to find anyone who knew what "macroses" meant. "I'll get to the bottom of it," she promised.

Two days later, she buttonholed me before rehearsal. "Macroses—it means 'pimps.' It's old Buenos Aires slang from the sixties, from the French word 'maquereau.'"

"Which means . . . ?"

"Pimp!"

"How did you find it?"

"I talked to the secretary of the governor of Buenos Aires. She knew. . . . Don't ask."

Lunfardo slang may have taken two decades to decipher, but it finally yielded its secrets. Basque proved even tougher. When preparing *Spanish Gold* with soprano Jennifer Aylmer in 2001 I didn't know any Basque speakers, and the Basque Center in New York was not answering the phone. Jen took on the task of landing word-for-word translations.

"I found a Basque restaurant in Newark, and they said they'd go over the songs with me. 'Come at 11:45,' they said—'we open at noon.'"

Jen obligingly sped across the George Washington Bridge with her scores, arriving on the dot. But she was in for a disappointment. They opened her music and read for a moment, then shook their heads. "I'm sorry. This is not our mountain."

"Pardon?"

"We don't know these words. They were not spoken where we come from. Oh, wait, now *this* one we know," pointing to the score. "It means 'fly.'"

"Fly?" she asked. "I looked it up and the glossary said it meant horse."

"Or horse," they agreed amiably.

Using a little ingenuity, a lot of ballsiness, and the help of a short synopsis of the song included in the sheet music, I cobbled together something close enough to pass muster. No one's objected—so far.

It took even more resources to deal with the Polish texts for *Warsaw Serenade* in 2014. One of my students, Szymek Kómasa, painstakingly took me through all the poetry and made recordings of the texts in tandem with his father, a distinguished Polish actor. Szymek also supplied me with music, gave me advice about composers, and held my hand every step of the way as I built the program. A small army of Polish speakers helped with the arduous task of translating the lyrics, which were filled with dialect and antiquated words. *Warsaw Serenade* proved to be the biggest linguistic challenge in NYFOS's history.

But there were delicious moments along the way. One of the numbers was a children's song about three magpies; the third magpie, according to Szymek, was seated on a rock, "holding little violins on his thong." Even while I prayed that would be the correct translation, something told me to ask around. Another team member, Basia Revi, clarified: the magpie was indeed sitting on a rock, playing little violin tunes—on the G string. It seems a computer thesaurus had turned the G string of a violin into the G-string of a stripper. With great sadness I bid farewell to my lap-dancing Polish magpie.

Warsaw Serenade stretched soprano Dina Kuznetsova and tenor Joseph Kaiser to their limits. "I speak Russian," said Dina, "and that helps me when I sing Czech. But Polish?" Her eyes widened. "It makes Czech look like baby-talk. It's as if they took Russian and put it through a meat-grinder." Joe would sometimes get caught on a consonant cluster and erupt into a string of profanities. But they mastered their songs, and the concert was one of our best.

After the concert I greeted friends and well-wishers. An elderly woman waited patiently to offer her congratulations. "You did a good job," she said in a vintage New York accent. "I liked the music, the singers were great. And you got the translations right."

I breathed a huge sigh of relief. You can't get away with anything in New York, and one of the Szymanowski songs had been in Kurpian, a rare dialect spoken in northern Poland. My translation had involved a fair amount of guesswork, even with my team of experts.

"Wow, thank you, I'm so glad to hear that. I really had to struggle with the Kurpian text..."

"Oh, the Kurpian? No, no, you totally screwed up the Kurpian. But everything else was okay." With that, she shuffled off.

I felt a brief bolt of shame, but euphoria soon returned. Every NYFOS concert lands me in the belly of the beast—pianistically, intellectually, musically, linguistically—and I'd rather be nowhere else. I've played Schubert at Carnegie Hall, but I am more interested in wrestling that Kurpian poem into submission. Which, one day, I will.

Rehearsing at Caramoor's Schwab Vocal Rising Stars program with Julia Bullock (*far left*), Sarah Larsen, and Tobias Greenhalgh. Their stars certainly did rise.

CHAPTER 12

Scheherazade Had It Right

ONE SUMMER WHEN I was teaching a master class at San Francisco Opera's Merola Program, a young soprano surprised me by offering an especially challenging aria: "Al dolce guidami," from Donizetti's *Anna Bolena*, a bel canto retelling of Anne Boleyn's sad fate. I knew this young woman as a delightful Puccini soprano and didn't think this would be a particularly suitable choice for her. Her first rendition of the piece didn't change my mind. She pretty much had the notes down—no mean achievement. But the sweet timbre of her voice suggested ingénue, not the Queen of England. Nor did she achieve the ineffable suspension of time that is the very heart of the aria. It didn't help that the music is closely associated with Maria Callas, and I irrationally expect every performance to replicate her crimson timbre and smoldering intensity.

I plunged in and tried to work directly on the phrasing, aiming for gravitas rather than sunshine. "Elongate the last four notes of that run ... more weight on when you say 'ei mi sgrida,' it means he's berating you ... turn up the heat with the trill...." She obliged, but we both knew I was just pushing the broccoli around on the plate. She seemed not to have the style in her blood and it would have taken more than twelve minutes to show her, particularly since I was not at the piano myself. If I had been, I might have found a way to ensnare her into the mood of the aria. Floundering, I resorted to an old standby: Talmudic questioning. I asked her how she envisioned the aria.

"Well, it's a mad scene..."

Ah. The problem revealed itself. "Are you sure?"

"Well, she's going to be decapitated and she goes crazy."

"She does? I'm not so sure. I know everyone calls it a mad scene" (I flashed back to the old LP containing the aria, which is indeed called *Callas Sings Mad Scenes*), "but I don't think she's losing her mind. She's the wife of Henry the Eighth, she's imprisoned in the Tower of London, she's retreating to fantasy just to survive. She says, 'Don't let me die alone, take me back to where I was born so I can forget this anguish. Give me back one day of my youth. In my mind I can create a safe haven for a few moments.' Not so crazy."

I looked over and saw that the singer had become very still. Some door had opened. "Look up," I said gently. "See the guillotine." She slowly raised her eyes to the back of the top balcony, and froze. She'd made the leap. I turned to the pianist and said quietly, "Okay, start the aria."

For the next four minutes, she gently spun out Donizetti's music as she stared up at the imaginary blade that would soon end her life. About twenty bars into the piece, tears started to roll down her face, but her voice remained steady. There wasn't a sound in the hall as the audience watched this woman bargain with death. The ovation at the end was staggering.

Did I somehow turn this lovely soprano into Donizetti's Anna Bolena? Not quite. But for those four minutes she *was* Anne Boleyn. And she took all of us hostage in the world of that doomed woman, lost in the sublimation of memory.

At the reception afterwards, a donor sidled up to me. "Mr. Blier, the word 'guillotine' was actually invented 250 years after the death of Anne Boleyn." "Oh, I know that," I replied (a half-truth). "But the word was also invented fifty years before the Donizetti opera. So we're both right. Hey, could you get me another glass of white wine?"

That master class made a deep impression on both student and teacher. Years later the soprano wrote me, "The 'guillotine moment' taught me just how powerful a good image can be in guiding interpretation. It has carried me forward ever since, and for that I have always been grateful."

PREPARING AN audition aria is one thing. But let's face it: coaching an opera role requires far more than inspiration and imaginative leaps. It inevitably includes a great deal of mechanical labor—there's a reason pianists who specialize in opera are sometimes referred to by their French name, *répétiteurs*. This type of work involves playing the score while belting out all the other parts as cues for prospective Mimís and Rodolfos, Otellos and Desdemonas. Singers will need to have total command of every entrance in every ensemble and every recitative, ready for the vagaries of temperamental conductors and stage directors. They will also need to be able to hold their own even when their onstage colleagues come in wrong or forget their words. An opera contract might provide the leisure of a long rehearsal period, but a singer might also get thrown onstage without having ever met their colleagues or walked the set. They have to be ready for anything.

The great opera coaches manage to combine deep artistic work with nuts-and-bolts practicalities. I revere colleagues like Diane Richardson and Bénédicte Jourdois who excel at this balancing act. I too can manage it—my first paid job in music, after all, was teaching Jeanette Walters the role of Alice Ford in *Falstaff*. But it's not my thing any more, and everyone seems to have realized that I'm a song-and-aria guy, not a recitative-and-ensemble jukebox.

Preparing solo repertoire, however, does not exempt me from *répétiteur* duties. Our work might have to begin by running a vacuum cleaner over the foreign language diction, or working out concrete details of style. Sometimes there are rhythmic issues—modern singers are increasingly prone to sing Romantic-era music with the square precision you would use for Stravinsky or Handel. Others attack Kurt Weill's astringent songs with the breast-heaving passion appropriate to Puccini. And if a singer is hell-bent on an outré tempo or oddball interpretation, they'd be wise to know the tradition of the piece first, before breaking it.

Coaching isn't an exact science, but an odd mix of fact and fancy, science and creativity, immutable laws and judgment calls. At work, I feel like a human Ouija board, channeling all the people with whom I have ever made music, all the performances and recordings I have ever heard. Everything is at the service of an elusive, subjective goal: the inner flame of a song. Performances don't coalesce into something communicative and immediate unless the singer's imagination has been groomed as carefully as their voice. Art and craft emanate from a single human being, not from separate silos.

When I do hear a glaring problem, I'm fairly sure that two dozen other coaches have already tried to work it out. Attempting tact, I might say, "The tuning in your middle voice sometimes shades the underside of the pitch." Translation: You're singing flat. The honest ones will reply, "Yeah, I know, I'm working on it"; the defensive ones might feign surprise—"I've *never* been told that!" And occasionally a singer will have a significant vocal issue that their teacher has not addressed. How could Professor X not be working to correct that alarmingly slow, wide vibrato in this guy's upper register?

Usually an oblique approach, rather than a full-frontal attack on the hot-button issue, works better as a starting point, and there are myriad options on the table. We could start by talking about diction, breathing, phrasing, translation, tempo, dynamics, or tone color. All these elements are bound together in that catch-all word "interpretation," but they can open the door to looking at the real technical issues. For that baritone with the wobble, though, there was no time to beat around the bush. If his teacher wasn't going to deal with it, I would. This singer trusted me, and we were able to smooth it out in a couple of sessions. Professor X, of course, was delighted.

Ultimately, coaching comes down to a metaphysical game of dominoes. I am looking for the one domino that will knock over as much of the stack as possible, and it might not be the obvious one.

For example, it can be hard to achieve authentic foreign vowels or native-sounding consonants if a singer's technique is built on certain fixed oral positions. Tempo is a matter of taste, but it's also a function of breath control, vocal size, energy, musical security—and age. Style emerges from what singers have in their throat, in their mind, in their ear, in their training, and above all in their lifelong musical culture. After listening to a young woman butcher a popular song at an audition some years ago, the director turned to me. "What a shame," he shrugged. "She was obviously listening to the wrong records when she was eleven." Many singers aspiring to operatic careers start with that deficit—they probably hadn't even heard operatic voices by age eleven. They usually discover that repertoire in their mid-teens, much later than instrumentalists, who begin their studies in childhood.

Of course, those metaphorical dominoes fall more quickly when the singer is talented, intuitive, and well-trained. When the baritone Tobias Greenhalgh was a master's student at Juilliard he brought in "Avant de quitter ces lieux," a baritone warhorse from Gounod's *Faust*. The aria was in decent enough shape vocally but it seemed static and plain, and the high phrases were somewhat labored. Instead of talking about the music, I reminded Toby about a basic tenet of French diction: the stress of the phrase needs to be directed away from the downbeat. There's a technical term for this—the *accent d'insistence*—and though I was sure Toby knew about it intellectually, he seemed not to have understood how important and pervasive it was. Time for a little tough love.

"No, not, Ô, SAIN-te mé-DAIL-le, QUI me vient de ma SOEUR," I sang with exaggerated squareness. "It's more like, "Ô, sain-te MÉ-daille, qui ME vient de MA soeur," I crooned, lightly leaning on the unaccented notes and pulling away from the strong beats. "It's kind of like clapping on two and four rather than one and three." Toby nodded, and launched into the aria again. I expected that he'd make a small adjustment, and that I'd need to keep pushing him for a more meaningful change in his phrasing. Instead, he eased into the piece with a kind of Gallic suavity any French baritone would envy. For once, "Avant de quitter" was an exalted prayer rather than a macho roar. The high notes sailed into the room with magisterial ease. I still think it was the most stylish rendition I ever heard, and one of the most beautiful. A lovely postscript: Toby wrote me recently to say that he'd sung the role with a French conductor, who observed after his aria, "Your French is perfect; and the style too!" Yet if Toby learned something from me that day, I also learned something from him: focusing on one thing can solve six problems, if it's the right thing for that artist.

Miracles like that don't happen every day, but I never stop looking for them.

They are particularly welcome in master classes, where I am given twenty minutes to effect some sort of transformation in front of an audience whose members range from opera insiders to music fans with no firsthand experience of the artistic process. I get only one chance to throw the bowling ball down the lane, so whatever I choose to focus on should be something that everyone in the hall can absorb intellectually and emotionally. I want to give the public a broad sense of how performances are built, rather than dwell on technical matters that are better left to the privacy of a studio. And it's crucial that singers leave the stage with a feeling of success; bad master-class encounters can cloud an artist's life for years. I think back to my experience in Elisabeth Schwarzkopf's class at the Mannes School in 1982. That half hour did more to destroy me than to educate me, and it took me a while to recover. But I did learn some unforgettable lessons from her, by negative example: never insult a student's intelligence, and don't kill his or her love for music.

For someone as empathetic as the young woman who sang Anna Bolena, imagery proved to be a direct path to the floodgates of emotion. But there are others. Specifying intention can turn the heat up quickly on a bland performance. At a master class some years ago in Hidden Valley, California, a young baritone and I were working our way through Samuel Barber's "Dover Beach." This song is often assigned to undergraduates because Barber keeps his vocal demands manageable, and the range isn't extensive. But the ideal interpreter is actually someone who's been around the block a few times. The sprawling imagery of Matthew Arnold's mid-nineteenth-century poem benefits from a dose of life experience.

Arnold paints a world of melancholy and rootlessness, as he broods over the erosion of bedrock religious belief by the incursion of science. At first the narrator appears to be musing to himself, but we soon learn that he is also speaking to a lover whom he entreats to watch the moonlight on the ocean with him. Since Arnold wrote the poem during his honeymoon on Dover Beach, the unseen woman is assumed to be his wife. Performers, of course, need to grasp the essential theme: anguish over the burgeoning conflict between science and faith. But I have always felt that the true dramatic energy of the song emerges from narrator's relationship with his offstage scene partner. Barber's musical climax arrives with an outburst, "Ah, love, let us be true to one another!" The entire work must coalesce in that moment, or "Dover Beach" risks turning into a nine-minute kvetch.

The baritone in that day's class had the pipes to sing it, but the piece as a whole seemed a bit shapeless. I call this type of performance "singing along with the song," a passive rendering of the text that avoids internalizing the music. In a private coaching I might have begun by discussing the poem's central idea, the slow, disturbing constriction of what Arnold calls the "sea of faith." But I had a hunch that that would only make this young man's performance more earnest. And, as an actor friend likes to say, "Sincerity is the booby prize."

Instead, I focused on the relationship of the man and woman. What could have happened between them that would give rise to this monologue? I had a sudden idea. When we got to the plea to be "true to one another," I asked him to sing it as if he had committed an infidelity and was pleading for another chance—knowing that this had absolutely nothing to do with the meaning of "Dover Beach," simply trying to light a fire. The young baritone erupted with an outburst of passion and shame unlike anything he had yet demonstrated, and the whole room came alive. I had hit the Master Class Jackpot.

I wasn't quite done. "Now sing it again," I suggested, "but this time she's the one who was cheating on you, and you are begging her not to destroy your marriage." He took a moment and launched the phrase once again, this time with a complex blend of vulnerability and accusation. The difference was startling. Clearly this guy was a talented actor, able to summon up inner objects—Uta Hagen's term for an actor's psychological triggers—on command. When he started the song again from the beginning, it was transformed. Barber's queasy sixteenth-note ostinato became an obsessive replay of the betrayal. Practically everything fell into place, and the poet's philosophical quandary seemed personal and urgent. Others have sung "Dover Beach" with more colorful voices and more musical nuance—the kid was twenty-two—but his rendition is the one I shall always remember.

It's exciting to wave the wand in a master class and produce the "wow" moment. But it isn't only about putting on a good show. Such lucky bolts of inspiration can fuel artists for years.

One-on-one sessions are a different matter entirely. There we have the freedom to stop and work on details I would never address in public. Vowels, for example. We want the widest possible spectrum so as to give the words plenty of color. But it's complicated: a vowel may be linguistically correct—that's how you would say it in everyday speech—but turn sour or spread or tight when sung accurately in that part of the voice. What we want is the "acoustical vowel": the precise version of a phoneme, the perfect oral space, that allows the voice its maximum freedom and resonance. When we find it, it is as though singers have unlocked their inner microphone. This takes patience, but the glorious moment when a voice releases and ricochets around the room is worth the wait.

Or tuning. Singers are always afraid of singing flat, and with good reason. Being under pitch is the kind of obvious flaw anyone can notice, even if it affects just a couple of notes. It's a deal-breaker in auditions—if you sing flat, you're out. On the other hand, singers don't worry so much about singing sharp. In the world of opera, being a little above the note doesn't bother auditioners or audiences nearly as much as being a fraction under pitch. For many people, singing sharp is akin to having too much frosting on a cake—and who ever complained about that? But it is one of my special aversions, often to the surprise of singers who are in the habit of hiking the pitch a bit simply to be sure they aren't singing flat.

It's painstaking work to get the details of a song right, and most singers, especially students, welcome specific instructions. "The general rule for cadenzas is slow-fast-slow—the slowdown is usually on the last four notes." Or "The grace note in this style comes before the beat, not on the beat." Or "The fermata means the whole phrase gets stretched, not just that one note where the typesetter put the fermata." But the secret of good coaching is to meld the technical with the artistic so that they become part of the same energy stream. We are building a personal connection to a work of art, and I never want to lose sight of the deeper artistic elements that bring songs and arias to life. First and foremost: What is the central event of this song? Who are you, to whom are you speaking, and why do you need to say this? Does the person you're addressing understand what you mean? How would your character stand? Where are you—what's to your left, your right, what's in front of you, over you, behind you? What story are you telling—and what are you concealing? (That question can lead to some most interesting answers.) Once singer and pianist are creating a scene, the music becomes vivid and expressive.

When rehearsing for a concert, on the other hand, I am more of a collaborator than a coach—at least with most of the artists with whom I work. Our initial task is to absorb each other's energy and get a sense of what kind of dish we are cooking together. If we've both done our homework and are on top of the piece's technical demands, we may not need to talk much. We're engaged in psychic, nonverbal communion, and while the first run of a song might bring a shock of warring musical impulses, a surprising amount of the time it is uncannily smooth.

Rehearsal sessions involve both deeper and shallower kinds of questions than coachings. There is the pure housekeeping level—"I need more time there," or "We're never together on the second beat of measure forty-four," or "I know it's marked *piano* but that's about as soft as I can manage right now," or "Darling, shouldn't there be a *liaison* between 'aux' and 'étés'?" But as always, I try not to neglect the broader questions: "What are we trying to express in this song? What are the sonorities that bring that feeling into the room?" Some singers want to tell me, while others prefer to keep their creative process to themselves. And sometimes secrets are for the best; I might disagree violently with how they describe their interpretation, while adoring the way they sing the piece. We don't need to be running the same inner narrative to make art together.

ULTIMATELY, THE delicate architecture of a NYFOS program depends on each song landing the way I envisioned when I was planning the playlist. Songs aren't just pieces of music. To me they are more like animals, and I am counting on the cats to purr, the tigers to roar, the dogs to bark, the snakes to slither. This song needs to be climactic, this one needs to be dapper, this one seduces, this one jolts. It can take the diplomacy of Eleanor Roosevelt to massage the song—and the singer—into place if they offer me a poodle when I was counting on a Great Dane. And as my former students transition into their roles as professionals, I've needed to find ever-subtler ways to keep control over my animal kingdom.

At NYFOS I am both pianist and musical director, so I usually feel I can speak up with confidence. I did not always have that kind of free exchange with the big-name singers I played for in the 1990s. When there was a window for offering a musical suggestion it was tiny, and I needed to be ready with just the right words—informative, inspiring, terse, nonconfrontational.

In one of her recital programs, June Anderson sang four early Debussy songs using lots of tempo variation, unwritten holds on high notes, and a healthy dose of portamento—sliding connections between notes. I felt her swoopy approach to the vocal line was off-kilter for songs that thrived on purity and rhythmic discipline, but our relationship was not especially collaborative. We made music at the same time, but we didn't exactly make music *together*. Psychologists call this parallel play, the way young children engage in the same activity without appearing to relate to one another. Eventually I worked up the courage to address the issue: "You know, I'm not used to playing the Debussy songs with so much rubato," using the musician's term for pulling a tempo faster and slower. "Oh!" she replied. "Well, I see them as great big Puccini arias." That explained everything. Except... what did this delicate French music have to do with the earthy throb of Puccini? I knew I had roughly ten seconds to make my case. "Um, what if they... *weren't*?" I proposed. And when I saw that a door had opened a crack, "I think they'd sound better if you kept a steadier tempo." June probably heard the implication of that sentence: I think *you'd* sound better if you kept a steadier tempo. She took my advice, and the Debussy songs stayed in their lane instead of careening all over the highway. We still lingered gently on a few of the arching high phrases, but the songs now exuded the glow of moonlight, not the glare of a pizzeria.

Although I enjoyed a warmer personal relationship with Renée Fleming, she also didn't look to me for musical advice. Why would she? She had already worked with every great coach and conductor in the world as well as a dazzling roster of star pianists. I was happy just to keep her show on the road.

Still, I was able to offer her one piece of guidance during our time together. On one of our tours, she ended the first half of her concert by pairing the Tin Pan Alley tune "Poor Butterfly" with the aria "Un bel dì," from Puccini's *Madama Butterfly*. When we came offstage in Santa Barbara, Renée muttered, "I get so tired singing 'Un bel dì,' I don't know what it is about that piece." I was surprised. I hadn't heard any strain in her Puccini, in fact it sounded gorgeous to me. Once again I knew I had about ten seconds in which to say something useful. Hmm, if she's getting tired, she must be overselling the piece. What's the solution? "But Renée, remember, Butterfly is only fifteen years old," I blurted. A brief silence. "Oh my god, you're right. Wow!" Then she turned and waved as she headed for her dressing room. "Okay, great, I've got to change my dress for the second half. See you out there!" Whether or not my observation helped her find a more innocent, less overwrought vocal approach for the aria, she never complained about it again. (Nor did I revise my comment when I later realized that by Act II, when she sings "Un bel dì," Butterfly is actually eighteen.)

MY COACHING has always sprung from the way I do my own work on songs. This, of course, has evolved over the years. When I was in my twenties, it was hammered into me that I needed to find something in my life that was similar to the song, and use that—Uta Hagen's "inner object"—to build an emotional relationship with the music and words. I became obsessed with Acting 101 techniques—"What is my objective? What is my obstacle?" Small wonder—I was spending about half of my time working with actors and directors, and I was swayed by their artistic vision. The pure-music people I knew seemed stuffy by comparison.

I became a zealot, and wouldn't start a song until I had properly motivated the first notes. This could get quite tiresome. An audience might have to wait for me to begin Kurt Weill's "Pirate Jenny" until I had dredged up my anger at the landlady who had raised my rent. Only then did I feel I had the right to kick off Weill's well-known song of revenge. When my landlady was no longer a hot-button issue, I'd have to drum up another inner object.

Everything changed one night in 1980, when Martha and Alvin and I were performing our Kurt Weill show at Harvard's Loeb Drama Center. I was on fire, aware that I was playing to a sold-out house that included luminaries (including the renowned director/producer Robert Brustein) and family (including my brother and sister-in law). When we came to "Pirate Jenny," I tore into it with a steely ferocity unlike anything I had felt before. It took me a moment to realize that I had not bothered with my usual inner-object prep to work up a head of steam. I didn't need it any more—the song was just *there*. Of course, I felt guilty, as if I had cheated on a diet. But after more than one hundred performances of "Pirate Jenny," the music itself had become a trigger for my feelings, stronger than any thoughts of my greedy landlady.

I still think it's important to encourage artists to tie their music to personal memories, particularly young singers at the beginning stages of their development. This gives them an emotional grounding that lifts them out of their usual preoccupations—vocal technique, diction rules, whatever their last coach told them to do—and reminds them that music is an act of expression, not a sports event.

As I was turning thirty I began to realize that acting technique—to the extent that I even understood it secondhand—left too many crucial issues unanswered. For one thing, it finally occurred to me that I was an instrumentalist, not an actor. I wasn't enacting a character so much as providing a colorful soundtrack for someone else to enact a character. My medium was vibration, not speech, not movement. If my music had a theatrical flair, great! But it expressed itself through the piano keys under my fingers—the precise pressure I placed on eighty-eight buttons.

And if I only thought about drama, I was tempted to play with an inappropriately feverish intensity that overwhelmed the music, raced the tempo, and made my body tense. To combat that impulse I would dial the fervor all the way back to zero—at which point I could sound as if I'd taken a horse tranquilizer.

Without consciously realizing it, I was developing a third path to bring songs to life: I began to hear them as soundtracks for an imaginary movie. My work with Martha Schlamme and my semester playing for Mark Zeller's class at NYU hammered home the importance of imagery in forging an interpretation, and each of them had different methods for harnessing the imagination. Building on my experience with them, I gradually became aware that I was the curator of a vast inner library of dream-like films conjured up by words and music.

One song might evoke a place where I was alone, another a scene with a cast of characters. Some were in suffused with an intense color, occasionally even an aroma. What was uncanny about these imaginary films was their staying power. When I returned to a song by Meyerbeer after a ten-year interval, after just the first four notes the old scene appeared again—that same seascape with grassy knoll and stone bollards, the same time of day (3 p.m.) and year (September) the music had evoked a decade earlier. This scene exists only in my mind, and only for this one song—but for me it's as intrinsic to the song as Meyerbeer's music and Rückert's words.

At first my fantasy scenarios took on so much reality that I assumed everyone else must be experiencing them as well. At the Aspen Festival in 1980, I was working with tenor Jon Humphries on Rachmaninoff's "What wealth of rapture," which I imagined as a fairly graphic scene of seduction. When Jon asked me to tone down my sforzando attack on an E-minor triplet tumbling into a cascade of major chords, I was dumbfounded. "But that's when he grabs her from behind!" I cried. "What? He does *what*? *Who*? What are you *talking* about?" I was so naïve that I assumed Jon knew I was engrossed in a bodice-ripper, and that the E-minor chord was exactly when the bodice got ripped. He, on the other hand, just wanted to make sure his Rossini-weight lyric tenor wouldn't be submerged by the clang of a nine-foot Steinway. I did my best to oblige, but of course that meant I had to reshoot my imaginary scene (in the new version, the guy slyly unhooked her bra at the E-minor chord).

Over the years my artistic process has become increasingly complex, a melding of opposites: both more technical and more intuitive; more historically informed and more fanciful; more objective and more subjective; more physical and more spiritual; and above all, more conscious. My mind is fielding a barrage of questions: What did the composer want? Do I trust his metronome marking? The composer plays it slower on the recording he made of this song, what does that mean? What do I want it to sound like in my mind? Given that I can't play like Horowitz, what can I actually achieve pianistically? What do my hands want to do (besides reach for the online crossword puzzle)? Who's right, my ear, brain, or hands?

Nowadays a single phrase might exist on three simultaneous levels: a series of seventy-two notes to be weighed and measured to a precise formula devised by my inner ear; a carefully crafted piece of manual choreography: and the underscoring for a movie scene I have imagined (let's say, a tense marital conversation between warring spouses). I make music in a constant eddy of technical oversight and cinematic imagination. But among these competing elements, narrative remains the most potent, the incontrovertible starting point for what follows. When used judiciously, it can transform a dutiful rendering of the words and notes into something magical. Everything springs from a simple question: what events would make someone—would make *me*—sing these words in this way?

Some years ago, I was working at Juilliard with a baritone named Jacob Scharfman who possessed a lovely gift for song. He'd been assigned Vaughan Williams's "The Water Mill," a three-quarter-time tune about the simple pleasures of English country life. The composer makes charming use of a lazy *perpetuo moto* motif, as well as pastoral, folky turns of harmony that some disdainfully call "British cow pat" style. I enjoy listening to Ralph Vaughan Williams's music—my local radio station WQXR often resorts to RVW during the breakfast hour to take the edge off the morning rush. But I don't program it very often.

Other people can give far more authentic renditions of these quintessentially British songs than I ever could.

By the time we'd finished reading through "The Water Mill," the song appeared to have sucked all the air out of the room. Neither of us East Coast city boys could relate to the piece at all. Yet he had sung it well, stayed in tune and in tempo, observed the dynamic markings. And I had dutifully chugged through Vaughan Williams's machine-like piano part, a musical portrait of the water mill. How were we going to bring this song to life? When would either of us ever say anything like this to anyone:

> The miller's wife and his eldest girl
> Clean and cook, while the mill wheels whirl.
> The children take their meat to school,
> And at dusk they play by the twilit pool.

Never, that's when.

I decided to go out on a limb. I knew he was gay, and was soon to move to Europe to start his career. "What if... okay, what if you were living in London, and you were dating a guy who appears to be a good prospect—you know, solvent, caring, handsome, treats the wait staff in the restaurant with kindness and respect, seems to be crazy about you." I had his attention. "But there's one problem."

"Oh dear! What?"

"Well, he was born in London, and he thinks it's okay to make jokes about where you come from—the countryside. You've come to love the city, sure, but you also love your father and your sister and your little hometown. It bothers you that he treats you like a bumpkin. So you form the idea of taking him home for a weekend, which will be a big deal since you've never brought a boyfriend home before. And this song is your way of saying, 'Wait till you actually experience the beauty of the countryside. I'm dying to share it with you.'" We looked at each other. "Whoa. Good," he said. "Let's try it."

Same notes, same voice, same dynamics, same tempo, same pianist.

Different song. He was now fired up by the images in the poem, warmed by the modal harmonies, filled with love for his family and for his imaginary paramour. The frumpy little art song stood revealed as a beauty.

I've spun tall tales like this for many a song, and remain surprised by how effective they can be at unlocking stylistic elements that had been elusive. An infusion of ardor and a jolt of expressive purpose lift a song off the ground. Sure, there might still be some lingering issues with diction and phrasing and tuning, but all those problems are more malleable when there is artistic flow. And it's not a cure-all: some singers can't work this way and require detailed, phrase by phrase guidance in order to get the song out of the garage—what I call color-by-numbers. For them, one domino won't knock over the stack. But no matter what, every song benefits from a backstory.

The soprano Elisabeth Schwarzkopf was a relentless stickler for detail, and much as I disliked her caustic approach to the performers in her master classes, I was in awe of her analytical ear. The problem was that even on those rare occasions when students managed to make the refined sounds she wanted, the song itself was turning to stone. Singers were trying to reproduce isolated details without penetrating to the heart of the material.

The real magic happened on those rare occasions when Schwarzkopf illustrated what she wanted by singing a phrase or two. Her middle voice, even in her late sixties, was still voluminous, with a dark, commanding beauty. I felt privileged to hear those few notes ring into the hall at the Mannes School. Working on Donna Elvira's Act II aria "Mi tradí" from Mozart's *Don Giovanni*, she sang a bit of the recitative. When she came to the line "Aperto veggio il baratro mortal," she stared down in horror at the ground in front of her, as if witnessing something so appalling she had to look away. "I see the deadly abyss opening before me," she sang—and she made the horror visible to us. You could practically smell the stench of sulphur.

I wondered, "How did she make that moment happen—out of thin air? Now, *that's* what she ought to be teaching!" But teaching magic isn't easy. And many accomplished sorcerers and sorceresses would rather not share their spells; they may not even know how the spells work.

There isn't a single formula. A suggestion that releases one artist's creative powers might be nothing more than an amusing public service announcement for another. But I've become convinced that Scheherazade had it right: stories are what keep us alive. The musical text is the powder, the story is the liquid. And when they combine just so, you've created the magic potion.

A concert with Paul Appleby in 2009 at Merkin Hall; against the wall, my first scooter.

CHAPTER 13

Arms and the Man

AFTER I OPTED for a life in a wheelchair I was in a haze of relief. No, I'd never be able to stand up again. But I would also not have to fall down again, and on the whole this seemed like a decent trade-off. I no longer needed assistance to traverse the short distance from my studio to the faculty lounge, or to go across West End Avenue, or to step off a curb. In my mind I had "graduated" to a wheelchair, and my diploma brought me a sense of independence I hadn't felt in years.

Sometimes it seems that the only way to live with a condition like FSH dystrophy is to maintain a healthy sense of denial. I remember thinking, "Well, that's the last inroad it's going to make on me—really, what else could it possibly do? I'm *already* in a wheelchair."

This is how I managed to avoid seeing for quite some time that something was going awry with my arms, and in the process my ability to make music.

Every musician remembers his or her worst concert. Mine was in Chester, Connecticut—a French program called *The Last Time I Saw Paris* with tenor Paul Appleby and mezzo-soprano Julie Boulianne. I lunged at the piano all afternoon, creating what sounded to me like a tangle of wrong notes and cacophonous tone clusters. Aiming for the marmalade of French music, I served up week-old haggis.

It began to dawn on me that my most perilous concerts seemed to be with Paul, which made the experience especially painful. I first met the young tenor when he arrived at Juilliard in the fall of 2006, a fresh-faced Midwestern guy who already had the musicianship and stage savvy of a seasoned artist. Paul had a disarming ability to seduce audiences with his sweet sound, his open connection to his feelings, his immaculate musicianship, and his unique blend of classical purity and renegade rascal. He was as touching in the sweetness of Schubert as he was in thickets of Roussel, as mesmerizing in Brazilian samba as he was tossing off a Springsteen tune. He was one of the most gifted balladeers I had ever met.

For a few years we concertized together often, with both NYFOS and outside presenters. We shared some unforgettable experiences onstage, particularly in low-pressure circumstances when we were at our most relaxed. A 2009 concert we did in a tiny Long Island barn, with a hundred people crammed into a space that seated seventy, remains one of my sweetest memories. But our timing was off: I was trying to learn how to contend with my diminishing resources just when Paul was ready to soar. We never discussed any of this openly, of course. But I became aware that after Paul graduated from Juilliard, he began to put distance between us. By then he had not only won the Metropolitan Opera National Council Auditions but also become a member of the Met's Lindemann Young Artist Development Program—tremendous achievements for a young singer. He now had his pick of high-level, able-bodied coaches and pianists. Our collaboration began to sour.

My second-worst concert also happened to be with Paul just a few short months after the Long Island gig, this time at Christ and St. Stephen's Church in New York. It was part of a recital series sponsored by Marilyn Horne called *On Wings of Song*. I began to have *shpilkes* about this performance weeks before it was slated to happen. It was to be taped for broadcast; I harbored a suspicion, perhaps paranoid, that Marilyn Horne disliked my work and thought I wasn't up to the challenge; and worst of all, I was getting spooked by some of the music's technical demands. Like any pianist, I can get physically tight when nervous. But now, muscular dystrophy was limiting my options for fighting back.

The songs that stayed in just one part of the piano were still comfortable, but I was terrified of passages that moved up and down the keyboard rapidly. A piece like Benjamin Britten's "Avenging and Bright"—a walk in the park when I had played it twenty years earlier with Peter Kazaras—evoked the anguish of a drive to the emergency room through a traffic jam. At the performance, my technique did in fact collapse, over and over again. Still, I held out hope that perhaps I'd only imagined how badly I'd played—until Marlena Malas, Paul's voice teacher and a friend for decades, walked up to me after the concert. I saw something in her eyes that I would now call compassion but at the time I registered as pity. She took my hands in hers and looked at me wordlessly as if we were at a funeral—the last rites for my career as a pianist.

With the distance of time, I now understand why my difficulties were at their most severe when I played for Paul. His ability to fill a room with musical vitality was on a par with the greatest singers I had ever worked with, like an artistic reincarnation of Lorraine Hunt Lieberson. I began to consider him a kind of muse, and was determined to hang onto our partnership. But I was facing not only the loss of physical strength, but also the cumbersome new logistics of my life in a scooter, which also included transporting my own piano chair to every gig. I had become a handful, and it fell to Paul to look after me, the scooter, and the piano chair at all of our non-NYFOS gigs. This was exactly the opposite of what I wanted.

Of course, there were other emotional complexities: I was gay, childless, and in my mid-fifties. For the first time in my life, my paternal instincts came roaring to life—but Paul didn't want another dad. The dilemma was new to me, and I didn't always handle it gracefully. I had to learn a difficult lesson: sons, even metaphorical ones, are prone to rebel against their fathers, especially over-protective ones.

Painful as it was, Paul and I had to go our separate ways for a few years. But eventually an emergency brought about our reunion: in September of 2014, a colleague had to cancel an important recital with me because one of his sons was very ill. Paul was the only singer who knew all the oddball French repertoire I'd programmed, and he happened to be in town and free to step in. During our time apart things had changed for me; I was finally learning to maintain healthy boundaries with my colleagues, and I'd also made some significant progress at the piano. We kept things businesslike, Paul sang brilliantly, and the concert was a success.

That 2009 concert with *On Wings of Song* had been my wake-up call. I couldn't dance around the truth when the radio station sent the recording to us. Paul and I had to approve the tracks for broadcast, and I winced as I listened to the playback. WQXR wanted fifty minutes of music; I could only find thirty-five minutes of the concert where I played acceptably. It was time to face down my demons.

I put myself into the hands of a series of piano teachers, all of them Israeli, all with helpful things to say. None had ever taught a guy with FSH dystrophy before, and I could see that my idiosyncratic difficulties were bewildering to Ilya Itin and Ronn Yedidia, the first two I worked with. Yet all three agreed on one thing: I still possessed the essential musculature needed to make music. Since it was becoming clear that I didn't have the bicep strength of a kindergartner, I was not so sure. But everyone assured me that the basic control of the piano comes from the forearms, and that happened to be the one area of my body I could legitimately call "burly." My wimpy upper arms lead down to a strangely meaty pair of forearms, the only part of my body I like to flaunt.

The lessons helped, but making music was still a confusing enterprise. In certain repertoire and certain situations, I could still sound recognizably like myself. But I couldn't be sure I'd come up with the goods when I ventured out of my comfort zone. Sometimes I would place my hands on the keys to play a phrase, only to manage 80 percent of the notes. In search of a floating, rose-colored tone, I'd produce a clunky sound in battleship gray. After a 2010 NYFOS concert called *The Voluptuous Muse* (songs from the late-Romantic era), I seriously thought about giving up concertizing altogether. I had bravely programmed the Rachmaninoff song that I'd played with relative ease at Aspen in 1980—"What Wealth of Rapture." This time I barely got to the double bar. Its strenuous demands used to be manageable, leaving me free to go off into one of my wild cinematic fantasies. Now my Hollywood romance had turned into *Alien 3*.

No longer was I able to pick up a piece of classical music and sight-read it with accuracy. The difficulties of getting around the keyboard were siphoning off too much attention. Every note needed to be massaged into place, every move had to be carefully choreographed, and every song required dozens of repetitions before my body would absorb the patterns.

IN THE late summer of 2010 I had lunch with a friend, David Younger. David was also living with FSH dystrophy, and we would get together a few times a year to compare notes. The disease was affecting us in very different ways: he was still walking (albeit with difficulty), but his forearms had lost too much muscle mass for him to continue playing classical guitar, one of his prized pastimes. I tended to be a bit passive about treatments—as the son of a doctor, I am patiently awaiting a medical cure for FSH, and the research scientists have as good as promised me a pink pill (I specified the color) that will reverse the atrophy. David, on the other hand, had delved into alternative medicine, even making a trip to India for prolonged work with an Ayurvedic specialist. At our lunch, David told me this doctor was making a rare visit to New York, and David thought I might benefit from seeing him. "Come with us—my wife and I are hosting him for a lecture. Then you can hear some of his ideas."

Since the doctor had a five-syllable last name, he went by just his first name, Manik, to put his American clients at ease. Dr. Manik was aptly named, a geyser of information and opinions whose energy flared up in unpredictable jolts. Punctuating his volley of advice was a recurring physical tic—a tiny jerk of his head accompanied sometimes by a little squeak, apparently a remnant of a serious childhood malady. Although I had no way to evaluate the doctor's philosophy, I craved direction. Traditional Western medicine had not offered me much guidance, and David felt certain that Dr. Manik had helped him.

I made an appointment to see Dr. Manik for a noon consultation a few days after the lecture. I had been told our appointment, in David's East Side apartment, would last about half an hour, and scheduled an afternoon of coachings at Juilliard starting at 2 p.m. After a twenty-minute wait I finally had audience with him. The doctor asked me what I did for a living, and what kinds of problems I faced. "Well, I'm a musician—I play the piano, I work with singers. I teach at a big conservatory, and—oh, I run a concert series here in New York. A successful one," I boasted shyly. "As for problems . . . I have trouble controlling my time. I feel that I'm constantly rushing to keep up with my schedule. It's kind of a common problem in New York, I think."

He took a beat, and then launched into a lengthy disquisition on how I ought to give my concerts. "In my country the musicians come onstage in front of the audience, and they are not warmed up. Then they play only one piece, over and over again. The first hour, ninety minutes, it sounds terrible. But after around two hours, it comes together, and then it is beautiful."

"And the audience . . . ?"

"They are patient. They wait for the music to sound right." A twitch. "And that is how you should give *your* concerts." I tried to imagine a New York audience glaring at the stage for two hours as we stumbled through a single song, struggling to come up with something listenable. It seemed unrealistic. Since Dr. Manik was as certain about concert programming as he was about treatments for muscular dystrophy, I began to have qualms.

As for time management, his advice took the form of chiding admonishment rather than deep philosophy. "You need to arrange your schedule more realistically and say no to things that do not lead to rewards. You need to be less passive with people who eat up valuable hours. It is up to you."

By this time it was already around 1:10, and I could see that his lecture on time management was about to make my afternoon skitter off the rails. Putting his advice to work, I gently cut him off. "Dr. M., this is absolutely fascinating. But I wonder if we could get to the point of this consultation: How do I best handle my muscular dystrophy?"

Picking up a black-handled instrument with a lens at the top, he bent over and looked into each of my eyes for a few seconds. Then the examination was over. "You must give up gluten and lactose in your diet. If you do that, you will be walking within two years. They are causing inflammation in your body. What is your diet now?" I explained that I had been put on a high-protein diet some years earlier, based on some research indicating that muscular dystrophy patients could not assimilate carbohydrates in a normal way.

"No. You are eating far too much protein." He glanced at my red scooter. "And where has this diet gotten you? In a mobility device. It is not working."

There was more to it, of course. The doctor handed me several pages of typewritten, Xeroxed instructions about which foods to eat and which to avoid—pages that had clearly seen decades of use, not tailored specifically to my condition. Perhaps he had different regimes for different biological types, but I was pretty sure I had heard him preach this particular one at his lecture two days earlier. It contained many twists and turns: raw tomatoes recommended, cooked tomatoes taboo; lemons prohibited, limes encouraged. The microwave was off-limits.

I thanked Dr. Manik and handed him the envelope of cash David had instructed me to bring. My afternoon was now a shambles: it was 1:35 and I had just twenty-five minutes to get to Lincoln Center, easily a forty-five-minute trek from the Upper East Side. Nevertheless, since being late because of a doctor's appointment is a "Get Out of Jail Free" card in most situations (especially if you're wheelchair-bound), I was able to reschedule my first appointment. I then made a beeline for an East Side patisserie, bought an expensive pastry with buttercream filling, and wolfed it down right in the store. If I was going to say farewell to wheat and dairy, I wanted one last blowout, my dietary bachelor party.

I decided to take Dr. Manik's recommendations in stages. I'd go gluten- and dairy-free first and tackle the intricate list of dos and don'ts later. While I held out little faith that I'd be dancing the samba in two years just by cutting out bread and cheese, it had been almost two decades since anyone had proposed a concrete plan for regaining physical strength. I was diligent about dairy and gluten, though I was never able to master the complicated dietary guidelines on those Xeroxed sheets. They encouraged me to eat foods I couldn't abide, and I did not believe that stuffing myself with lentils would lead to salvation. Months went by and I began to wonder whether or not I was on the right path.

When I shared my concerns with David Younger, he suggested I see a nutritionist for a second opinion, and recommended a doctor named Peter Bongiorno. Even his name inspired optimism.

This exam was the diametric opposite of the time I'd spent with Dr. Manik. Dr. Bongiorno was low-key, he had a receptionist, his office had the familiar fluorescent lights and acoustical ceiling tile I was used to, and he ran a tight ship. Above all, he was an approachable person with a warm, welcoming manner. Needless to say, his method of examination was entirely different from Dr. M's Ayurvedic approach: using a small appliance he quickly drew a drop of blood from my hand. His analysis was based on my blood type.

"Well, Dr. Bongiorno, what's your recommendation?" His answer was immediate. "Steve, the important thing is no gluten and no dairy. Your body cannot process them; it has enough to deal with as it is." He went on to recommend various supplements, and I dropped over a hundred dollars on a satchel of pills before I left his office. Having been down that road before with other practitioners of alternative medicine, I was skeptical. Most of the herbal remedies I tried in the past had had little effect, and some expensive products recommended by an acupuncturist had once caused me to erupt in violent coughing night after night—I had to down those pills with a double NyQuil chaser to get to sleep.

But one message from both doctors came through loud and clear: stay away from gluten and lactose. I recommitted to the new diet, though I still wasn't seeing significant improvement. True, my energy was on a more even keel, without spikes and valleys. And my digestion seemed calmer. I realized that I had lived with a very slight stomachache for a long time, a discomfort so continuous that I ceased to register it. But these changes seemed fairly subtle.

In March 2011 I traveled out to San Francisco to play a concert of Spanish and Latin American song. The first rehearsal was scheduled very soon after the end of a previous project, and I was resigned to the fact that I'd have little time to prepare. In earlier years this wouldn't have posed a problem—I'd played all the songs at one point or other, and that would have been enough to see me through the week. No longer. Songs that used to roll out of me easily could feel abruptly unfamiliar, and I couldn't rely on muscle memory any more.

At the first rehearsal, the singer and I began work on "Desdichas de mi pasión," a song by an Argentinean composer I love, Carlos López Buchardo. I hadn't touched it in eight months. Though not an especially difficult piece, it begins with a bouncy, vigorous motif that suddenly looked treacherous. "Here goes nothing," I thought as I prepared to splatter the opening bars.

I played it perfectly.

While attempting to appear calm, a triumphal ticker tape parade was exploding inside my head. How was it possible that this tricky passage had just emerged so elegantly from these hands? Why was I not screwing up as expected? We moved on to "Las puertas de la mañana" by Carlos Guastavino, a song that held no physical terrors, no darting movement or rapid scales, but required a radiant color and a flowing line. That kind of beauty had been in short supply for a while, so I steeled myself for the bumpy, mouse-colored phrase I expected to produce. Instead, the room was filled with the silky sweetness of Grand Marnier, a liquid, shimmering melody that actually sounded melodious. My sound had not floated into space like that for some time. Another ticker-tape parade, this time with streamers and a motorcade.

After rehearsal I tried to make sense of what had just happened. "This feels... neurological," I thought to myself. It was as though the pathway from brain to fingertips had cleared. My eye registered the printed music; my brain formed a desire to produce certain sonorities; nerve impulses traveled down my arms; my fingertips touched the keys in the precise way I intended. That's how it's supposed to work. But for years there had been interference every step of the way, like a series of lane closings on a highway. It had been six months, practically to the day, since I had begun my gluten- and dairy-free regime. Was I finally reaping the rewards? Here was the first glimmer of hope I had felt in some time.

It would be nice to report that everything was smooth sailing from then on, and that I never had another day's worry about making music. But the following years have provided plenty of fresh setbacks, necessitating fresh solutions. FSH dystrophy is a progressive disease, always looking for new ways to put you to the test. I continued to lose strength in my arms and hands and, as always, refused to admit it to myself for as long as possible.

The attrition was slow, and it manifested in strange ways. For example, the farther my hands got from the center of the piano, the easier it was to play. As they approached middle C, my arms rebelled. They seemed to dislike the very idea of making music so close to my belly button, and they went on "Power Saver" mode, a trickle of energy that restored itself to full blast when I could make my way back to the higher and lower ends of the instrument. A wide-spaced chord that my right hand could span easily in the upper octaves seemed like an impossible stretch in the middle of the piano. A fast scale passage rippled faultlessly with my arm extended out from my body only to get tangled as my hands descended the keyboard. To compensate for my physical limitations, I grabbed onto whatever muscles were working—mainly my beleaguered forearms and thumbs.

In 2012, on the advice of several friends, I sought help from my third Israeli piano teacher: Edna Golandsky, a New York guru and Juilliard graduate famous for her expertise with injured pianists. I played a bit for her, expecting to hear a scream of "Oy vey" as she watched me lumber around the piano in my extremely idiosyncratic way. But Edna was kind, calm, and helpful. She identified the areas of tension, she guided me to healthier hand positions, she suggested techniques for moving around the keyboard, and she showed me how much more movement I could access in my hands and arms. You don't know how locked up you are until you zero in on your tensions.

On my own, I couldn't always replicate everything Edna showed me—or rather, I couldn't sustain the positions and the flow we found at the best moments of our lessons. I suspected they required more bicep support than I could supply, and I tired quickly when I tried to reproduce those glimpses of piano bliss. Another subtle disagreement cropped up between us over time: whenever my hands were able to follow Edna's instructions, I sensed that the change originated from a spot higher in my arm, or even in my torso. This was important because technical changes are cemented partially through muscle memory (what your body remembers) but largely through verbal instructions (what your mind tells you to do). Edna wanted me to stick to her vocabulary verbatim and speak only to my hands and wrists, while I wanted to bring my shoulders and chest into the discussion. She was a brilliant elbow-to-fingertip teacher—admittedly the areas that needed the lion's share of adjustments. But as someone who had originally gotten his act together with a major infusion of Alexander Technique, I knew that I had to deal with *all* the quirky compromises of my FSH musculature.

Whatever our differences of philosophy, Edna pulled me out of the muck and reorganized my physical approach to the piano, and I am extremely grateful to her. The tools she gave me corrected some of the bad habits that had crept in over the years, particularly my tendency to let my elbows splay out as if I were doing the Funky Chicken. While I could implement some of her advice immediately, my body was putting up a good fight when it came to the more egregious infractions of piano law. (I had played with a flat hand and a low wrist ever since I was five years old, two huge no-nos at the keyboard.)

When she came to hear a concert in 2013, I was nervous that she'd flip out when she watched me in action. I warned her: "Now Edna, you're not going to like what you see."

"At a concert I go to listen, not to watch. Just play. Let the music lead you."

Afterward she came up to me. "It was absolutely beautiful."

"In spite of . . . ?"

"Not in spite of anything. Your music is all there."

Edna confirmed what I sensed: I was making progress. So two years later, when the New York Philharmonic asked NYFOS to produce a Rachmaninoff concert as a tie-in with a festival they were planning, I agreed. It was an act of faith: Rachmaninoff was a virtuoso pianist with a formidable technique and huge hands. His piano concertos demand the physical strength of Johnny Weissmuller and the finesse of Rudolf Nureyev. And while his songs are less athletic than the solo piano works, they still present enormous challenges—he premiered many of them himself. Even the dreamy, floated phrases require a big stretch and rapid lateral movement.

I offloaded two big knuckle-busters onto Michael Barrett, who was sharing the program with me. I still had my hands full with the more lyrical pieces, several of which took me to the limits of my dexterity. In my mind this program would serve as the test of my future as a pianist. If I could play Rachmaninoff songs, I was still in the game. I practiced for weeks, working out ways to play like a tiger even though I felt more like a kitten on the keys. Would my Popeye arms be up to the task?

Every song included one or two phrases for which I could not find a work-around. But I soon realized that all I needed to do was leave out just one note in a widely spaced chord, or occasionally move a bass note up an octave. No one would notice the shortcut, and I would be able to sleep at night. (At a party some months earlier, I'd asked the pianist Inon Barnatan if he ever altered the score slightly at nasty spots to make his life easier. "Of course! *Everyone* does that! No one cares, and no one knows. The public winces at wrong notes, not missing notes.")

The Rachmaninoff rehearsals went pretty well, and it looked as though I might have tamed the beast. But I was still nervous about the first performance, at the Gardner Museum in Boston. Having used beta-blockers a few times in the past, I decided to take one at the performance—just a half dose to give me that longed-for Zen calmness. By way of preparation, I also took a half dose before the dress rehearsal. Alas, I played quite badly at the dress, utterly flummoxed by all the difficult passages I'd worked out so carefully. This was not very comforting, but I blamed it on having to go directly to the piano after a long drive with no time to warm up; I was under pressure, and I reminded myself that I often have problematic dress rehearsals. Certainly, everything would be better tomorrow.

The performance the next day was, if anything, worse. In my pantheon of horrible afternoons at the piano, it took third place, after those concerts with Paul in Connecticut and *On Wings of Song*. Too late, I remembered why I'd stopped taking beta-blockers: I don't have the margin of strength to overcome the feeling of lethargy they produce. That tiny half pill relaxed my arms so much that when I attempted a leap from a bass note to a chord in the middle of the piano, I crashed into a spray of black keys en route—my arm was flying too low to clear the keyboard. It affected my concentration as well—in my search to stay calm I became a space cadet, unable to lock into the patterns I'd learned or the passion I felt for the songs.

After the concert people came up to congratulate me and compliment my playing, but I knew I had tanked. When I finally got to my dressing room I burst into tears. It was the first time I ever cried after a performance. I have rarely felt so demoralized.

I gathered my forces during the car ride home, and resolved to man up and address the problems the next morning. I'd go to the piano first thing and wrestle into submission every phrase that had gone down in flames at the Gardner Museum. After all, there was still the New York concert to play. I sat myself down at 10 a.m. to put Humpty Dumpty back together again. But there was a problem—or rather, the problem was that there *was* no problem. Everything sounded great. Rachmaninoff is never going to be effortless, but the songs were pouring out of me with nary a chipped note. Nothing to fix.

It began to dawn on me that the beta-blocker was only partially responsible for the Boston debacle. The real culprit was my motivation for taking the pill in the first place: fear. I had allowed my anxieties to dominate me, then self-medicated to protect myself. In the process I essentially disconnected my internal piano-machine. An odd, intermittent stage fright has dogged me over the years. The moment I imagine that a piece of music holds an insurmountable technical challenge, or that a colleague has doubts about my ability to play, my confidence can erode. In the past, the fear evaporated once I got onstage and I reassured myself I could still find middle C. With age, though, the problem has worsened.

That Monday morning I felt reassured that the Rachmaninoff songs were still in my neural memory, at least when I was at home. But how about in the hall? What if I suffered another attack of the Holy Terrors on Tuesday at the New York performance?

Two very ordinary circumstances came to my aid. The dress rehearsal was scheduled for noon on concert day, and I knew that no one else in the cast would want to stay in the hall for more than forty-five minutes of our three-hour call. It was rainy outside, particularly unpleasant weather for wheelchair travel. I resolved to move into Merkin Hall for the entire day, sparing myself an unnecessary, wet round-trip voyage. I packed all the items I needed for a concert, plus tea bags, a blanket, a pillow, and my computer.

As I predicted, all my colleagues cleared out by about 12:45. I stayed at the piano until the stage manager kicked me offstage at 3 p.m., by which point I was a little tired and, blessedly, a little bored. There was plenty of time to recover before the show, and boredom is the perfect antidote to nerves. I napped in my dressing room, did a bit of email correspondence in the fourth-floor library, rippled through a second warm-up at 6:30, then wolfed down some sushi. By the time 8:00 rolled around, I had made Merkin Hall into my second home. I was impatient to get onstage and play my songs.

That night, I nailed it.

Upstairs at the reception after the concert, Karen Koch, a NYFOS board member, brought me a glass of white wine. As she leaned in to hand it to me, she said, "Well, it's obvious *you've* been working hard at the piano!" She knew I'd been taking lessons, and she heard the difference. A few minutes later one of my dearest friends, the coloratura soprano Cyndia Sieden, came up to greet me. She hadn't heard me play for a while, but earlier in our lives the two of us had shared the stage for many concerts. Again just a brief comment, murmured in a low, confidential voice: "Well, *you* certainly can still play the piano!" There was a bittersweet quality to both compliments—sweet to hear that I had run the Rachmaninoff gauntlet successfully, a tad bitter that this might have been in question. I decided to take a leaf from Martha Schlamme, my beloved old colleague, and bask in the triumph. She knew how to accept praise.

I remembered something Ned Rorem had told me a year earlier. The *New York Times* was doing a preview piece before NYFOS's tribute concert, *Ned Is Ninety*, and we were in a Juilliard hallway waiting for the photographer to show up. Ned had always been the master of the unanticipated aperçu, but his capacity for epigram had slowed down considerably in his later years. By 2013 he spoke quietly and tersely when he spoke at all, as if it cost him a bit of effort to pull his thoughts together. I had become accustomed to his long silences, and felt he might be worried that he no longer had the razor wit he'd commanded until recently.

Without warning he broke the silence. "Steve, you're a natural pianist." I was too flabbergasted by his comment to formulate a response, but Ned continued, "So am I." In all the years I'd known Ned, he had never said a word about my playing. This unsought moment of affirmation, wrapped in Ned's characteristic self-regard, blew away some clouds. If I might possibly have deserved to be called "natural" when younger, I was now struggling to keep my head above water as my body changed. I'll always need to outsmart my muscular dystrophy. All of us with FSH learn that adaptation is the name of the game, and you have to accept the joy of the chase. But with those brief words, Ned reminded me of who I am.

Another piano teacher of mine, Ronn Yedidia (Israeli No. 2), put it more bluntly. "Steve, you're how old? In your late sixties? You don't sight-read like you did when you were twenty? You're not as strong? Everyone slows down as they age. Get used to being human. Stop using your muscular dystrophy as an excuse." He paused. "You can do this."

I'm working on it.

At Caramoor with Amy Burton, the soprano who not only helped unlock the mysteries of Barber's "Nuvoletta" but also sang it superbly.

CHAPTER 14

Across a Crowded Room

I WAS HAVING DRINKS one evening with a composer friend of mine, a man of lofty ideals and strong opinions about music—let's call him Javier. He gravitates to music with thick textures and dark colors—*Boris Godunov*, maybe Scarpia's torture and murder in Act II of *Tosca* for something more madcap. After a few glasses of wine, I worked up the confidence to profess my enthusiasm for the Spanish composer Enrique Granados.

My friend was dismissive. "Granados? he sniffed. "He's okay, I guess. But he won't change your life."

I didn't rise to the bait, and in any case my friend was too late: Granados had already changed my life. With his subtle interplay of major and minor keys, his unique balance of lament and dance, Granados evokes the drama of the abject lover and the haughty beloved with breathtaking insight. And he was not the only so-called minor composer who has invaded my soul; among the Spaniards alone, I've reveled in the beauties of Eduardo Toldrà, Federico Mompou, and Xavier Montsalvatge—each a master of the deft, small stroke that unlocks a wellspring of emotion.

Another glass of wine brought me around to the point of our conversation: a possible commission to write some songs for NYFOS. But when I popped the question, Javier instantly demurred. "No. I don't think I want to write for voice and piano."

"Why not?" I asked, crestfallen.

"Because with just those two elements every detail has to be perfect. There's nowhere to hide."

I exercised tact and did not mention that this was precisely Granados's genius. With his magisterial command of melody, harmony, rhythm, and word-setting, even his three-page songs conjure up a complete world.

The story has an interesting epilogue. A few years later, Javier attended NYFOS's twentieth-season celebration, during which Susan Graham sang "Chère nuit" by the one-hit wonder Alfred Bachelet. This hyper-Romantic warhorse has always seemed more like a full-out aria than an intimate art song. It begins with an introductory section that's like a sustained recitative, then launches into a broad tune over a burbling piano accompaniment. The poem is standard-issue stuff: a woman waits expectantly for nightfall, when her lover will visit her under the protective veil of darkness. For me, "Chère nuit" falls into the category of delicious guilty pleasure, like a vanilla Carvel dipped in chocolate syrup. Still, with its appealing tune, pleasantly predictable structure, and well-placed high notes—sure-fire ingredients for anyone who loves singing—the piece works like a charm. And Susan delivered it to perfection that night.

Javier came backstage after the concert. "Steve, thank you for the ticket. And, wow, that song!"

"Which song?" There had been a lot of great tunes on the program.

"The French piece! The one Susan Graham sang!"

"*Chère nuit*?" I was incredulous that my avant-avant-garde, Granados-disparaging colleague would warm to that nineteenth-century bonbon.

"Oh, it's an amazing song! You know, it made me want to write some songs myself."

Post scriptum: a few years later he did, and very effective songs they are. But true to his earlier verdict, they're scored for voice with instrumental ensemble, rather than just piano. And of course he didn't attempt the concision of Granados or the melodic grace of Bachelet. Instead, he opted for something more abstract and coloristic, using ostinatos (repeated rhythmic phrases), improvisation, and the enhancement of digital interplay with the instrumentalists, filtering their sound through a laptop during the performance. The result was a more like a movie score for the poems rather than the psychological monologues of the old-school composers. It was all very twenty-first century.

How had the Barricini candy of "Chère nuit" inspired the futuristic paëlla of Javier's song cycle? Why it was that piece and not a "better" one by an acknowledged master? For that matter, why do three notes in a Toldrà phrase sound like the beating of my heart, whereas a canonic masterwork like Beethoven's *An die ferne Geliebte* sounds like someone else's longing, nothing like my own?

Pauline Kael once wrote, "Sex is the great leveler, taste the great divider." And of course, taste is part of the answer. But there are many other factors, and context plays a large role in how we experience music.

Renée Fleming once told me that she was excoriated by the London press in 2000 when she sang an aria by Erich Korngold, "Marietta's Lied," from *Die tote Stadt*. The critics' reaction came as a shock, an unanticipated slap in the face. Not only is that aria part of the standard repertoire, recorded by some of the greatest sopranos of the last four decades, it is also stunningly beautiful, in a high-cholesterol way. At that time, though, the British reviewers lit on the Korngold piece as a pretext for attacking Renée as a purveyor of sentimental kitsch. How dare she subject her London audience to such bargain-basement treacle?

A year later, Renée sang the same aria to an audience of grieving survivors at the site of the devastated World Trade Center towers. The lyrics speak of lovers who are torn apart by death, but the last stanza promises a reunion: "We will not be separated. If you must leave me one day, believe me—there is an Afterlife." For that audience, "Marietta's Lied" brought a kind of celestial consolation. In the space of four minutes, Korngold's music and Renée's sublime singing reassured a sea of mourners that they would once again see their loved ones and find peace. And this time, the critics praised her for offering the most beautiful solace imaginable to a traumatized city.

Sometimes songs can morph before your very eyes. A few years ago a student brought in Richard Strauss's "Säusle, liebe Myrthe," the third song of a 1918 cycle set to poems by Clemens Brentano. Light sopranos are drawn to this piece because it shows off the voice without imposing any great difficulties. It's a bit like wearing a pretty polyester party dress that doesn't need ironing. And Strauss came up with a nice tune that meanders through a variety of episodes in ever-shifting modulations. The music strikes me as aimless, but the real stumbling block is Brentano's poem. The writer, an icon of German romanticism, was not at the top of his game here. He encourages the myrtle to rustle as he apostrophizes all the usual suspects: the clouds, the turtledoves, the moon, the crickets, the fountains. Unlike the palpitating protagonist of "Chère nuit" waiting for sexual congress, this lover seems blandly passive. At the end of the song's four and a half minutes, he blurts out, "I'll wake you soon, and I'll be glad." With this inane comment the song seems to be limping to a conclusion. But Strauss throws in one final appeal to the myrtle, this time including an awkward hiccup up to a high B—the piece's one clumsy vocal moment. And finally the musical strudel is done.

Whenever I've played this song, I've always felt I was on a Bridge to Nowhere, scenic but pointless. And now I was faced with a talented soprano, Deanna Breiwick, who wanted me to coach her on it. She already sang the piece gracefully and in excellent German; nothing needed to be corrected. But how was I to help her make sense of something essentially trivial and ornamental? I could hear Martha's voice saying, "Stevie, no one needs to hear a song like this."

I decided to tell the truth. "Look, I don't think this song is really about anything. Sure, it's pretty, and skillfully written, but empty. The character doesn't seem to want anything, and her relationship to nature strikes me as insipid and clichéd."

Deanna knew me well enough to take this in stride. "Oh! Well, that's... *interesting*." She didn't say anything more, but I knew what she was thinking: "Now what? We have forty-five minutes to fill, and I didn't bring anything else."

I wracked my brains for a minute.

"Okay, I have an idea. This song is sectional, and each part has its own character, its own 'color.' Let's assign an actual color to each one, OK? Got a pencil? The beginning will be aqua, then on page two—second line, second measure—we'll go to pink. Page three at the very top—cobalt. On the fourth page, yellow." I color-blocked the entire song, we each notated it in our scores, and I struck up the introduction.

The result was one of the best readings of that song I'd ever heard—and certainly the best I'd played. There was a magic moment when both of us switched from cobalt to yellow at the same moment, and we both heard it happen. How? Brighter vowels from her, less weight in the left hand from me? I really couldn't say. All I know is that those colors gave "Saüsle, liebe Myrthe" a foundation garment. No longer an amorphous blob, it suddenly boasted an hourglass figure. The song still didn't have anything much to say, but it was dancing, not doddering. And that was the most I could have hoped for.

Yet if some songs from the classical canon, like "Saüsle, liebe Myrthe," don't carry much expressive weight, a simple folk tune can move—and even repair—mountains. It was one of these, "Joe Hill," that brought one of the longest ovations I can remember in recent years at NYFOS.

I'd known about "Joe Hill" since I was a kid—it was in the *Fireside Book of Folk Songs*, a volume I perused on a daily basis when I was in grade school. Of course, I had no understanding of what the song was about at the time, and I didn't hook onto its full meaning even by the time Joan Baez famously sang it at Woodstock in 1969. I had a vague sense it was about a historical injustice in America.

A pair of catastrophes brought "Joe Hill" back into my life. The first was comparatively minor: in October of 2016 I abruptly had to cancel my annual show at Juilliard when a snowballing series of scheduling problems derailed my annual January concert. But my annoyance ramped up to full-out terror when Donald Trump won the presidential election a month later. We New Yorkers were all too familiar with his modus operandi, his outsize selfishness, and blatant mendacity. The future of our nation looked dark.

I met with Mary Birnbaum, who was to have directed the now-canceled show. "What are we going to do?" she wondered bleakly. With barely a thought, I replied, "We're going to do a program of protest songs. It may not solve anything, but it will give us courage. And that is something we could use right now."

The result was a show simply called *PROTEST* in March 2017, cast with seven singers and three players. I knew exactly which students to recruit for it, and every one of them jumped on board without hesitation. Since the concert was to play in a small recital venue, it remained an in-house event, available only to Juilliard students, faculty, donors, and invited guests. But we dug in as though we were preparing for Madison Square Garden. Our multinational playlist included "The Lavender Song" from Berlin's Weimar years, the first known song about gay liberation; Fats Waller's "Black and Blue" and Stevie Wonder's "Big Brother," two fierce pieces about racial inequality; and "Como la cigarra," an Argentinean tune about resilience in the face of fascism. In spite of the cramped black box hall and its limited audience capacity, PROTEST provided the cathartic experience Mary and I had envisioned. The minute I played the last note I was determined to bring it back the next season for the entire NYFOS audience.

That concert took place in February 2018. In the intervening eleven months, the administration at the White House had not magically turned into a garden of earthly delights, and our concert was even more potent. We just needed to add a few more songs to the original hour-long runtime for the new venue. One singer, Dimitri Katotakis, came up with a rarity by American balladeer Woody Guthrie called "Old Man Trump." The lyrics, dating from 1954, had been found among Guthrie's papers, and since there was neither a lead sheet nor a recording, a modern songwriter, Ryan Harvey, supplied a Guthrie-esque melody. The song details the racist policies of an apartment complex in Brooklyn called Beach Haven, owned and operated by Donald's infamous father, Fred Trump. Reading the opening lyrics still sends my blood pressure skyrocketing:

> Now gather around people,
> This story I will tell,
> of a hateful racist landlord
> with a name you all know well.
> I'll tell you of his tale,
> and I think that you'll agree
> When the rotten apple falls
> It doesn't roll far from the tree.

Dimitri, accompanied by guitarist Jack Guglielmetti, delivered a red-hot performance, and the audience was electrified. To this day, people stop me on the street to thank me for presenting that song, a lightning rod for their frustration.

Bass Andrew Munn also lobbied for a song—"Joe Hill." Joe Hill was a union organizer who rose to prominence in the early years of the twentieth century as a political songwriter. Framed on a murder charge in 1914, he was executed the following year. Two decades later, Earl Robinson and poet Alfred Hayes wrote a commemorative song that overshadowed anything Hill himself had written, and it became an anthem for the labor movement, for outsiders, for all Americans who felt the system was rigged against them.

The Woody Guthrie song had been a shoo-in, but I was more skeptical about this tune. Andrew is a deep, meditative person, and I feared "Joe Hill" might be too somber and antique to stand up to the neon colors of the other material. But he was calmly insistent about including it on the program, bringing it in to coaching after coaching. He had a personal reason. After his undergraduate years, Andrew had spent half a decade in West Virginia as an environmental activist. When he told me of his time in the mining towns, all my doubts melted away. The rest of us were talking the talk, but this young man had literally walked the walk. "Andrew," I said, "you have to tell that story. And then sing the song."

He drafted a spoken introduction that we rehearsed as much as the song itself. When he took the stage toward the end of the program, the audience found themselves face to face with a tall, somewhat shy, blond basso who thus far had not been featured as much as the other performers. With unassuming authority, Andrew described his efforts to organize against mountaintop-removal coal mining, "which is exactly what you think it is." He worked alongside miners, other young radicals, and Appalachian environmentalists.

"And that's where I really learned 'Joe Hill,'" Andrew quietly told the audience, "as I heard it sung in union halls and around campfires, and yes, sometimes with moonshine in hand. I was a young rabble-rouser with a few arrests under my belt for civil disobedience on mine sites, working side by side with retired union coal miners and their families," he continued. "It wasn't just a fight for fair wages, or black lung benefits, or mine safety. These mine workers were alarmed about the fate of the planet and coastal communities around the globe. And they knew that the coal industry was no friend of theirs."

He then read the names of his mentors and friends who had died during the struggle, and launched into the song:

> I dreamed I saw Joe Hill last night,
> Alive as you or me,
> Says I, "But Joe, you're ten years dead."
> "I never died," says he,
> "I never died," says he.

When he had finished the last verse, Jack concluded with a short postlude on his guitar. For several moments the hall was silent, and then the audience exploded in cheers. After a while I gestured for Andrew, who had remained seated, to take another bow. It was clear the show couldn't continue until he had accepted their applause one more time.

PROTEST was a watershed moment for me. From the beginning of

The *PROTEST* cast, 2017. *Upper row:* Mary Birnbaum, Andrew Munn, Jacob Scharfman, Christine Price, Amanda Lynn Bottoms, Joshua Blue, Dimitri Katotakis; *bottom row:* Jack Guglielmetti, Mikaela Bennett, me.

my career I had been indoctrinated to think about the moral, philosophical, and psychological value of songs. Working with Martha Schlamme and Alvin Epstein I became aware that that there were many ways that songs could speak to the burning issues of the day. But as I watched my country struggle to remain a functional democracy in the wake of the 2016 election, I felt a greater-than-ever urgency to use music as a way to heal and connect. In the right hands, under the right circumstances, a simple song like "Joe Hill" can pack the wallop of the weightiest German art song.

THE LAST piece I played before the world shut down in March 2020 was an American hymn tune, "How Can I Keep from Singing," in a gorgeous setting by Broadway arranger David Krane. At that moment all of us onstage, four singers and three pianists, were facing a bleak future where a deadly virus was snaking its way around the world, and our professional lives would be on ice for an indeterminate amount of time—assuming we survived at all. The song is about the power of music to sustain us in times of adversity—not as a luxury, but as sustenance for the soul. And it sent us into our year-long exile with a message of tenacity and endurance.

Songs take possession of our hearts in many ways, for reasons so personal that they are nearly impossible to explain. What makes us think a song is good? In my own case, sometimes a beguiling turn of melody seduces my ear. Or there might be a lyric that could have sprung from my very soul. Given my childhood roots in Gilbert and Sullivan, I am a sucker for clever rhymes and verbal dexterity. When Stephen Sondheim is on his game, his songs ravish me with an artistic sugar high—"I'm Still Here," from *Follies*, dazzles every time, especially on those rare occasions when the singer remembers all the lyrics.

I can point to two specific metrics that attract me to a song. The first is what might be termed the "Across a crowded room" factor: a melding of words, melody, and harmony that combusts into eloquence. That famous phrase from Rodgers and Hammerstein's "Some Enchanted Evening" is the paradigm. You probably remember that the song begins with three rather square musical phrases, all with the same melody except for the last note, which climbs higher each time:

> Some enchanted evening
> You may see a stranger
> You may see a stranger

Rodgers then breaks the pattern with the sensual swoon of "across a crowded room," a perfect musical evocation of desire. In just eight bars, his music lifts us from the humdrum of social conventions to the unexpected awakening of love. This blend of squareness and sensuality is part of Rodgers's genius for songwriting—think of the title song from *The Sound of Music*, which boasts a similar mix of purity and fervor.

Many famous songs score 5 out of 5 on the "Across a crowded room" meter, works as disparate as "Gretchen am Spinnrade" by Schubert and Goethe and "Skylark" by Hoagy Carmichael and Johnny Mercer. "Night and Day" by Cole Porter is another 5, as is "En sourdine" by Fauré and Verlaine. It's all about the unique way music can blast a lyric into orbit.

My other acid test is the "Nuvoletta" factor, named after Samuel Barber's setting of an excerpt from James Joyce's *Finnegans Wake*. The novel is a lengthy, experimental work as famous for its verbal brilliance as for its difficulty. A dream landscape composed of wordplay and puns, it draws on multiple languages, private jokes, portmanteau words, and nonlinear narrative. At Princeton, the poet Paul Muldoon needed a two-semester course to finish reading and analyzing the book.

For his song, Barber took 226 words from *Finnegans Wake* and set them as a loopy waltz, the sound of a stoned merry-go-round. Toward the end he interrupts the dance with a mysterious interlude and a wailing cadenza; then the waltz returns and wafts the song away like a soap bubble. I've studied those 226 words with two scholars—first with William Herman, a Joyce expert and at the time the Dean of Humanities at City College; and later with Muldoon, who had been poetry editor of *The New Yorker* before joining the Princeton faculty.

The meeting with Paul Muldoon was fortuitous. We had programmed Russell Platt's *Muldoon Songs* at Caramoor, and were able to entice both Russell and Paul to come up to Katonah for a rehearsal. Once we had Paul in the room, there was no way we were going to let him go without helping us with *Finnegans Wake*. Opportunities like that don't come round very often.

With charming dexterity, Muldoon dissected the complex words, executing a brilliant dive into Joyce's fountain of puns. I marveled as he revealed the names of sixteen rivers and pulled apart the portmanteaus hidden in this short paragraph. His expertise was mind-boggling, but I must admit that his incisive literary analysis didn't give us much to work with as performers. We can't act a list of rivers. What we need is a story.

Luckily Bill Herman had already provided me with that crucial but elusive narrative some years earlier. Soprano Amy Burton introduced us in 1993 when she and I were working on the song. She was already singing "Nuvoletta" with great beauty and fluidity, no mean feat in itself. Barber had written the song for the young Leontyne Price, exploiting the floating freedom of her voice. Amy was tossing it off with ease—even the crazy cadenza that mounts to an exposed high C was perfect every time. Still, both of us were flummoxed by the very strange text.

Bill, who was also a poet, helped us with the wordplay. "'Sisteen shimmers' is Joyce-talk for 'sixteen summers,'" he began.

"Ah, so . . . she's a teenager!"

He went on to explain that Joyce had a schizophrenic daughter named Lucia. "She had multiple personalities," he said. "That's why it says at the end, 'And she made up all her myriads of drifting minds in one.'" Lucia's idiosyncratic way with English delighted her father, who considered her a genius. She was also prone to sudden shifts of mood, abruptly breaking into keening tears until the clouds would lift and she became placid once more. Joyce nicknamed her "Nuvolucia"—Lucia of the clouds. At the end of the song, Nuvoletta climbs over the "bannistars" and . . . wait, does she jump? It's not clear. "A light dress fluttered. She was gone,"

writes Joyce.

"Does that mean she . . . kills herself?" we asked.

"No. Well, not really," said Bill. "Everyone in *Finnegans Wake* goes through transformations and comes back as someone else." He paused. "It's more as if she's jumping into the great Stream of Consciousness."

By unlocking the mysteries of a song we loved, Bill Herman provided Amy and me with a precious gift. Yet the genius of Barber's music is that in its span of four minutes it already captures everything Bill told us that day: the fanciful charm, the mood swings, the wailing tears, the spaced-out dissociation. Expert scholarship gives you grounding, a feeling of ownership. But if a song is well-written it isn't absolutely necessary—the composer has already supplied it.

The ability of music to elucidate poetry, even the most difficult poetry, is what I call the "Nuvoletta" factor. It's what humanizes a song, lifting it from the abstract to the actable. When the "Nuvoletta" factor" is high, the composer has provided the sets, costumes, stage directions, and expert line readings for the performers. I am always hungry for scholarly background, but first and foremost I want the words and music to create an immediate spark of their own. While "Nuvoletta" is about as obscure as a song text can be, Barber gives the performers the essence of the title character—enough words-and-music vitality for a convincing performance without any research.

Words may not be the highest priority for all composers, or all singers, or for that matter all listeners. A prominent theater director who is known for his productions of recherché European plays once shocked me when he declared that he never looks at the texts and translations at my recitals. He's only there for the music; the poem is a distraction.

By the same token, some composers are happy to write music that blows a dense fog around the poem. The modernist giant Milton Babbitt unleashed his full twelve-tone arsenal on Shakespeare's Sonnet 71, with the result that I could barely follow the poem's basic idea. The high-concept jabs of his duo-piano accompaniment and the angular leaps of his vocal line put a tall, protective fence around the words, securely barring them from the listener's understanding. As a work of music-as-mathematics, the song may well be brilliant. Expressively, it gives me a migraine.

In 2001 NYFOS commissioned Milton to write a song for a composite cycle of twenty premieres, a musical greeting to the new century.

Since we knew that Milton had once aspired to be a Broadway composer, things seemed promising when he said he was going to write us a "torch song." Alas, the piece he gave us, called "Pantun," was an atonal dirge similar to that Shakespeare sonnet.

"Um, Milton," said Michael Barrett, "I thought you were going to write us a torch song."

He gave a wry smile. "Michael, this *is* a torch song."

The only lyrics I remember from "Pantun" are "Do not write, do not send a gift." To which I always added, "Do not pass go, do not collect 200 dollars," which I would sing in faux-Babbitt style.

Thankfully, composers are continuing to push the boundaries of vocal music into new territory, and we're hearing new creative voices in the concert hall from an ever more diverse cross section of musicians. Pioneers are vital to the art form. I take pride in the fact that NYFOS was already kicking doors down decades ago, mixing genres, exploring beautiful material that time had forgotten, and always programming contemporary song alongside the older material.

Yet I find myself in sympathy with what the great Francis Poulenc, one of my favorite songwriters, said toward the end of his life (1960): "I write as I want, as it comes to me. Some composers *innovent* [innovate], but some great composers do not *innovent*. Schubert did not *innove*. Wagner, Monteverdi, they *innovent*. Debussy *innove*; Ravel did not *innove*. It is not necessary that one *innove*."

When I consciously try to *innove*, I usually fall on my face. This happened in 2006, at a time when I was on a mission to gain street cred with the critics. Perhaps programming something thorny and intellectual, I reasoned, might counteract the criticism I occasionally received, that I was an audience-pleasing lightweight. No matter that NYFOS had found a way to delight audiences with unfamiliar songs by Alexander Zemlinsky, or Wilhelm Stenhammar, or André Caplet. Or that we commissioned a diverse crew of composers season after season. I felt I had something to prove, and it didn't matter whether I actually liked the music as long as it was definitively non-pretty.

That was why I programmed a cycle by the mid-century modernist Luigi Dallapiccola for a concert called *Brava Italia: Songs by Italians and Italian-Americans.* Now, I reasoned, I could show everyone my all-embracing command of style and establish myself as a serious musician, not just a clever entertainer. What could affirm this better than the *Quattro liriche de Antonio Machado*? They are atonal and spiky, and in no way do they fall gratefully on the ear. Since I was accused of gravitating to flowers, I'd serve up a plate of thorns.

Unfortunately, I made three huge errors. First off, I assumed I still remembered the songs from twenty-two years earlier, when I'd learned them in a hurry for an Ohio recital. No surprise—not a single note had stuck in my memory or hands. I would have needed weeks to get a handle on the composer's six minutes of bleeps and blorps, but I had only a weekend. Second, I assigned the cycle to a soprano with a big-boned Puccini/Wagner voice, while the piece requires a light, pointed sound to negotiate the tricky leaps into the high register and the jagged intervals. Even so, we both threw ourselves into the music and everyone, including Dallapiccola, somehow survived.

But my third error—the idea of using Dallapiccola to spruce up my image—brought the bitterest revelation: no one cared. After all that drama I expected to be lionized for my musical acumen, but my efforts went unnoticed by both critics and audiences. Since there was a lot of opulent music in *Brava Italia*—including songs by Catalani, Pizzetti, John Musto, and John Corigliano—the Dallapiccola cycle came off as a homely intruder on a gorgeous banquet. I'm scarcely averse to compliments, but I did a slow burn as everyone gushed over the encore, Henry Mancini's "Moon River," after I'd bashed my head against the *Quattro canzoni*. The truth was I'd programmed it for the wrong reasons—my ego. I learned my lesson.

These days my overriding goal is to offer music as a counterweight to the perilous state of our world. Humanity seems to be set on a lemming's course off a high cliff, and I feel the need to give listeners something of value, something I believe in and that I think will nourish them. I'm thrilled when a song written two weeks ago can do the trick—and equally happy to find strength in the vast vocal repertoire of the past four centuries.

In 2017, after a performance of a wide-ranging program of songs from Ireland, Cuba, Madagascar, and Manhattan called *Four Islands,* the soprano Teresa Stratas came running down the aisle to speak to me. I hadn't even gotten offstage. It was clear that the program had moved her deeply. "That was wonderful," she said, her eyes fastened warmly on mine. "The thing is, Steve, you give us hope." Though gratified, I was a bit surprised. The show had no express political content, no axe to grind, no specific intention to uplift. Yet somehow its immersion into four different cultures had made the world seem more safe, more connected, more colorful for Stratas. I know that the sheen of the singing and playing also had a powerful effect on her.

YOU CAN never predict where people will find their inspiration. Granados, one of classical music's most distinctive songwriters, leaves Javier cold, yet he heard something in "Chère nuit," a superficial work of art, that inspired him to *innove*. Babbitt's music might do the same for another listener, while someone else might discover the secret of life in a song by Adele. The human soul is complex and hungry. And music is the food of love.

Curtain call for the 2023 concert commemorating the fiftieth anniversary of my professional debut. *Left to right:* Lucia Bradfordx, Federico De Michelis, Will Socolof, John Musto, Shawn Chang, and Michel Spyres.

CHAPTER 15

Iolanthe 3

I SIFT THROUGH MY mail and notice a flier for a recital series at the Park Avenue Armory. These concerts are held in one of their elegant side rooms, and the tickets don't come cheap. I see with pride that all three singers are people I've taught and accompanied in earlier days when they were just getting their feet wet. Now they're big stars. In recent years I have hired two of them for NYFOS programs.

What I do not see on the flier is my own name next to theirs. For a moment I am crestfallen. This was my earliest dream: to be at the top of the voice-and-piano food chain, alongside some A-list singer who commanded a fancy ticket price at a major New York hall. If I had stayed in that end of the business I would have reaped the benefits of the new respect given to members of my profession. When I started out, the pianist's name was all too often left off the publicity for vocal recitals. My frustration mounted decade by decade, coming to a boil in the year 2000 when I saw a poster outside the 92nd Street Y for my upcoming concert there with tenor Paul Groves and mezzo-soprano Charlotte Hellekant. It bore their names and photos—and no mention of me. Half-seriously, I threatened to cancel ("There's no pianist listed, so clearly you won't be needing my services") until the singers' manager simultaneously sweet-talked me and bullied me into sucking it up and playing the performance.

All that is behind me now, a tempest in an old teapot, and even my sadness about the Armory only lasts a moment. A quick reality check reminds me that my duties at Juilliard and New York Festival of Song keep me much too busy to run around playing on the concert circuit. And I remember how uncomfortable I had become in the role of pianist-for-hire. I admit to myself, with a touch of chagrin, that I didn't actually want those gigs, or even the fee. All I really wanted was the publicity.

All this Sturm und Drang turned out to be irrelevant. I learn from Matthew Epstein, who had actually wanted to engage me for one of the concerts, that the stage at the Armory is on a raised platform reached by several steps off a narrow hallway, and there isn't enough room to install a ramp. Since the piano is not wheelchair-accessible, there is no way I could ever play there anyway. Should I be pissed off that the Armory, recently and expensively renovated, had failed mobility-impaired performers? Life is too short. I soothed myself with a glass of Albariño.

In any case, my feelings about performing have changed since I started out. Back then, playing concerts was the driving force of my life, and my self-esteem was based on my identity as a professional pianist. For the first seven years after college, I said yes to every single offer that came my way. Occasionally there would be something wonderful: after all, at age twenty-five I got to play at Tully Hall with Patricia Brooks. But a lot of my time was spent cranking out recitals in out-of-the-way libraries, shows at less-than-sanitary cabarets, cocktail music on upright pianos where the babble of the crowd rendered me utterly inaudible, and enough auditions and voice lessons to win me the Croix de Guerre. At one of my more memorable nightclub gigs I looked over to see a monkey staring up at me expectantly—the simian pet of the owner. Hell-bent to prove myself a working musician, I was willing to step around monkey droppings just to settle the score with the Yale School of Music, who thought they had consigned my music career to the junk heap.

Eventually it dawned on me that I could pick and choose my engagements, and I finally began to fulfill my real dream: a public love affair with my singer colleagues, with music lovers, and with the songs that animated my spirit. It can take years for a collaborative pianist to understand his artistic nature, since our stock in trade is to blend our sound seamlessly with a wide variety of musicians. In those early decades, having an overly defined artistic personality was practically a liability. Our job was to take someone else's musical impulses and turn them into gold, and if gold is not a possibility, then at least stainless steel. What color is a chameleon? Whatever color he needs to be.

With NYFOS I created a laboratory where I could experiment musically without the fear that I might be fired or—the more usual sign of failure—simply not re-engaged. And I finally had an arena for sharing the music I loved with an audience on a regular basis. My father had an expression he used whenever one of his friends cooked a great meal or sewed a button elegantly in place. "You missed your calling," he would murmur in an ironic tone that mixed admiration with mock regret. I am happy to look back on a half century of concertizing and know that I did not miss my calling.

These days, I am not as addicted to being onstage as I was a few decades ago, and the Covid pandemic further hastened the shift in my priorities. For most performers, those eighteen months on the sidelines were a painful period of silence. I was as terrified as everyone else about the plague that raged all over the world, washing my hands like a deranged Lady Macbeth while singing "Happy Birthday" twice, as the folks on public radio counseled. Yet that long period of isolation had an unexpected silver lining: I was at a point where I needed a retreat, and the world forced me into a semi-sabbatical.

With no live performances on my calendar, I had a chance to meditate on the all-too-predictable emotional roller coaster that plagued me as I got ready for my concerts: the days of mounting dread before the event, the total absorption with the task at hand while onstage, the euphoric high right after, and the plunge of self-doubt afterwards. If a review appeared with even a whiff of criticism it would disseminate its poison at my most vulnerable moment, stoking self-doubt and feeding my suspicion that my work sucked.

All this drama began to seem like a high price to pay for a few hours of musical communion, and particularly excessive for a collaborative pianist like me. Traditionally we are seen as not merely the second fiddle, but the last chair in the second violin section. There's an old joke about the perfect lover: someone who services you perfectly for two hours, and then turns into a pizza. For some, this also describes the ideal accompanist. With NYFOS, of course, I was in a far more prominent role—not merely pianist, but also the front man, host, arranger, and producer. Still, my tendency to be a skittish pile of nerves was of interest to absolutely no one.

Music was my private world as a child, and during the long, enforced isolation of the pandemic music once again became my retreat. But this was no Zen garden. As I've aged, my practice time has become an increasingly tumultuous summit meeting between my ear, my brain, and my body. My ear can imagine colors and shapes, sounds that usually range far beyond the scope of what eighty-eight keys and hammers are capable of producing. My brain is aware of not only the printed text at hand, but also the history of the work and the performance traditions attached to it.

And my body... well, it's always been quirky, as John Kirkpatrick tactlessly noticed way back in 1968 at our fateful piano lesson.

My body has only gotten quirkier over time. I long for the days when I wasn't so aware of my physical limitations nor of the emotional baggage I carry around. But while it is a struggle to overcome the ongoing challenges of FSH dystrophy, it has also become a source of pride. Music has powers to charm not only the savage breast, but also the savage thumb, wrist, forearm, and shoulder. I work every day to assert myself over my weaknesses. Sometimes I succeed. Often I am tempted to give up. But I never do.

When it became clear that NYFOS would not be able to give live concerts for a while, I made a snap decision to create a season of video concerts which we would stream on our website. I felt a responsibility to the NYFOS audience, who had been faithful to us for three decades. Surely they would appreciate having our music to sustain themselves through the tough times. I also saw it as an opportunity to make new connections with musicians I admired (no hassles with visas or flights), and to expand the reach of NYFOS from Manhattan to Mandalay. It took me no longer than five seconds to come up with a name—"We'll call it NYFOS@Home."

Looking back on that moment, I realize that I might have been channeling Martha Schlamme once again—"I wouldn't want to rob them of my 'Surabaya Johnny'!" she had wailed to me backstage before she sang it as her eighth encore. At the time, her audience's need to hear her sing a long, sad Kurt Weill song had seemed delusional. Decades later, I finally understood Martha's impulse. I, too, didn't want to "rob them" of my songs. And my audience, like hers, actually did relish the gift of our music.

I couldn't have foreseen that this was going to lead NYFOS—and me—into a new burst of creativity.

But first I needed to deal with my lifelong terror of being filmed. Having shunned the camera for decades, I assumed I would need to learn to relax for a video. Alas, when I tried that, I was abashed to learn that my "resting pianist face" bore more than a passing resemblance to the red snapper I saw on a bed of ice at the fish market: blank eyes, gaping mouth. And the deeper my emotional connection to my songs, the more glassy-eyed I looked. Occasionally my tongue would make a cameo appearance between my front teeth.

My former student, baritone John Brancy, taught me a trick: he told me to keep my tongue permanently in the "ng" position. "Just do it, you'll see!" he said with his typical enthusiasm. He was right—when I remembered to do it, my face settled into something between "pleasant bland anchorman" and "Mona Lisa contemplating a Dove Bar." It was a vast improvement on "dead snapper."

During that first Covid year, I had to film my piano accompaniments alone as I tried to conjure up the phrasing and vocal colors of my absent partners. They, of course, were also holed up all over the map. In a kind of transcontinental karaoke, they filmed their half of the song later, using an earbud to sync themselves to my prerecorded track. Julia Bullock crooned an exquisite rendition of Billy Strayhorn's "A Flower Is a Lovesome Thing" from her perch in Norway, while Sasha Cooke lifted a glass of champagne as she swung into Kurt Weill's "One Life to Live" from her home in Texas. Thomas Hampson sang William Grant Still's "Grief" from a hotel room in Germany, and Corinne Winters breathed Iberian fire while tucked away at home in Philadelphia.

There were new things to think about, the kind of musical detailing that I would do automatically if I were actually in the room with my colleagues. I had to allow space for tiny consonant clusters—the "ng-b" of the words "coming back," for example, dictated a minuscule amount of extra stretch in the phrase. At the same time, I needed to establish a more solid rhythmic groove for my absent partners—while still allowing room for breathing and the natural expansion of the phrase. But squareness doesn't come easily to me—I'm a pretty curvy player. Still, the ensemble was often astounding. You'd never guess Kate Lindsey was singing 3,500 miles and two weeks away from me; her performance of Hollander's "Black Market" sounded as commanding and spontaneous as the Marlene Dietrich original. How did she follow my supple, undulating tempo? For that matter, how did I manage to anticipate her supple, undulating phrasing?

Though NYFOS@Home only lasted one season, it was a watershed moment. For the first time in years I was repeatedly forced to confront the reality of my pianism, never as smooth and elegant as I wanted, but also never as clunky as I feared. I heard its beauty. I observed its pockmarks. And I began to make peace with myself.

Fortunately, the video project started after I had spent the entire spring and summer of 2020 at the piano alone. When the pandemic hit in March, I made a resolution to play the piano every single day. Without any performances on the horizon I had no immediate reason to practice, and I tend to shun the piano unless I've got to get music ready for something—which has included pretty much every day of the last fifty years. Practicing makes me face my demons, and who wants to do that if they don't have to?

For once, my inner adult prevailed, and I kept to my commitment. I played Bach, I played Mozart, I played Albéniz (the easy pieces, not the gnarly ones), I played blues. I worked on jazz improvisation with a wonderful teacher, Jason Yeager. In all my adult years I had never been through such a long period of musical solitude. Locked in a room with my hands day after day, I got to revisit the vagaries of every knuckle and joint from my shoulder to my fingertips. When they were uncooperative, I looked for new ways to outsmart them. I felt like a deprogrammer going to work on a teenager wrested from a commune.

I would never have been able to get through that initial video season without the support of Jonathan Estabrooks, whom NYFOS hired to produce the series. Jonathan had been my student at Juilliard in the early 2000s, at which time he had the makings of a fine singing actor. But in recent years he had turned videography, which had been his side job, into his main gig, and he was developing extraordinary expertise in filming, recording, and editing. He also had a fourth area of expertise: handling me. When he was a master's student, I was his coach. Now he was mine, instilling confidence, marshaling my resources, and holding up a finger when I slipped back into "dead fish face."

I imagined that it would be a breeze to move from live performances to videos created at home on my beautiful piano. I discovered at the first couple of sessions that I had stepped from the frying pan into—well, another frying pan. In a live show, you want to be note-perfect and artistically spot-on. But the concert stage is a bit more forgiving of small slips. If the audience is swept away on the tides of emotion and musical verve, if the singer is in the zone, you can usually get away with a clam or two at the piano, no harm no foul. Who's keeping score, besides me?

On video you cannot afford any obvious errors. (Hidden ones are fine.) True, you have the luxury of repeated takes and editing. But at some point you're going to have to come up with the notes, preferably before you go crazy. Factor in my longstanding twin phobias—microphones and cameras—and you'll understand why I constantly froze in those first sessions. Mic test: beautiful! Take one: oy gevalt.

It took me a while to learn to let go at the keyboard, while maintaining the bland facial expression of a 1950s hostess offering a tray of canapés. Full disclosure: we took some footage of me looking beatifically calm as I pretended to play. We occasionally used those clips to edit out dead-fish moments. (Mona Lisa, meet Milli Vanilli.)

Jonathan proved to be an important partner in the next Covid-era project: NYFOS Records, our own label. This was a dream I'd had for decades, but I had never been able to persuade the board of its value. Certainly I had been complicit, caving in to their lack of enthusiasm too easily. Now, as my seventieth birthday approached, I felt emboldened to the point of belligerence, demanding what I wanted. I was tired of spending months creating concerts that would turn into a blip, at best a vague memory for the audience that was present on the night. NYFOS@Home had given me a taste of playing to a worldwide audience, as well as the experience of producing something that would last. Those videos were posted for a month online. Our recordings would be available indefinitely.

I'm not a complete Luddite, but I have only the most rudimentary understanding of playlists and algorithms—vital elements in the commerce of an online record label in 2021. I didn't even know how to spell "algorithm" until spellcheck gave my first attempt ("algorhythm") the red underline. This is another benefit of having Jonathan on your team. He straddles the world of art and the world of tech, and he's constantly honing his skills. By November of 2021 we were off and running, with monthly online singles and a series of albums. And NYFOS Records means as much to me as any concert I have ever played. At the time of writing, we have put out six albums, with two more in various stages of completion; our tracks have been streamed several million times worldwide.

Another bulwark of my current life is my physical therapist, Lawrence Harding. Since December of 2010 Lawrence has been devising exercises, educating my body, and building strength. Edna Golandsky had given me valuable tools for correcting many of my lifelong bad habits, but I feared I lacked the stamina and coordination to sustain the hand and arm positions she advocated. I explained my dilemma to Lawrence, who listened carefully and nodded understandingly.

We started our sessions and it eventually dawned on me that he was working on the very movements Edna had been teaching me. Isolating the various components of my arms, fingers, and shoulders, he subtly began to build back the mobility I would need to keep playing the piano.

"Now—Lawrence—I don't exactly understand what we're doing all the time. I'm kind of dumb when it comes to my body. I don't really remember from session to session."

"Doesn't matter, Steven," he said in his rich bass-baritone. "I'm mostly talking to your body and your nervous system. They're the ones that remember. It's good if you can grasp it mentally. But it's not necessary."

Lawrence's words resonated deeply within me. The body has its own logic and its own memory. I am constantly amazed by the way it figures out how to solve problems, usually far more effectively than when I order it around from Command Central. And my piano lizard brain has saved my butt on several notable occasions.

In 2014 I was set to record a piece by Narcís Bonet for an all-Spanish album with Corinne Winters called *Canción amorosa*. The cycle sounded better in her voice transposed down a step, but the new key was creating problems for me. A few of the chords in the original score that allowed the pianist to grab two white keys with the side of the thumb had now morphed into awkward clumps of badly placed black and white keys. Try as I might, I could not figure out how to form those shapes on the keyboard. Screwing my fingers up to play the chords, my hand twisted and locked. On recording day I headed down to the studio as if I were about to walk the gangplank, knowing I had to expose my unsolved technical snag to the scrutiny of a microphone.

But when we got to the spot I was dreading, the strangest thing happened: my hand spontaneously found a way to play the previously unplayable. I still have no idea how this happened—which tendon, which knuckle, which neuron came to its senses. I was so shocked that I looked down at my hand to confirm that it was indeed I who had just tamed measure 63, the bane of my life for an entire month.

Since that day I've had other moments when a physical block abruptly vanished into thin air with no explanation. I wish I knew the formula to coax my body into this kind of release, but it seems to be utterly resistant to intellectual analysis. The experience falls into the category of spiritual alchemy, a moment of enlightenment that bypasses the mind. I know of only one way to induce it: after working industriously on a passage, sometimes failing five hundred times in a row, I give up. Eventually my mind goes blank, and that's when the magic spell takes hold—look, there's the phrase, note-perfect. I would never give this advice to another musician. "Screw up, screw up, screw up, and then space out" is scarcely the foundation for any kind of technical command. But it can create astounding breakthroughs. I live for them.

As any musician will tell you, the opposite is just as likely to happen: a phrase that has been trouble-free for weeks will fall apart without warning, and it can be tough to glue the shards back together. These secret battles fill my days and nights. But in spite of all the struggles, music remains my primary way of connecting to the world. I know I am not alone in this—many musicians would say the same thing. Music is the one invisible art form, constructed out of pure vibration. The ability to blend my sound waves with those of another person—and send them into the world—still seems like a miracle to me.

These connections are multifaceted. I have a deep, daily communion with the composers and poets whose songs I attempt to bring to life. Sometimes I feel more intimacy with a long-dead composer than one I know in my everyday life. I am obsessed by harmony and in thrall to rhyme. A beautiful chord can melt me, a perfectly turned couplet is like an aphrodisiac. And I fall in love with the artists who join me in bringing this beauty into the world.

Until the pandemic I had an easy, willing connection to audiences, the voyeurs of my soul. But after a season away from the concert hall, I suddenly found myself less comfortable about sharing my private musical world with a crowd of people. For the first time in my life it felt unnatural to be so vulnerable in a public space, and my body rebelled. The 2021–2022 season was filled with enough Hail Mary moments—my arms as stiff as the Bride of Frankenstein—that I began to wonder if I should still be playing in public. After a lot of work, both technical and psychological, I began to re-harness the energy flow necessary for making music. I almost divorced the piano, but we're OK for now. Still, I know that the contract will need to be renegotiated every year.

Inner harmony is only one of the things I need in order to make outer harmony on the piano. These days I also require a lot of equipment.

The muscle that flexes my foot is a lazy bastard—it was the one that made me fall on my face over and over again back in the 1990s. My legs do retain some strength, but they're no great shakes. As a result, I've been a side-pedaler for many years, using the ball of my foot to toggle the corner of the sustaining pedal on a diagonal. To make my life easier, a piano technician named Manuel Buri built me a pedal extender, a second pedal mounted on a metal box that slips over the one on the piano like a condom. (Appropriately enough, it is fixed in place by a couple of screws.) Meanwhile, farther north on my body, I use a back support that Lawrence Harding constructed for me, made out of acrylic and a variety of different rubber foams. And finally, I now avail myself of a seat belt at the piano—not to stop me from running away from the keyboard, which I want to do a lot of the time, but to keep me from sliding off the bench.

Yes, it's a lot of equipment, but it has kept me playing. I've come to realize that music is not only my connection to beauty and expression, but also my fundamental connection to that noble, flawed structure that I call home—my body. I chucked sports and dancing from my life years ago, but my daily encounters with the piano keyboard take the place of both. Music may be invisible, but it is created by real muscles and tendons that move flesh and bones. Playing the piano is a contentious negotiation between my will, my imagination, and my corporeal reality. All three parties are fierce bargainers, and the discussion sounds something like, "DO it! "DREAM it!" "DAMMIT, no!"

Each party is yelling at the top of its lungs. Of the three, the body requires the most coddling—it's always ready to shut its metaphorical attaché case and leave the table. But when all of them reach an entente cordiale, ah, how sweet it is. It can take days. It can take two months. It can arrive out of the blue while I am totally spaced-out, or emerge from slow, methodical repetition. But eventually mind, fantasy, and technique link arms, and the result is the music that has given me a sense of purpose for almost all my born days.

I KNOW I have paid a price for not going to music school—I have no training, for example, in dealing with large groups of musicians like orchestras or choruses. And I lack the type of analytic skills that I would have acquired in advanced music theory courses. I am expert at perceiving detail—after all, I'm a song guy, a kind of musical jeweler—but I don't have a conductor's understanding of larger musical structures or massive layers of sound. Still, I did emerge with my intuition unharmed, and that has been my greatest source of strength as a teacher and performer. I do not believe I would have survived the onslaught of a conservatory. In my studio I am at my most creative, a gestalt therapist for the voice.

By now, so many of the people who helped set this journey in motion are no longer here to guide me—but surely Dan Ferro, Martha Schlamme, Alvin Epstein, and Martin Isepp are taking it all in from some celestial parterre box. Meanwhile, some of my most venerable teammates remain steadfastly by my side. My college piano teacher Alex Farkas drops by for a visit every few months. Simply being in his presence calms my mind, opens up my voice, and eases my breathing. Five decades ago Alex steadied me when I was first dealing with my sexuality. Not that we ever discussed it openly—I was too freaked out to tell anyone about my tortured love affair with a guy whose interest in me began to plummet twelve minutes after he got my cherry. But there was no need to explain anything; Alex registered my distress, probably figured out the cause, and for one hour a week put a soothing cold compress on my anxiety. Wordlessly, he kept me from going to pieces. Recently I've been able to return the gift he gave me half a century ago. Not long ago Alex's wife Toni died, and he told me that our time together is a comfort to him.

I no longer study piano with Alex in any conventional sense. But he never stops teaching me. Over the years Alex has become one of the world's premiere instructors of Alexander Technique. I know that he can observe the inroads FSH dystrophy has made on me, and just before he leaves he always offers me a gentle bit of advice—the man is a walking koan. When I complained about my thumbs, the bane of my piano existence, his advice was typically brilliant and indirect. He is a master of enlisting one part of the body to free tensions elsewhere.

"The thumb is related to the jaw. When your hand gets tight, check in with your jaw. See if you can release it. And then notice what's going on with your thumb. After that, release your foot." He lets a moment pass, and then says, "Give me your arm." He cradles my forearm gently in the air, and I feel a rush of warm energy and a release of muscular tightness I didn't even know I was carrying. "There you go," Alex says with quiet satisfaction. "Plenty of chi. You have what you need." He turns again. "Don't try so hard. Trust." Once again I am filled with the same sense of wonder and gratitude I felt when we met in 1969.

Alex has not changed with the decades. Nor has my friend Matthew Epstein, who at seventy-six continues to be the same blustery force of nature he was at age eighteen. Over the years, he has sometimes provoked a fight-or-flight response in me (I always chose flight), but I recently made peace with his need for control. Matthew has dominated all our conversations for nigh unto sixty years, why should he stop now? Anyway, you have to let Matthew have the floor, with all his convictions and contradictions. There's really no other way to be his friend.

It was Matthew who first engaged me as an accompanist a few months after my bar mitzvah, and it was Matthew who introduced me to Valerie Masterson later that year. During a recent encounter he mentioned that he had been in touch with her, and by some miracle I managed to get a brief word in edgewise. "My book starts with Valerie—" "It does?" he breaks in. "You should write her. She does email—I'll send you her address."

I had a crush on Valerie when I was eleven, and I still do. When I tune her in on YouTube, my heart skips a beat at the sight of those uncannily bright blue eyes and that incandescent smile. Her Mozart, Massenet, and Handel opera arias are wonderful, but predictably it is the Gilbert and Sullivan clips from her early years that reduce me to a blubbering mess. Over the years I made sporadic efforts to contact her, but as each one foundered I finally gave up. With Matthew's encouragement, I screwed up my courage and dropped her a note, enclosing the opening chapter of this book.

When I saw Valerie's name in my inbox, I smashed my trackpad to pick up her message with such force that I nearly dented my computer. I feared I would receive a polite, pro forma response to my letter. I was not ready for her to share a memory that practically knocked me off my chair:

> *How clearly you revisited that (although the three of us did not know at the time) truly life-changing night when all of us saw our future desires and hopes taking shape. I, for one, was so encouraged to fur-*

ther my dream of becoming an opera singer, even though I was being fêted at that time with very lucrative contracts to be the next Julie Andrews—and I had even been invited for screen tests in Hollywood! After that fateful night, even though I had signed with them, I told them I wanted to further my operatic career—and nothing they offered would interfere with that. I don't think even Matthew knew about that!

I can only hope and pray that young people with ambitious desires find two friends like I did to give them the thrill and encouragement at the right time to follow their dreams.

I will never forget that night or my two dear friends Matthew and Steven to whom I owe so much. If only I had known then that two of the world's greatest talent/coaches were there I would probably not have been able to sing a note.

I knew that Valerie's reminiscences probably required some adjustment for inflation—I was a five-foot, five-inch prepubescent boy at the time, scarcely a source of life-changing encouragement. Nevertheless it seemed as if the long-ago night that changed my life might truly have changed hers as well. In this revised version of the story, I become the knight-errant who rescued his damsel from distress: Valerie had been in thrall to the evil wizards of Tinseltown, locked in the dungeon of operetta, but I, empowered by my recent bar mitzvah, manage to lift her into the realms of high art where she became one of its stars.

I heard Valerie in all of the G&S roles she sang in New York, but never saw her in *Iolanthe*—she didn't perform the ingénue lead, Phyllis, very often with the company. They probably knew that her best qualities would have been wasted on the role: Phyllis is a brittle character with nothing showy to sing, and her one, somewhat drab solo song comes in the middle of the first-act finale where there is no break for applause. On the other hand, Phyllis's swain, my alter ego Strephon, is a uniquely interesting character—ardent, naïve, and (fascinatingly) half-mortal, with a man's legs and a fairy's torso and brain. The Act II curtain comes down, of course, on a happy ending, and we never get to see what would happen to him when he became a senior citizen. In the show all the male chorus members become head-to-toe fairies, but it isn't made clear whether Strephon acquires supernatural haunches to go with his magical upper body.

Conjuring up an image of Strephon as a half-human seventy-year-old, I compare the two of us. All in all, I think I come out ahead. Strephon struggled with being "half a fairy," while I am blessedly a Kinsey 5 in the age of Gay Pride. His upper body was immortal, which sounds like fun until you think through the ramifications. Mine might be a flukey mixture of brawn and bog, but it is functional enough to fulfill my dreams, even though it sometimes drives me crazy. True, we both have lower bodies that are destined to decline precipitously with the years. But when I die, at least I won't leave behind a youthful, legless, fairy torso. This, I decide, is a point in my favor.

I try to imagine my present-day life as written by Gilbert and Sullivan, the *Iolanthe 3* I once dreamed about. But much as I love them, they probably aren't the right artists to script and score an operetta about my current existence. That work would have to be by writers like Stephen Sondheim and Tony Kushner, or Pedro Almodóvar and Adam Guettel, with contributions by Mel Brooks, Colm Tóibín, and Randy Rainbow.

At the end, the audience would see me seated at a piano, surrounded by my extended family—relatives, colleagues, friends, and, most important, my husband Jim. Through some kind of stage magic, there would be a bolt of light and a puff of smoke, and the entire company would sail upward through the open ceiling of the theater. Our destination: that region where the body encounters no physical barriers, the place I dream about night after night.

The show ends with the plummy contralto voice of the Queen crying out, "Then away we go to Fairyland!"—as I ascend, grinning from ear to ear.

Outside in Riverside Park on my seventieth birthday.

ACKNOWLEDGMENTS

THE IMPETUS FOR writing *From Ear to Ear* began with a series of lunches with Julia Reidhead, President of W. W. Norton, and Susan Gaustad, a seasoned editor of music books there. Both were regular (and enthusiastic) audience members at my New York Festival of Song concerts, and avid readers of my program notes; they were certain I had a story worth telling. I was far less certain, so at lunch number four they brought along a man I did not know at all, Robert Weil, the Editor-in-Chief of Liveright, one of Norton's imprints. Where Susan and Julia had tried to persuade me to write about my life in music, Bob dispensed with the niceties and addressed me bluntly: "I've read your stuff. You have to write this book." He then told me how. "Don't get bogged down in 'and then I did this, and then I did that.' Boring. Make an outline and write fourteen essays. You know how to write an essay, right?" If Susan and Julia's fireside chats hadn't quite done the trick, Bob's ice bucket challenge was my wake-up call.

His marching orders were echoed verbatim by my husband, James Russell. Jim is a brilliant writer himself, and also a professional editor—my live-in blue pencil. His support and savvy fill every page of this book, not to mention every corner of my life. I owe a debt of gratitude to my agent at Calligraph, Lucy Cleland, who added me to their illustrious roster much the way Zeus scooped up Ganymede. She too sent valuable suggestions, and provided a welcome blend of warmth and objectivity as the book reached the double-bar.

I received some expert advice from a variety of people along the way. Manuela Soares, a professor at Pace University and the director of Pace University Press, gave me some excellent early guidance: to sit down and let it rip, waiting to edit later in the process. D. P. Snyder, a world-class author and translator (and my Spanish teacher) was a constant source of perspective and encouragement, as well as the kind of early reader every author longs for. And Jonathan Galassi, executive editor at Farrar, Straus, and Giroux, gave me a few suggestions that sliced through some of my most troubling Gordian knots during the writing process.

Many people read individual chapters as they emerged from my computer, and a few people went the whole nine yards and read the entire book. Margaret Crane served as a much-needed interim editor, and Jeanne Betancourt offered her own uniquely helpful perspective. Philip Stoddard, once my student and now my friend and colleague, gave it a read too; his response set me up perfectly as I prepared to send the manuscript to Norton. At Norton, Caroline Adams, associate editor, cheerfully helped me with the photo selection and guided me through the book-making process.

Lots of other people read parts of the manuscript, among them Jason Yeager, Peter Kazaras, Stephen Wadsworth, Kurt Ollmann, Greg Feldmann, Jamie Bernstein, Andrew Altenbach, Sasha Cooke, Carll Tucker, Sylvia Smith, Gordy Slack, Jonathan Estabrooks, Francis Raeside, Bénédicte Jourdois, S. J. Rozan, Susan Chin, Robert Hughes, Paul Gruber, Evan Rogister, Steven Cole, Lela Love, Linda Viertel, and Jack Viertel. Each of them provided me with the kind of insight that extended far beyond the chapters they read.

Special thanks to my brother and sister-in-law, Malcolm and Vicki Blier. I could never have published *From Ear to Ear* without their careful reading, their wisdom, and their stamps of approval. Finally, I owe a debt of gratitude to Adam Gopnik, whose generosity and guidance culminated in the book's beautiful foreword.

I feel like one kind of person when I sit at a computer or go out shopping for food, and another, more vibrant kind of person the minute I am in the presence of a singer. I close with a deep bow of thanks to the composers and poets whose songs line the library shelves of my soul; to everyone I ever accompanied; and all the singers I heard in concert halls and opera houses, on the grooves of records and over the airwaves. I spring to life in the presence of singing, and those voices have sustained me since the day I came into this world.

INDEX

TK

ABOUT THE AUTHOR

Steven Blier is the artistic director of the New York Festival of Song (NYFOS), which he co-founded in 1988 with Michael Barrett. Since the festival's inception, he has programmed, performed, translated, and annotated more than 160 vocal recitals with repertoire spanning the entire range of American song, art song from Schubert to Szymanowski, and popular song from early vaudeville to Lennon-McCartney. NYFOS has also made in-depth explorations of music from Spain, Latin America, Scandinavia, and Russia. *New York* magazine gave NYFOS its award for Best Classical Programming, while *Opera News* proclaimed Blier "the coolest dude in town" and in December 2014, *Musical America* included him as one of thirty top industry professionals in their feature article, "Profiles in Courage."

Blier enjoys an eminent career as an accompanist and vocal coach. His recital partners have included Michael Spyres, Julia Bullock, Renée Fleming, Cecilia Bartoli, Samuel Ramey, Lorraine Hunt Lieberson, Susan Graham, Jessye Norman, and José van Dam, in venues ranging from Carnegie Hall to La Scala. He has also been on the faculty of The Juilliard School since 1992, and has been active in encouraging young recitalists at summer programs, including the Wolf Trap Opera Company, the Steans Institute at Ravinia, Santa Fe Opera, and the San Francisco Opera Center. Many of his former students, including Stephanie Blythe, Sasha Cooke, Paul Appleby, Corinne Winters, Will Liverman, and Kate Lindsey, have gone on to be valued recital colleagues and sought-after stars on the opera and concert stage. In keeping the traditions of American music alive, he has brought back to the stage many rarely heard songs of George Gershwin, Harold Arlen, Kurt Weill, and Cole Porter. He has also played ragtime, blues, and stride piano evenings with John Musto. A champion of American art song, he has premiered works of John Corigliano, Paul Moravec, Ned Rorem, William Bolcom, Mark Adamo, John Musto, Richard Danielpour, Tobias Picker, Robert Beaser, Lowell Liebermann, Harold Meltzer, and Lee Hoiby, many of which were commissioned by NYFOS.

Blier's many recordings include the premiere recording of Leonard Bernstein's *Arias and Barcarolles* (Koch International), which won a Grammy Award; *Spanish Love Songs* (Bridge Records), recorded live at the Caramoor International Music Festival with Lorraine Hunt Lieberson, Joseph Kaiser, and Michael Barrett; the world premiere recording of *Bastianello* (John Musto) and *Lucrezia* (William Bolcom), a double bill of one-act comic operas set to librettos by Mark Campbell; and *Quiet Please*, an album of jazz standards with vocalist Darius de Haas. On the NYFOS Records label, he has released *From Rags to Riches*, a journey through the twentieth century in American song featuring Stephanie Blythe and William Burden; Paul Bowles's surprising masterpiece *A Picnic Cantata*; and *Black & Blue*, with tenor Joshua Blue. September 2023 saw the release of *Mi país: Songs of Argentina*, with bass-baritone Federico De Michelis; in 2024, an album entitled *NYFOS Records: Vol. 1*, with repertoire ranging from Rossini to Duke Ellington. In 2025 he added a pet project, *Schubert/Beatles*, with Theo Hoffman and Julia Bullock, to his expanding discography. His writings on opera have been featured in *Opera News* and the *Yale Review*. A native New Yorker, he received a bachelor's degree with honors in English literature at Yale University, where he studied piano with Alexander Farkas. He completed his musical studies in New York with Martin Isepp and Paul Jacobs.

Blier lives with facioscapulohumeral muscular dystrophy and supports fundraisers for the FSHD Society. He lives in Manhattan with his husband James S. Russell, an architectural writer and journalist.